FAMILY GUIDE TO PRESCRIPTION DRUGS

**Gillian Martlew N.D.
and Shelley Silver**

Edited by Ann Rushton

DIAMOND BOOKS

This edition published 1995 by
Diamond books
77–85 Fulham Palace road
Hammersmith, London W6 8JB

First published as *The Medicine Chest, Your Family's Guide
to Prescription Drugs* by Thorsons in 1988

ISBN 0 261 66577 4

Printed and bound in Great Britain

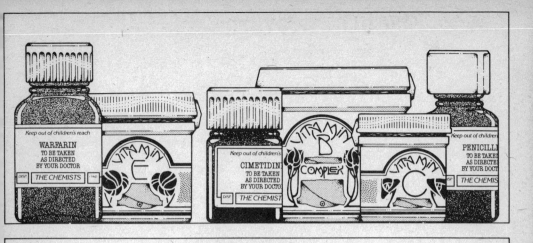

FAMILY GUIDE TO PRESCRIPTION DRUGS

PRACTICAL ADVICE ON HOW TO GET THE BEST FROM MEDICINES AND HOW TO AVOID POTENTIALLY HARMFUL COMBINATIONS OF DRUGS AND FOODS

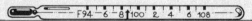

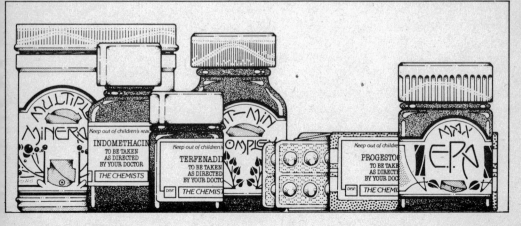

CONTENTS

DEDICATION

This book is dedicated to our families, who with their total support made this project possible. It is also dedicated to the memory of family members who will always remain close to our hearts.

DISCLAIMER

No statement contained in this book shall be construed as a claim of cure or palliative for any condition of ill health. The natural remedies and nutritional information found throughout this book are not intended as medical advice or to replace any information given to you by a doctor. Every effort has been made to produce accurate information, but neither the authors nor publishers accept any liability, however arising, from the use of any of the information by any person whatsoever.

PREFACE

While working with natural healing methods it became clear to us that people needed accessible information about the drugs they were taking. Every year, an increasing number of prescriptions are dispensed but most of the information about drugs is written for doctors or pharmacists, not for the patients.

When you take home a new car or appliance you probably consult the instruction manual in order to find out how to use it and get the most benefit from it. When you arrive home with your medicine there is no manual to consult so you have to rely on what you were told and what you happen to remember.

The aim of this book is to provide information which can help promote safer and more informed use of drugs; to look at the relationship between medicines, nutrients and health and the potential of natural healing and its partnership with orthodox medicine. It provides you with a body owner's manual, to help you find out how to work with your doctor to receive the most beneficial treatment, not just to get better, but to really get well.

FOREWORD

Over £2 billion per annum, or £30 per person per year, is spent on drugs, more than double that spent on the whole of the General Practitioner services. Then there are the hidden costs — adverse reactions to drugs account for over 10 per cent of all hospital admissions — 40,000 admissions alone for overdoses of psychotropic drugs leading to 2,000 drug-induced suicides. The Thalidomide, Opren scandals are but the tip of the iceberg — there are thousands of patients who have been affected by the side-effects of steroids and the psychoactive drugs, yet as a nation we take fewer pills than our European neighbours and American cousins. On average, British citizens receive six to seven prescriptions a year, the Germans ten, and the Americans at least sixteen a year.

The pharmaceutical industry is one of the largest and most successful in this country, spending over £7,000 per doctor per year on advertising alone. Yet it would be simplistic and inaccurate to blame these multi-nationals and look for sinister motives. We need look no further than ourselves. The nature of our health service is a reflection of the culture we live in. If we insist on renewing our cars every 2-3 years, buying the latest electronic toy and responding to the dictates of fashion, we then also demand new drugs, the miracle cure and the magic bullet. In this most consumer of ages, we prefer to take tablets for our high blood pressure, tablets to counteract the effect of over-acidity, and demand antibiotics for our three-day cold.

The fact that our high blood pressure might just as easily respond to a relaxation exercise practised daily, or our ulcer symptoms to a change of diet, and that colds are not responsive to antibiotics, does not impress us because it is much easier to take a pill than to address our life-style. It is far easier to place the causes of much of our illnesses on external factors than to accept some responsibility for their occurrence.

However, there are clear signs we are beginning to change, and that we are demanding a different sort of health-care. The sort of health-care that accepts the necessity for drugs but one that also appreciates that 'time may be an even greater healer', that many of our ailments may respond equally to some of the complementary therapies, be it homoeopathy or herbal medicine. The sort of health-care we are demanding involves us in being better informed ourselves, accepting that we may need to address some aspect of our life-style and that we should not place our health-care

FOREWORD

practitioners, be they doctors, osteopaths or Yogis, on some kind of pedestal.

To be better informed requires us to read or listen to those who are prepared to share their knowledge. In health-care, knowledge is power, and what we are observing is a necessary and healthy redistribution of the power between doctor and patient. The information provided in this book is invaluable to both doctor and patient. I wish I had learnt my pharmacology and therapeutics as it is presented in the following pages. It is often said that a little knowledge is a dangerous thing — I would add that no knowledge is even more dangerous.

Radical changes in health-care have almost always occurred as a result of consumer pressure. Using the information provided will allow you to ask your doctor the right questions, but more importantly, it may drive you to ask yourself — should I really be taking this drug? — is there an alternative and what do I need to change to enable me to live my life without requiring another prescription?

PATRICK C. PIETRONI, F.R.C.G.P., M.R.C.P., D.C.H.
Chairman
The British Holistic Medical Association
London, 1988

ACKNOWLEDGEMENTS

We would like to acknowledge the efforts of the dedicated people who helped turn this book from an idea into reality.

Very special thanks are due to our editor, Ann Rushton, for her sound editorial and textual advice, guidance and creative input. In addition, we would like to thank her for the great patience she has shown in dealing with the enormous number of amendments and tidying of loose ends necessary in a book of this scope.

This book's visual image was created by David Fairbrother-Roe whose imaginatve design and illustrations are an integral part of the *Family Guide to Prescription Drugs*. We also wish to thank Ann and David for their encouragement and their enthusiasm when we first proposed the idea to them.

Behind the scenes various people have played important roles in this book's evolution. Valerie, Tony, and Neil Martlew, and Amy and William Davis have provided a liberal supply of constructive criticism, encouragement and confidence during this project. In addition Valerie's encyclopaedic knowledge has been invaluable. She has offered many important leads for us to follow and has tirelessly proof-read countless drafts of the manuscript. Thanks are due to Stephen Crane who provided us with help, advice, and an office. His sense of humour helped us through some difficult times.

Our sincere thanks to Dr Laurence Gerlis for his medical and pharmacological advice and comments, and to other medical practitioners for their important input.

INTRODUCTION

This book is designed as a guide to help you work with your doctor to obtain the most beneficial treatment for your disorder. It is not intended as a DIY book for health or medical treatments, or as an alternative to consulting your doctor. The natural remedies are offered as suggestions, not treatment, and should only be used after consultation with a doctor — especially if you are already taking any medication. No attempt has been made to include full or complete information on any drug or drug group and the ones given in this book are only those which are commonly prescribed.

WHERE TO START

Before you visit the doctor it would be a good idea to read the section on Getting The Most From Your Medicine. When you have your prescription you need to look up the name of the medicine you have been given. There are two ways to do this, either in the drug index where you will find a list of generic names and brand names or in the index of ailments and illnesses. Because pharmaceutical manufacturers quite frequently bring out new versions of drugs the brand names are often changed and you may discover that your particular brand name is not listed. If you ask your doctor or chemist for the drug's generic name then you may look it up under the generic category instead.

The drug fact sheets in this book are grouped into seven sections and include the major body systems whose ailments they are most frequently used to treat. The fact sheet on ulcers for example will be found in the chapter on the Digestive System, and so on. Many drugs are prescribed for numerous conditions and in order to avoid confusion and repetition the information on them will be found in the section where they are used most commonly, and cross references will be made to other sections where they may be used less often. The fact sheet will give you information on a group of drugs, including their contra-indications, side-effects and interactions. There are special sections for children and the over-sixties as there is a possibility of increased drug reactions within these two groups. At the end of each group of fact sheets is a section on natural healing, including suggestions on diet and alternative medicine and therapies.

INTRODUCTION

Diet and nutrition are an important part of being well. When a vitamin or mineral is referred to in the text, you can check in the chapter on Vitamins, Minerals and their Food Sources for more information on nutrition and a complete analysis of what part each vitamin and mineral plays in the nutritional cycle. In the natural healing sections natural practitioners are suggested and you will find details about individual therapies in the chapter on Alternative and Complementary Medicine and Therapies. Finally if there are any medical or natural terms that you are not sure of you can look for them in The Fact Finder.

GETTING THE MOST FROM YOUR MEDICINE

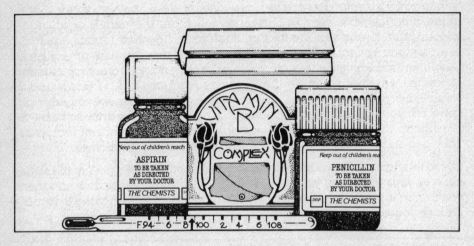

Over 400 million prescriptions are dispensed each year in Great Britain, but many of them will be wasted if the medicine is not taken properly or a prescribed course of drugs is not completed. The information which follows will help you use your medicine more safely and obtain the most benefit from it.

WHAT TO ASK YOUR DOCTOR

The average consultation with a doctor lasts for around five minutes and we tend to remember what we are told earlier rather than later. It is helpful to ask your doctor for the following information and to make a note of the answers you are given.

First you need to know what type of medicine you have been prescribed, its name and how it is going to help you. You should get very clear instructions on how and when to take it; how long the course should last; what to do if you should miss taking a dose and when the doctor will need to see you again. Ask if there are any possible side-effects, what they might be and how quickly they could develop. You may also need to know if the medicine will affect your ability to work normally or drive a vehicle.

GETTING THE MOST FROM YOUR MEDICINE

WHAT TO TELL YOUR DOCTOR

When you visit your doctor, see a new one, or even another doctor in the same practice, it is very important to tell them the names of all non-prescription drugs you are taking, such as indigestion tablets, aspirin, cough mixtures etc, as they may interact with a drug you are prescribed. Also mention any side- effects you are experiencing from your current medicine, whether you have shown severe reactions to ANY drugs and if you have any allergies. If you are pregnant, or even suspect you are, you must tell your doctor as some medicines may harm your unborn baby. A change in diet, heavy drinking or smoking are also important factors as they can increase or decrease the effects of certain medicines.

If you intend to use any alternative or complementary therapies at the same time as your treatment you should discuss this with your doctor and then make sure that full details of your medication are passed on to the therapist before you begin any treatment.

WHEN YOU HAVE YOUR PRESCRIPTION

Studies have shown that different people will interpret the instructions printed on a medicine label in varying ways and this can lead to drugs being taken incorrectly and even dangerously. If you are unsure of any instructions on the medicine label then ask your pharmacist for help. Even if you think you understand it perfectly it can still be a good idea to confirm the instructions while you are there. If you have trouble reading small print then do ask for the instructions to be written so that you can read them clearly.

If you have been given several prescriptions, or if other members of your household keep their medicines together with yours, it could be very easy to take the wrong tablets. To prevent any possibly fatal mistakes, each person should label their own medicines so they can be easily recognized, perhaps with different coloured stickers or marking the label with coloured pens. All instruction labels should be read in a good light to ensure that you take the right medicine and the right dose.

Make a note of any medicines you are taking and carry it with you at all times, in case of accident. This information could prevent any possibly dangerous interactions between your own medicine and anything you may be given as emergency treatment. Always carry your drug warning card on you if you have one.

Drugs and anaesthetics used in dentistry may react dangerously with other medicines. You must tell your dentist about anything you are taking, any illnesses you have, if you are pregnant or have any allergies, particularly to antibiotics.

WHILE TAKING YOUR MEDICINE

If you become pregnant or suspect pregnancy whilst taking any drug contact your doctor immediately to check on the suitability of your medicine.

Any symptom which arises after you start taking a drug could be a side-effect and must be reported to your doctor as soon as possible. If you experience either a headache which lasts for more than three days, have serious indigestion which has lasted more than one week or have diarrhoea lasting three days then you must contact your doctor immediately.

Medicines prescribed for other people should never be taken and do not share yours with anyone else. Transferring drugs from one container to another could contaminate them and they may lose some of their effectiveness. Household spoons are not accurate enough for measuring liquid medicines so check that you have been given a measuring spoon or cup and shake all liquids well before taking them. If you have any old or out of date medicines do not try to use them as they are liable to be ineffective, dangerous or contaminated. If you miss taking your medicine, or have to change the time that you usually take it then you should contact your doctor or pharmacist as soon as possible. Always complete a prescribed course, especially antibiotics, unless advised otherwise. If you want to stop your treatment before it is finished you should always consult your doctor first because many medicines need to be gradually reduced.

Exercise is generally a good thing, but if you are taking any form of medicine, and especially heart medicines, you must contact your doctor before embarking on any strenuous exercise programme. Check also if you intend taking saunas, or are going to an extremely hot or cold climate.

GETTING THE MOST FROM YOUR MEDICINE

SWALLOWING TABLETS AND CAPSULES

Many people have difficulty swallowing tablets and this can be made worse by the fear of discomfort if the tablet does not go down. Tablets or capsules which get stuck in the throat can be very uncomfortable and if they begin to disintegrate in the gullet they may cause a burning sensation, heartburn or nausea. It is easier to swallow if you are relaxed, and if you have a technique which works for you. Taking tablets whilst standing up can help to prevent them getting stuck in the gullet and it is best to remain standing for up to two minutes after swallowing them. Always take tablets with at least a FULL glass of water, it not only helps you swallow them but in many cases may help the medicine work better.

STORING AND DISPOSING OF MEDICINES

A medicine chest should be secure and childproof with all medicines stored away from moisture, direct sunlight and heat; bathroom cabinets or cupboards above a cooker or sink are unsuitable for this purpose. If a medicine needs refrigeration make sure you do not actually freeze it. Unused drugs should be returned to a pharmacist and not flushed down the lavatory or sink as they may cause eventual contamination of the water supplies. Never put them in the dustbin where children or animals may find them.

WHERE TO GET MORE INFORMATION

Any questions you have about your medicine should be directed to your pharmacist or doctor. Pharmacists are highly trained in many aspects of drug use and chemists which have a registered pharmacist on the staff display a green and white cross on the window or door.

DRUG
FACT
SHEETS

CARDIOVASCULAR SYSTEM
CONTENTS

CARDIOVASCULAR

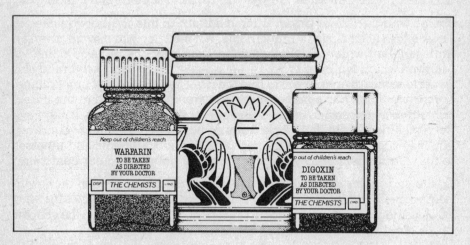

The heart is a muscle which weighs under a pound and is about the size of your clenched fist. It has the ability to respond to increased activity, nervousness or excitement with changes in its rate, force or contraction. Each day it pumps a total of two thousand gallons of blood around a distance of sixty thousand miles of blood vessels, and every cell in the body depends on the life-giving blood that the heart pumps to it. The cardiovascular system is an extremely intricate collaboration between the heart (cardio), miles of veins and arteries (vascular), and the bloodstream.

In 1785 the English physician, William Withering published the *Account of the Foxglove* after distinguishing it as the active ingredient in a potion for dropsy made by a Shropshire woman known as Old Mother Hutton. He discovered that it slowed the pulse rate and helped the body remove excess fluids. As a medicine, foxglove is now better known for it's extracted cardiac glycosides or digitalis drugs. Digoxin and digitoxin are extracted from the dried leaves of the foxglove and used to treat heart failure.

There is a great variety of medicines used for the cardiovascular system; some treat the heart's rhythm, contraction or pumping ability; others affect blood pressure, cholesterol levels, clotting and circulation.

Although there is not total agreement as to why heart disease has been

CARDIOVASCULAR

increasing every year, it is generally believed that stress, diet, smoking, and lifestyle all influence the way the cardiovascular system functions.

To find your particular prescription medicine in this chapter you need to know either its generic or brand name. For instance you may be given an anticoagulant which is labelled either warfarin, the generic name, or Marevan which is a brand name. The index of drugs lists both brand and generic names to enable you to find the right fact sheet for your medicine. If your medicine has a name which you are unable to find in the index, contact your dispensing chemist and ask for its generic name. It may have been included under that name. If you do not know the name of your drug, you may prefer to check in the separate index of ailments and illnesses to find the drugs that may be prescribed for your particular complaint.

At the end of this group of fact sheets you will find a section on how to help yourself, with suggestions for natural remedies and therapies that may be of assistance. Information about practitioners will be found in the chapter on Alternative/Complementary Medicine and Therapies.

If you come across a particular word or term that is unfamiliar to you, please look in The Fact Finder for an explanation; information on food and nutrition will be found in the chapter on Vitamins and Minerals.

PRESCRIPTION NAMES

MEDICINES FOR HEART RHYTHM DISORDERS

Antiarrhythmics are usually prescribed for heart rhythm abnormalities and work by relaxing the heart muscle and nerves. A local anaesthetic action returns the over-active heartbeat and rhythm to normal and improves the efficiency of the heart's pumping action. Other medicines for heart rhythm disorders prolong the resting phase of the heart.

NAMES OF PRESCRIPTION MEDICINES

The following are commonly prescribed antiarrhythmics and are shown with the generic name first, followed by the brand name. If your medicine is not listed by name you should follow the information for the generic, if you know it, as the information given will still apply to your particular medicine. If you are not sure of the generic name your pharmacist will be able to advise you. Please note that ALL the information on this fact sheet applies to antiarrhythmics generally, not specifically to any one medicine.

Generic	Brand Name
amiodarone	Cordarone X
disopyramide	Dirythmin/SA, Rythmodan/Retard
flecainide	Tambocor
lignocaine	Xylocard
mexiletine	Mexitil PL
procainamide	Procainamide Durles Pronestyl
quinidine	Kiditard, Kinidin, Quinicardine
tocainide	Tonocard

WHAT TO TELL YOUR DOCTOR

It is important to make sure your doctor or doctors are given as much information as possible. If you are aware that you are allergic to any antiarrhythmic drugs, local anaesthetics or quinine, then do tell them so. Information on other medication is vital so if you are taking any other medicine, including non-prescription drugs, then they must know that too. Additionally, make sure they know if any of the following apply to you:

Acute infection	Low blood pressure
Breast feeding	Lupus erythematosus
Glaucoma	Myasthenia gravis
Heart disorders	Pacemaker
Kidney disorders	Parkinson's disease
Liver disorders	Pregnancy

If you will be having surgery or dental treatment which requires anaesthesia it is important to tell the person in charge that you are taking antiarrhythmic drugs.

CARDIOVASCULAR

SIDE-EFFECTS AND CAUTIONS

SIDE-EFFECTS It is impossible to predict how any medicine will affect a particular individual because everyone's metabolism is so very different. Sensitivity or reaction to drugs can vary greatly from one person to another and side-effects can be related to dosage. It is important to pay close attention to any changes you may notice either when starting, or during, a course of treatment.

The following are some of the side-effects reported within this group of drugs. Some of the disorders listed under Infrequent or Rare may occasionally be the symptoms of overdose and not always those of side-effects.

COMMON

Difficult urination
Dizziness

Dry mouth
Vision changes

INFREQUENT OR RARE

Bitter taste in mouth
Blood disorders
Blood pressure drop
Confusion
Depression
Diarrhoea
Difficulty in breathing
Digestive upsets
Drowsiness
Fainting
Fatigue or weakness
Fever or shivering
Hallucinations
Headache

Heartbeat changes
Joint pain
Loss of appetite
Low blood sugar
Pins and needles
Skin rash
Sleeping difficulties
Sore throat
Tremors
Unusual bleeding or
 bruising
Vomiting or nausea
Yellow skin or eyes

If you experience any of the listed side-effects, or any other unusual symptoms, you should consult your dispensing pharmacist or doctor immediately.

CAUTIONS It is important that this medicine is taken exactly as your doctor's instructions indicate so that the heart can be kept beating at a normal rate. The tablets are best taken with food to reduce the possibility of any stomach upset.

If sunbathing, or using a sun-bed or lamp whilst taking amiodarone, then a rash or increased tendency to burn may occur so it may be advisable to avoid exposure or to take extra precautions.

One of the side-effects can be a dry mouth and this may contribute to the chance of tooth decay or gum disease. If this occurs, your doctor will probably advise you to clean your teeth frequently and to use dental floss.

INTERACTIONS

INTERACTIONS WITH OTHER MEDICINES AND SUBSTANCES

No medication works in isolation but is affected to a greater or lesser extent by many other factors such as general fitness, diet and lifestyle. The action of antiarrhythmic drugs can be interfered with if taken in combination with alcohol, caffeine, iced drinks and tobacco.

It is also possible to unintentionally combine antiarrhythmics with other drugs and this could be dangerous. Check with your doctor or pharmacist before taking any other medication, including non-prescription items, and if you are taking anything from the list below then look at the key to find out what effect they may have.

1 Other antiarrhythmic drugs

3 Digitalis drugs
3 Some anticoagulants**
3 Some antihypertensives
3 Some antinauseants**

5 Antacids

Digitalis taken with propranolol may excessively slow the heartbeat in combination with antiarrhythmics.

Diuretics taken with laxatives may cause potassium loss which could affect the heartbeat.

**Often drugs within the same group differ in formulation and may or may not interact with antiarrhythmics. Your pharmacist can tell you which specific drugs within a group do interact.

KEY

1 INCREASES the effects of antiarrhythmics
3 ANTIARRHYTHMICS INCREASE the effects of these drugs
5 UNPREDICTABLE reactions

INTERACTIONS WITH VITAMINS, MINERALS AND FOODS

Large doses of vitamin C can decrease the effects of quinidine.

Food may become harder to swallow if you suffer from a dry mouth while taking these medicines, and the ability to digest starches and carbohydrates will be affected. An important element in this digestion is the enzyme ptyalin, which is present in saliva, and in order to stimulate its flow all food should be chewed extremely well before swallowing.

CHILDREN, OVER SIXTIES AND PROLONGED USE

CHILDREN Because the safety for children has not been established in some of the brand name antiarrhythmic medicines, they are generally not recommended for the young.

OVER SIXTIES As part of the ageing process the body begins to metabolize and eliminate drugs more slowly and so there may be the possibility of more frequent or severe side-effects or interactions with other medicines. With some of the drugs in this group there may be an increased possibility of urinary difficulty, constipation or a drop in blood pressure.

PROLONGED OR CONTINUED TREATMENT In susceptible people some of the drugs in this group have been found to increase the possibilities of blood disorders when used for prolonged or continued treatment.

STOPPING THE TREATMENT Do not discontinue or attempt to reduce the drugs without consulting your doctor as the dosage may need to be gradually withdrawn to prevent complications.

PERSONAL MEDICINE NOTES

CARDIOVASCULAR SYSTEM
ANTICOAGULANTS

PRESCRIPTION NAMES

MEDICINES FOR VASCULAR BLOOD CLOTS

Anticoagulants prevent blood clots from forming, or existing ones from increasing in size, and are used to treat forms of thrombosis or embolism. They do not dissolve blood clots but slow the clotting process by interfering with the action of vitamin K which is important in the formation of blood clotting factors. They may also be prescribed in the treatment of some heart disorders.

NAMES OF PRESCRIPTION MEDICINES

The following are commonly prescribed anticoagulants and are shown with the generic name first, followed by the brand name. If your medicine is not listed by name you should follow the information for the generic, if you know it, as the information given will still apply to your particular medicine. If you are not sure of the generic name your pharmacist will be able to advise you. Please note that ALL the information on this fact sheet applies to anticoagulants generally, not specifically to any one medicine.

Generic	Brand Name
nicoumalone	Sinthrome
phenindione	Dindevan
warfarin sodium	Marevan, Warfarin WBP

WHAT TO TELL YOUR DOCTOR

It is important to make sure that your doctor or doctors are given as much information as possible. If you are aware that you are allergic to anticoagulant drugs then do tell them so. Information on other medication is vital, so if you are taking any other type of medicine, including non-prescription drugs, then they must know that too. Additionally, make sure they know if any of the following apply to you:

Breast feeding
Blood or bleeding disorders
Diabetes
Heart disorders
Heavy menstruation
High blood pressure

Kidney disorders
Liver disorders
Peptic ulcer
Pregnancy
Ulcerative colitis

If you will be having surgery or dental treatment which requires anaesthesia it is important to tell the person in charge that you are taking anticoagulants.

CARDIOVASCULAR

SIDE-EFFECTS AND CAUTIONS

SIDE-EFFECTS It is impossible to predict how any medicine will affect a particular individual because everyone's metabolism is so very different. Sensitivity or reaction to drugs can vary greatly from one person to another and side-effects can be related to dosage. It is important to pay close attention to any changes you may notice either when starting, or during, a course of treatment.

The following are some of the side-effects reported within this group of drugs. Some of the disorders listed under Infrequent or Rare may occasionally be the symptoms of overdose and not always those of side-effects.

COMMON Unusual or unexpected bleeding or bruising

INFREQUENT OR RARE

Appetite change
Back pain
Black or dark red bowel
  movements
Bleeding gums
Blurred vision
Chills
Coughing up blood
Diarrhoea
Discoloration of the toes
Dizziness
Fever
Hair loss

Headache
Liver disorders
Nausea
Skin itching
Skin rashes or irritation
Stomach bloating
Swollen feet or legs
Urine cloudy
Urine pink or brown colour
Vomit containing blood
Vomiting
Weakness

If you experience any of the listed side-effects, or any other unusual symptoms, you should consult your dispensing pharmacist or doctor immediately.

CAUTIONS If you experience dizziness or drowsiness do not drive, operate machinery or work high above the ground, and try to avoid situations with a high risk of injury. Alcohol can increase the effects of dizziness or drowsiness and should be avoided during treatment.

Any rise in body temperature, whether from a fever or environmental factors such as very hot sun or sauna, can increase the effect of anticoagulants and this could be dangerous.

If your weight has increased or decreased at all during treatment, or you have stomach upsets or acute illness, you should tell your doctor because they can alter the effectiveness of the medicine.

If you suspect that you have become pregnant since beginning treatment with anticoagulants tell your doctor immediately.

INTERACTIONS

INTERACTIONS WITH OTHER MEDICINES AND SUBSTANCES

No medication works in isolation but is affected to a greater or lesser extent by many other factors such as general fitness, diet and lifestyle. Alcohol can increase or decrease the anticoagulant effects of these medicines.

It is also possible to unintentionally combine anticoagulants with other drugs and this could be dangerous. Check with your doctor or pharmacist before taking any other medication, including non-prescription items, and if you are taking any of the drugs listed below look at the key to find out what effect they may have.

1 Anabolic steroids
1 Antibiotics
1 Antidiabetic drugs
1 Antiplatelet medicines
1 Aspirin and other salicylates
1 Cimetidine
1 Gout medicines
1 Paracetamol in large doses only
1 Quinidine antiarrhythmics
1 Some antihypertensives**
1 Tricyclic antidepressants

2 Antifungals
2 Barbiturate sleeping tablets
2 Beta blockers

4 Digitalis drugs

5 Antacids
5 Anticonvulsants
5 Contraceptive drugs and oestrogens
5 Corticosteroids
5 Indomethacin
5 Lipid lowering drugs
5 Some diuretics**
5 Some tranquillizers**
5 Thyroid hormones
5 Urinary tract anti-infectives

**Often drugs within the same group differ in formulation and may or may not interact with anticoagulants. Your pharmacist can tell you which specific drugs within a group do interact.

KEY
1 INCREASES the effects of anticoagulants
2 DECREASES the effects of anticoagulants
4 ANTICOAGULANTS DECREASE the effects of these drugs
5 UNPREDICTABLE reactions

INTERACTIONS WITH VITAMINS, MINERALS AND FOODS

The action of anticoagulants can be quite seriously affected when taken with some vitamins, minerals or foods. If large supplemental doses of vitamin E or magnesium are taken in conjunction with anticoagulants they could dangerously increase the effect of the medicine. Extremely large doses of vitamin C and bioflavonoids and/or calcium if taken in supplement form could decrease the action of the drugs.

A large or inconsistent intake of vitamin K rich foods or supplements, or a large intake of fats and oils, could cause an imbalance of the drug and nutrients in the body and may decrease the anticoagulant effect. See the chapter on Vitamins and Minerals for which foods are rich in vitamin K.

CHILDREN, OVER SIXTIES AND PROLONGED USE

CHILDREN

Anticoagulants may occasionally be prescribed for children and the dosage will be scaled down accordingly.

OVER SIXTIES

As part of the ageing process the body begins to metabolize and eliminate drugs more slowly and so there may be the possibility of more frequent or severe side-effects or interactions with other medicines.

PROLONGED OR CONTINUED TREATMENT

If there is a predisposition to diabetes then prolonged treatment with anticoagulants may precipitate its onset.

STOPPING THE TREATMENT

Do not discontinue or reduce the drugs without consulting your doctor as the dosage may need to be gradually reduced.

PERSONAL MEDICINE NOTES

PRESCRIPTION NAMES

MEDICINES FOR HIGH BLOOD PRESSURE

Antihypertensives are used mainly to reduce blood pressure and they do this by causing the walls of the blood vessels to expand. Some antihypertensives inhibit the conversion of those substances in the body which cause contraction of the blood vessels, thus leaving them more relaxed and enabling the blood to flow with more ease. Others cause the blood vessels to expand by affecting the part of the brain which controls the muscles in the walls of the blood vessels. These medicines may also be prescribed for heart failure, disorders arising from decreased circulation and for migraine prevention.

NAMES OF PRESCRIPTION MEDICINES

The following are commonly prescribed supplementary antihypertensives and are shown with the generic name first, followed by the brand name. Other drugs used for hypertension are beta blockers, calcium antagonists and diuretics, and fact sheets on these will be found separately in this section. If your drug is not listed by name you should follow the information for the generic, if you know it, as the information given will still apply to your particular medicine. If you are not sure of the generic name your pharmacist will be able to advise you. Please note that ALL the information on this fact sheet applies to these antihypertensives generally, not specifically to any one medicine.

Generic	Brand Name
captopril	Acepril, Capoten
clonidine	Catapres
enalapril	Innovace
hydralazine	Apresoline
indapamide	Natrilix
indoramin	Baratol
methyldopa	Aldomet, Dopamet, Hydromet, Medomet
minoxidil	Loniten
prazosin	Hypovase

WHAT TO TELL YOUR DOCTOR

It is important to make sure that your doctor or doctors are given as much information as possible. If you are aware that you are allergic to antihypertensives then do tell them so. Information on other medication is vital so if you are taking any other type of medicine, including non-prescription drugs, then they must know that too. Additionally, make sure they know if any of the following apply to you:

Allergies	Diabetes
Blood disorders	Gout
Breast feeding	Heart disease or pains

CARDIOVASCULAR

Kidney disorders
Liver disorders
Lupus erythematosus

Peptic ulcer
Pregnancy
Stroke

If you will be having surgery or dental treatment which requires anaesthesia it is important to tell the person in charge that you are taking antihypertensives.

SIDE-EFFECTS AND CAUTIONS

SIDE-EFFECTS It is impossible to predict how any medicine will affect a particular individual because everyone's metabolism is so very different. Sensitivity or reaction to drugs can vary greatly from one person to another and side-effects can be related to dosage. It is important to pay close attention to any changes you may notice either when starting, or during, a course of treatment.

The following are some of the side-effects reported within this group of drugs. Some of the disorders listed under Infrequent or Rare may occasionally be the symptoms of overdose and not always those of side-effects.

COMMON

Constipation
Cough
Diarrhoea
Dizziness
Drowsiness
Dry mouth
Frequent urination

Headache
Lack of energy
Metallic taste in mouth
Nausea or vomiting
Rapid heartbeat
Urine retention

INFREQUENT OR RARE

Appetite change
Bloating
Blood sugar disorders
Chest pain
Chills or fever
Depression or anxiety
Difficulty swallowing
Flatulence
Flushing of skin
Impotence*
Inhibition of ovulation*

Joint pains
Low blood pressure
Menstrual cramps
Muscle cramps
Nightmares
Skin rashes
Skin sensitive to sunlight
Sleeping difficulties
Sore throat
Weight change

*These particular side-effects apply only to methyldopa and are not relevant to the other drugs in this group. The other listed side-effects still apply to methyldopa.

CARDIOVASCULAR SYSTEM
ANTIHYPERTENSIVES

If you experience any of the listed side-effects, or any other unusual symptoms, you should consult your dispensing pharmacist or doctor immediately.

CAUTIONS If you begin to suffer from water retention or swelling of the ankles it is advisable to tell your doctor.

If you experience dizziness or drowsiness you should not drive, operate machinery or work high above the ground. Alcohol can increase these effects and should be avoided during treatment.

Strenuous exercise and temperature extremes should be avoided and your skin may be more sensitive to burning from exposure to the sun or sunlamps.

One of the side-effects can be a dry mouth and this may contribute to the chance of tooth decay or gum disease. If this occurs, your doctor will probably advise you to clean your teeth frequently and to use dental floss.

If you are considering using a salt substitute it is important that you discuss this with your doctor first.

INTERACTIONS

INTERACTIONS WITH OTHER MEDICINES AND SUBSTANCES

No medication works in isolation but is affected to a greater or lesser extent by many other factors such as general fitness, diet and lifestyle. Alcohol can increase drowsiness or dizziness and may lower blood pressure. Smoking may cause chest pains.

It is also possible to unintentionally combine antihypertensives with other drugs and this could be dangerous. Check with your doctor or pharmacist before taking any other medication, including non-prescription items, and if you are taking any of the drugs listed below look at the key to find out what effect they may have.

1 Beta blockers
1 Calcium antagonists
1 Other antihypertensives
1 Other vasodilators
1 Some diuretics**

3 Anticoagulants

5 Antidepressants including MAOI's
5 Non prescription cold remedies

**Often drugs within the same group differ in formulation and may or may not interact with antihypertensives. Your pharmacist can tell you which specific drugs within a group do interact.

CARDIOVASCULAR

KEY 1 INCREASES the effects of antihypertensives
3 ANTIHYPERTENSIVES INCREASE the effects of these drugs
5 UNPREDICTABLE reactions

**INTERACTIONS WITH
VITAMINS, MINERALS
AND FOODS**

Large supplemental doses of vitamin E can slightly raise blood pressure in susceptible people and should not be taken with the drugs in this group unless specifically advised by a doctor. Niacin and nicotinic acid, which are forms of vitamin B3, when taken in supplement form can produce a vasodilatory effect and may dangerously increase the effects of these medicines.

A high salt intake may decrease the effect of these medicines and foods which contain dopamine or tyramine can increase blood pressure and may also decrease the effectiveness of the medicine if taken in large quantities. Further information on these foods can be found in The Fact Finder and the Vitamins and Minerals chapter.

DLPA is an amino acid supplement used for pain relief, depression and weight control. It can increase blood pressure and might decrease the antihypertensive effect of the drugs in this group. If you are pregnant or suffer from phenylketonuria or are taking MAOI's then DLPA must only be taken under supervision.

Natural liquorice, as found in certain sweets and herbal teas, contains a chemical called glycyrrhizic acid which can elevate blood pressure by causing salt and water retention. Because some of these medicines have diuretic action there may be depletion of some minerals and water soluble vitamins due to increased excretion. A feeling of 'pins and needles' in the toes or fingers may be caused by a vitamin B5 or B6 deficiency.

Food may become harder to swallow if you suffer from a dry mouth while taking these medicines, and the ability to digest starches and carbohydrates will be affected. An important element in this digestion is the enzyme ptyalin, which is present in saliva, and in order to stimulate its flow all food should be chewed extremely well before swallowing.

CARDIOVASCULAR SYSTEM
ANTIHYPERTENSIVES

CHILDREN, OVER SIXTIES AND PROLONGED USE

CHILDREN Can occasionally be prescribed antihypertensive medicines and the dosage may be scaled down accordingly.

OVER SIXTIES As part of the ageing process the body begins to metabolize and eliminate drugs more slowly and so there may be the possibility of more frequent or severe side-effects or interactions with other medicines. With some of the drugs in this group there may be an increased possibility of depletion of some minerals and water soluble vitamins.

PROLONGED OR CONTINUED TREATMENT In susceptible people some of the drugs in this group have been found to produce loss of appetite or joint pains. On rare occasions there has been a link with blood disorders when used for prolonged or continued treatment.

STOPPING THE TREATMENT Do not discontinue the treatment without consulting your doctor as the dosage may need to be gradually reduced. If other drugs are being taken at the same time then their dosage may also need to be adjusted.

PERSONAL MEDICINE NOTES

CARDIOVASCULAR

35

CARDIOVASCULAR

PRESCRIPTION NAMES

MEDICINES FOR HIGH BLOOD PRESSURE, VASCULAR CONSTRICTION AND THE HEART

Beta blockers interfere with the action of stimulating hormones on receptors in the nervous system. This slows down the strength of the heart's contraction and reduces its oxygen requirements and the volume of blood it has to pump. High blood pressure may be treated with these drugs because of their ability to increase the diameter of the blood vessels thus allowing blood to flow under less pressure. Some of these medicines include a diuretic to help reduce blood pressure by increasing the body's excretion of excess fluid. Beta blockers are also used to treat heart attack and rhythm disorders, angina pains, and disorders arising from decreased circulation and vascular constriction, including migraine.

NAMES OF PRESCRIPTION MEDICINES

The following are commonly prescribed beta blockers and are shown with the generic name first, followed by the brand name. If your medicine is not listed by name you should follow the information for the generic, if you know it, as the information given will still apply to your particular medicine. If you are not sure of the generic name your pharmacist will be able to advise you. Please note that ALL the information on this fact sheet applies to beta blockers generally, not specifically to any one medicine.

Generic	Brand Name
acebutolol	Sectral, Secadrex
atenolol	Tenormin, Tenoret, Tenoretic, Kalten
betaxolol	Kerlone
labetalol*	Trandate, Labrocol
metoprolol	Co-Betaloc, Betaloc/SA, Lopresor/SR, Lopresoretic
nadolol	Corgard, Corgaretic
oxprenolol	Apsolox, Slow-Trasicor, Trasicor, Trasidrex, Laracor, Slo-Pren
penbutolol	Lasipressin
pindolol	Viskaldix, Visken
propranolol	Apsolol, Berkolol, Inderal/LA/Half, Inderex, Inderetic, Spiroprop, Angilol, Bedranol, Sloprolol
sotalol	Beta-Cardone, Sotacor, Sotazide, Tolerzide
timolol	Betim, Blocadren, Prestim/Forte

CARDIOVASCULAR SYSTEM
BETA BLOCKERS

*These drugs are a mixture of an alpha blocker and a beta blocker.

WHAT TO TELL YOUR DOCTOR
It is important to make sure that your doctor or doctors are given as much information as possible. If you are aware that you are allergic to beta blockers, sulphonamides or diuretics then do tell them so. Information on other medication is vital so if you are taking any other type of medicine, including non-prescription drugs, then they must know that too. Additionally, make sure they know if any of the following apply to you:

Asthma	High uric acid condition
Blood sugar disorders	Kidney disorders
Breast feeding	Liver disorders
Breathing difficulties	Low blood pressure
Bronchitis	Pregnancy
Circulation disorders	Prolonged fasting
Diabetes	Raynaud's disease
Gout	or phenomenon
Heart rhythm disorders	

If you will be having surgery or dental treatment which requires anaesthesia it is important to tell the person in charge that you are taking beta blockers.

SIDE-EFFECTS AND CAUTIONS

SIDE-EFFECTS
It is impossible to predict how any medicine will affect a particular individual because everyone's metabolism is so very different. Sensitivity or reaction to drugs can vary greatly from one person to another and side-effects can be related to dosage. It is important to pay close attention to any changes you may notice either when starting, or during, a course of treatment. The following are some of the side-effects reported within this group of drugs. Some of the disorders listed under Infrequent or Rare may occasionally be the symptoms of overdose and not always those of side-effects.

COMMON

Abnormal fatigue after exertion	Dizziness*
Cold hands and feet	Drowsiness
Constipation	Low blood pressure
Diarrhoea	Nausea or vomiting*

CARDIOVASCULAR SYSTEM
BETA BLOCKERS

INFREQUENT OR RARE

Blood sugar disorders
Breathing difficulties
Depression
Difficult urination**
Digestive upsets
Dry eyes
Dry mouth
Excessive slowing
    of heart rate
Fluid retention

Headache
Impotence
Muscle fatigue or cramps
Sensitivity to cold
Skin rashes
Sleep disturbance
Stomach pains**
Tingling scalp**
Vision disturbances

*These side-effects are uncommon with labetalol.

**These particular side-effects apply only to labetalol and are not relevant to the other drugs in this group. The other listed side-effects still apply to labetalol.

If you experience any of the listed side-effects, or any other unusual symptoms, you should consult your dispensing pharmacist or doctor immediately.

CAUTIONS

If you experience dizziness or drowsiness do not drive, operate machinery or work high above the ground. Alcohol can increase these effects and should be avoided during treatment.

One of the side-effects may be a dry mouth and this can contribute to the chance of tooth decay or gum disease. If this occurs, your doctor will probably advise you to clean your teeth frequently and to use dental floss.

If you intend using a salt substitute you should discuss this with your doctor first.

INTERACTIONS

INTERACTIONS WITH
OTHER MEDICINES AND
SUBSTANCES

No medication works in isolation but is affected to a greater or lesser extent by many other factors such as general fitness, diet and lifestyle. Alcohol may cause a dangerous drop in blood pressure and smoking could lead to irregular heartbeats.

It is also possible to unintentionally combine beta blockers with other drugs and this could be dangerous. Check with your doctor or pharmacist before taking any other medication, including non-prescription items, and if you are taking any of the drugs listed below check the key to find out what effect they may have.

1 Other antihypertensive vasodilatory drugs
1 Other diuretics

3 Antihypertensives
3 Some antidiabetic drugs**

4 Anticoagulants
4 Anti-inflammatory drugs
4 Cortisone drugs

5 Antacids
5 Anticonvulsants
5 Antidepressants including MAOI's
5 Aspirin or NSAI's
5 Digitalis drugs
5 Heart rhythm drugs
5 Medicines for asthma
5 Nitrite vasodilators
5 Sedatives and tranquillizers

If calcium antagonists are taken with beta blockers this may cause irregular heartbeat, or even heart failure in extreme cases. If you are also taking Lithium with beta blockers then Lithium toxicity is possible, or the diuretic effect of some of the drugs in this group may be decreased.

**Often drugs within the same group differ in formulation and may or may not interact with beta blockers. Your pharmacist can tell you wich specific drugs within a group do interact.

KEY 1 INCREASES the effects of beta blockers
3 BETA BLOCKERS INCREASE the effects of these drugs
4 BETA BLOCKERS DECREASE the effects of these drugs
5 UNPREDICTABLE reactions

INTERACTIONS WITH VITAMINS, MINERALS AND FOODS

Niacin and nicotinic acid supplements, which are forms of B3, produce a vasodilatory effect and may detrimentally increase the effects of these medicines. Large supplementary doses of vitamin E should not be taken with the drugs in this group as it may cause unpredictable reactions. For important warnings on the use of vitamin E please see the Vitamins and Minerals chapter.

Foods which contain dopamine and tyramine can increase blood pressure if eaten in very large quantities and may decrease the effectiveness of beta blockers. Your doctor may also suggest following a low salt diet. Because some beta blockers contain diuretics there may be a loss of minerals and water soluble vitamins due to the increased excretion.

CARDIOVASCULAR

Food may become harder to swallow if you suffer from a dry mouth while taking these medicines, and the ability to digest starches and carbohydrates will be affected. An important element in this digestion is the enzyme ptyalin, which is present in saliva, and in order to stimulate its flow all food should be chewed extremely well before swallowing.

CHILDREN, OVER SIXTIES AND PROLONGED USE

CHILDREN Beta blockers are not recommended for children.

OVER SIXTIES As part of the ageing process the body begins to metabolize and eliminate drugs more slowly and so there may be the possibility of more frequent or severe side-effects or interactions with other medicines. With some of the drugs in this group there may be an increased possibility of mineral and water soluble vitamin deficiencies.

PROLONGED OR CONTINUED TREATMENT In susceptible people some of the drugs in this group have been found to weaken the heartbeat when used for prolonged or continued treatment. There may also be a possibility of nightmares, hallucinations or sleep disturbances.

STOPPING THE TREATMENT Do not discontinue or attempt to reduce the drugs without consulting your doctor as the dosage may need to be gradually withdrawn to prevent complications such as heartbeat irregularities or angina. If other drugs are being taken at the same time then their dosage may also need to be adjusted.

PERSONAL MEDICINE NOTES

CARDIOVASCULAR SYSTEM
CALCIUM ANTAGONISTS

PRESCRIPTION NAMES

MEDICINES FOR HEART PAINS, CIRCULATION, AND HEART RATE

Calcium antagonists are mainly used for angina pectoris, a heart pain which occurs when the heart's supply of oxygen is too low for its requirements. Calcium antagonists slow the entry of calcium into the heart and blood vessel muscles, thereby opening the blood vessels, and improving blood flow. Blood pressure is reduced and the heart relaxed thus lowering its oxygen requirements. Calcium antagonists are also prescribed for high blood pressure, obstructive circulatory disorders and for increased heart rate.

NAMES OF PRESCRIPTION MEDICINES

The following are commonly prescribed calcium antagonists and are shown with the generic name first, followed by the brand name. If your medicine is not listed by name you should follow the information for the generic, if you know it, as the information given will still apply to your particular medicine. If you are not sure of the generic name your pharmacist will be able to advise you. Please note that ALL the information on this fact sheet applies to calcium antagonists generally, not specifically to any one medicine.

Generic	Brand Name
diltiazem	Tildiem
lidoflazine	Clinium
nicardipine	Cardene
nifedipine	Adalat/Retard
prenylamine	Synadrin
verapamil	Cordilox, Securon/SR
	Berkatens

WHAT TO TELL YOUR DOCTOR

It is important to make sure that your doctor or doctors are given as much information as possible. If you are aware that you are allergic to calcium antagonists then do tell them so. Information on other medication is vital so if you are taking any other type of medicine, including non-prescription drugs, then they must know that too. Additionally, make sure they know if any of the following apply to you:

Breast feeding	Kidney disorders
Diabetes	Liver disorders
Heart disorders	Pregnancy

If you will be having surgery or dental treatment which requires anaesthesia it is important to tell the person in charge that you are taking calcium antagonists.

41

SIDE-EFFECTS AND CAUTIONS

SIDE-EFFECTS It is impossible to predict how any medicine will affect a particular individual because everyone's metabolism is so very different. Sensitivity or reaction to drugs can vary greatly from one person to another and side-effects can be related to dosage. It is important to pay close attention to any changes you may notice either when starting, or during, a course of treatment.

The following are some of the side-effects reported within this group of drugs. Some of the disorders listed under Infrequent or Rare may occasionally be the symptoms of overdose and not always those of side-effects.

INFREQUENT OR RARE

Chest pains
Constipation
Digestive upsets
Dizziness
Drowsiness
Excess saliva*
Flushing skin
Headache
Increased urination*

Irregular or slow heartbeat
Low blood pressure
Nausea
Nightmares
Ringing in the ears
Shakiness
Skin rash
Tiredness
Water retention

*These particular side-effects apply only to nicardipine and are not relevant to the other drugs in this group. The other listed side-effects still apply to nicardipine.

If you experience any of the listed side-effects, or any other unusual symptoms, you should consult your dispensing pharmacist or doctor immediately.

CAUTIONS Some people may experience heart pain shortly after taking the first dose of medicine and if this does occur then contact your doctor immediately for instructions.
If you experience dizziness or drowsiness do not drive, operate machinery or work high above the ground and try to avoid strenuous exercise or exertion whilst taking this drug. Alcohol can increase the effects of dizziness and drowsiness and should be avoided during treatment.

INTERACTIONS

INTERACTIONS WITH OTHER MEDICINES AND SUBSTANCES

No medication works in isolation but is affected to a greater or lesser extent by many other factors such as general fitness, diet and lifestyle. Drinking alcohol may lower the blood pressure and increase side-effects such as dizziness or drowsiness and smoking could increase the heartbeat.

It is also possible to unintentionally combine calcium antagonists with other drugs and this could be dangerous. Check with your doctor or pharmacist before taking any other medication, including non-prescription items, and if you are taking any of the drugs listed below look at the key to find out what effect they may have.

1 Cimetidine
1 Other anti-anginal drugs
1 Other vasodilators

3 Antacids
3 Antiarrhythmics
3 Anticoagulants
3 Anticonvulsants
3 Digitalis drugs
3 Other vasodilators

In combination with calcium antagonists, some diuretics and laxatives may cause a potassium loss which could affect the heartbeat. Other antihypertensives may cause a dangerous drop in blood pressure and beta antagonists used at the same time may cause irregular heartbeat or even heart failure in extreme cases.

KEY 1 INCREASES the effects of calcium antagonists
3 CALCIUM ANTAGONISTS INCREASE the effects of these drugs

INTERACTIONS WITH VITAMINS, MINERALS AND FOODS

Foods which contain dopamine and tyramine can increase blood pressure and may decrease the effectiveness of the medicine if eaten in very large quantities. Vitamin D and calcium supplements can decrease the effects of calcium antagonists as could an extremely high intake of both from the diet. See The Fact Finder and the chapter on Vitamins and Minerals for more information.

Niacin and nicotinic acid supplements produce a vasodilatory effect and may dangerously increase the effects of these medicines. DLPA, an amino acid supplement used for pain relief, depression and weight control, should be used with care if you have high blood pressure as it may be increased in

CARDIOVASCULAR SYSTEM
CALCIUM ANTAGONISTS

CARDIOVASCULAR

susceptible people. Children under the age of eight should not be given DLPA unless recommended by a practitioner, because although it is not thought to be dangerous, its safety in the young has not yet been established. If you are pregnant or suffer from phenylketonuria or are taking MAOI's then DLPA must only be taken under supervision.

Natural liquorice, as found in certain sweets and herbal teas, contains a chemical called glycyrrhizic acid which can elevate blood pressure by causing salt and water retention.

CHILDREN, OVER SIXTIES AND PROLONGED USE

CHILDREN When calcium antagonists are prescribed for children the dosage will be adjusted accordingly.

OVER SIXTIES As part of the ageing process the body begins to metabolize and eliminate drugs more slowly and so there may be the possibility of more frequent or severe side-effects or interactions with other medicines.

PROLONGED OR CONTINUED TREATMENT No data found.

STOPPING THE TREATMENT Do not discontinue or attempt to reduce the drugs without consulting your doctor as the dosage may need to be gradually withdrawn to prevent complications. If other drugs are being taken at the same time then their dosage may also need to be adjusted.

PERSONAL MEDICINE NOTES

CARDIOVASCULAR SYSTEM
CARDIAC GLYCOSIDES, DIGITALIS DRUGS

PRESCRIPTION NAMES

MEDICINES FOR HEART FAILURE AND ATTACK

Cardiac glycosides are commonly known as digitalis drugs and are based on substances extracted from the foxglove and related plants. They are used for atrial fibrillation, which is arrhythmia characterized by rapid and irregular heart and pulse rate, and when the heart is pumping inefficiently. Their action helps to strengthen the force of the heart's contractions which helps improve the blood flow and relieve the accumulation of fluids in the lungs and other areas of the body.

NAMES OF PRESCRIPTION MEDICINES

The following are commonly prescribed digitalis drugs and are shown with the generic name first, followed by the brand name. If your medicine is not listed by name you should follow the information for the generic, if you know it, as the information given will still apply to your particular medicine. If you are not sure of the generic name your pharmacist will be able to advise you. Please note that ALL the information on this fact sheet applies to digitalis drugs generally, not specifically to any one medicine.

Generic	Brand Name
digitoxin	Digitaline Nativelle
digoxin	Lanoxin
lanatoside C	Cedilanid
medigoxin	Lanitop

WHAT TO TELL YOUR DOCTOR

It is important to make sure that your doctor or doctors are given as much information as possible. If you are aware that you are allergic to digitalis drugs then do tell them so. Information on other medication is vital so if you are taking any other type of medicine, including non-prescription drugs, then they must know that too. Additionally, make sure they know if any of the following apply to you:

Breast feeding	Pregnancy
Kidney disorders	Slow heartbeat
Liver disorders	Thyroid disorders
Other heart disorders	

If you will be having surgery or dental treatment which requires anaesthesia it is important to tell the person in charge that you are taking digitalis drugs.

CARDIOVASCULAR SYSTEM
CARDIAC GLYCOSIDES, DIGITALIS DRUGS

SIDE-EFFECTS AND CAUTIONS

SIDE-EFFECTS It is impossible to predict how any medicine will affect a particular individual because everyone's metabolism is so very different. Sensitivity or reaction to drugs can vary greatly from one person to another and side-effects can be related to dosage. It is important to pay close attention to any changes you may notice either when starting, or during, a course of treatment.

The following are some of the side-effects reported within this group of drugs. Some of the disorders listed under Infrequent or Rare may occasionally be the symptoms of overdose and not always those of side-effects.

COMMON

Diarrhoea	Nausea
Loss of appetite	Vomiting

INFREQUENT OR RARE

Blood disorders	Heart disorders
Confusion	Leg or ankle swelling
Depression	Pins and needles
Digestive disorders	Shortness of breath
Drowsiness	Skin rashes
Excessive saliva	Tiredness or fatigue
Facial pain	Vision disorders
Headache	

If you experience any of the listed side-effects, or any other unusual symptoms, you should consult your dispensing pharmacist or doctor immediately.

CAUTIONS If you experience dizziness or drowsiness do not drive, operate machinery or work high above the ground. Alcohol can increase these effects and should be avoided during treatment.

INTERACTIONS

INTERACTIONS WITH OTHER MEDICINES AND SUBSTANCES No medication works in isolation but is affected to a greater or lesser extent by many other factors such as general fitness, diet and lifestyle. Alcohol, smoking and caffeine could all cause irregular heartbeat.

It is also possible to unintentionally combine digitalis with other drugs and this could be dangerous. Check with your doctor or pharmacist before taking any other medication, including

CARDIOVASCULAR

non-prescription items, and if you are taking any of the drugs listed below look at the key to find out what effect they may have.

1 Antiarrhythmic drugs
1 Calcium antagonists
1 NSAI's

2 Antibacterial drugs
2 Antibiotics
2 Anticonvulsants
2 Lipid lowering drugs

5 Antacids, indigestion and ulcer drugs
5 Antifungals
5 Beta blockers
5 Corticosteroids
5 Diuretics
5 Laxatives
5 Lithium

Some diuretics may cause depletion of potassium which could sensitize the heart to these medicines, see Interactions With Vitamins, Minerals and Foods which follows.

Non-prescription cold remedies could cause irregular heartbeat if taken with the drugs in this group.

KEY   1 INCREASES the effects of digitalis drugs
2 DECREASES the effects of digitalis drugs
5 UNPREDICTABLE reactions

INTERACTIONS WITH VITAMINS, MINERALS AND FOODS   Levels of vitamin K, magnesium, zinc and potassium may be decreased by the drugs in this group so you should ensure that your diet supplies plenty of these nutrients. They should come from foods and not from supplements. See the chapter on Vitamins and Minerals.

Salt should be restricted in the diet as it can decrease the medicine's ability to prevent water retention in the body and this should be discussed with your doctor.

Niacin or nicotinic acid should not be taken with these medicines as there could be unpredictable effects. Supplements of vitamins D and E, and the minerals calcium and magnesium, should be taken only under medical supervision as they can affect the action of the drugs.

CARDIOVASCULAR

CHILDREN, OVER SIXTIES AND PROLONGED USE

CHILDREN These medicines may be prescribed for children and their dosage will be scaled down accordingly.

OVER SIXTIES As part of the ageing process the body begins to metabolize and eliminate drugs more slowly and so there may be the possibility of more frequent or severe side-effects or interactions with other medicines.

PROLONGED OR CONTINUED TREATMENT No data found.

STOPPING THE TREATMENT Do not discontinue or attempt to reduce the drugs without consulting your doctor as the dosage may need to be gradually withdrawn in order to prevent complications.

PERSONAL MEDICINE NOTES

PRESCRIPTION NAMES

MEDICINES FOR HIGH BLOOD PRESSURE AND WATER RETENTION

Diuretics are among the most frequently prescribed medicines and are often referred to as 'water pills' because they help the body eliminate excess water and salt via the urine. They are used mainly in the treatment of high blood pressure because their action helps relax and expand the blood vessels and reduces the volume of fluid in the body. They are also used in the treatment of pre-menstrual syndrome, congestive heart failure and water retention caused by disease or other drug therapy. They may also be used during toxaemia in pregnancy or to help stop lactation.

NAMES OF PRESCRIPTION MEDICINES

The following are commonly prescribed diuretics and are shown with the generic name first, followed by the brand name. If your medicine is not listed by name you should follow the information for the generic, if you know it, as the information given will still apply to your particular medicine. If you are not sure of the generic name your pharmacist will be able to advise you. Please note that ALL the information on this fact sheet applies to diuretics generally, not specifically to any one medicine.

THIAZIDE DIURETICS

Generic	Brand Name
bendrofluazide	Aprinox, Berkozide, Centyl, Centyl-K*, Neo-NaClex, Neo-NaClex-K*, Abicol
chlorothiazide	Saluric
chlorthalidone	Hygroton, Hygroton-K*, Kalspare+
clopamide	Brinaldix-K*
cyclopenthiazide	Navidrex, Navidrex-K*
hydrochlorothiazide	Hydrosaluric, Esidrex, Esidrex-K* Moducren+, Moduretic+, Moduret+, Normetic+
hydroflumethiazide	Hydrenox, Rautrax
mefruside	Baycaron
methyclothiazide	Enduron
metolazone	Metenix
polythiazide	Nephril
xipamide	Diurexan

NON THIAZIDE DIURETICS

Generic	Brand Name
amiloride	Midamor+
bumethanide	Burinex

CARDIOVASCULAR SYSTEM
DIURETICS

ethacrynic acid	Edecrin
frusemide	Dryptal, Lasix*, Aluzine, Lasikal*, Frumil, Diumide-K*
piretanide	Arelix
spironolactone	Spiroctan+, Spirolone+, Spiroprop+, Aldactone+, Aldactide+, Lasilactone+, Diatensec+
triamterene	Dytac+, Dytide+, Frusene+, Dyazide+

*Diuretics which contain potassium.
+Diuretics which conserve potassium.

WHAT TO TELL YOUR DOCTOR It is important to make sure that your doctor or doctors are given as much information as possible. If you are aware that you are allergic to diuretic drugs, sulphur antibiotics, or medicines for diabetes, except insulin, then do tell them so. Information on other medication is vital so if you are taking any other type of medicine, including non-prescription drugs, then they must know that too. Additionally, make sure they know if any of the following apply to you:

Actor or singer*	History of depression
Addison's Disease	Kidney disorders
Asthma	Liver disorders
Blood disorders	Pancreas disorders
Breast feeding	Peptic ulcer
Diabetes	Pregnancy
Gout	Prolonged fasting
Hearing disorders	Prostate disorders
Heart disorders	Urinary problems

*Some of the drugs in this group may affect the voice.

If you will be having surgery or dental treatment which requires anaesthesia, or will be having thyroid or glucose tolerance tests, it is important to tell the person in charge that you are taking diuretics.

CARDIOVASCULAR SYSTEM
DIURETICS

SIDE-EFFECTS AND CAUTIONS

SIDE-EFFECTS It is impossible to predict how any medicine will affect a particular individual because everyone's metabolism is so very different. Sensitivity or reaction to drugs can vary greatly from one person to another and side-effects can be related to dosage. It is important to pay close attention to any changes you may notice either when starting, or during, a course of treatment.

The following are some of the side-effects reported within this group of drugs. Some of the disorders listed under Infrequent or Rare may occasionally be the symptoms of overdose and not always those of side-effects.

COMMON

Appetite loss
Drowsiness

Headache
Nausea or vomiting

INFREQUENT OR RARE

Altered potassium and
   sodium levels
Blood sugar disorders
Blue tint to urine*
Breast enlargement in males
Diarrhoea
Dizziness when rising
Dry mouth
Flatulence
Gout
Impotence

Irregular heartbeat
Irregular menstruation
Irritability
Light sensitivity
Low blood pressure
Mental confusion
Muscle pains
Skin rashes
Stomach cramps
Tremors
Vision disorders

*This particular side-effect applies only to triamterene and is not relevant to the other drugs in this group. The other listed side-effects still apply to triamterene.

If you experience any of the listed side-effects, or any other unusual symptoms, you should consult your dispensing pharmacist or doctor immediately.

CAUTIONS Contact your doctor if you experience fever, diarrhoea or excessive perspiration as they can cause dehydration which may lead to a drop in blood pressure and the loss of nutrients.

If you are using a diuretic which contains or conserves potassium you should not use a salt substitute without informing your doctor as many of these contain potassium chloride which could detrimentally increase potassium levels.

If you experience dizziness or drowsiness do not drive, operate machinery or work high above the ground. Alcohol can increase these effects and should be avoided during treatment.

CARDIOVASCULAR

One of the side-effects can be a dry mouth and this may contribute to the chance of tooth decay or gum disease. If this occurs, your doctor will probably advise you to clean your teeth frequently and to use dental floss.

If sunbathing, or using a sun-bed or lamp whilst taking these medicines, then a rash or increased tendency to burn may occur so it may be advisable to avoid exposure or to take extra precautions.

INTERACTIONS

INTERACTIONS WITH OTHER MEDICINES AND SUBSTANCES

No medication works in isolation but is affected to a greater or lesser extent by many other factors such as general fitness, diet and lifestyle. Alcohol can cause an excessive drop in blood pressure and smoking may cause a decreased diuretic effect.

It is also possible to unintentionally combine diuretics with other drugs and this could be dangerous. Check with your doctor or pharmacist before taking any other medication, including non-prescription items, and if you are taking any of the drugs listed below look at the key to find out what effect they may have.

1 Other antihypertensive drugs
1 Other diuretics
1 Some sleeping tablets** -

2 Aspirin, NSAI's and other analgesics
2 Lipid lowering drugs

3 Beta blockers
3 Lithium
3 Other antihypertensives
3 Tranquillizers

4 Antiarrhythmics
4 Antidiabetic drugs and insulin
4 Gout drugs

5 Anticoagulants
5 Digitalis drugs
5 Ulcer medicines

**Often drugs within the same group differ in formulation and may or may not interact with diuretics. Your pharmacist can tell you which specific drugs within a group do interact.

If antidepressants and some calcium antagonists are taken in combination with diuretics they may cause an extreme drop in blood pressure.

KEY
1 INCREASES the effects of diuretics
2 DECREASES the effects of diuretics
3 DIURETICS INCREASE the effects of these drugs
4 DIURETICS DECREASE the effects of these drugs
5 UNPREDICTABLE reactions

INTERACTIONS WITH VITAMINS, MINERALS AND FOODS

Diuretics may deplete water soluble vitamins such as B complex, vitamin C and bioflavonoids and minerals such as potassium, sodium, zinc, magnesium, calcium, phosphorus and iodine. The drugs ethacrynic acid and frusemide do not deplete zinc. If your medicine is not potassium containing or conserving then your doctor will probably give you dietary instructions or supplementation to counteract its loss. Do not take potassium supplements without medical supervision.

Unless directed to do so by your doctor do not change the amount of salt you usually use in your diet. Foods which contain tyramine and dopamine can increase blood pressure if eaten in very large quantities.

There are some cautions to be noted with DLPA, an amino acid supplement used for pain relief, depression and weight loss. It should be used with care if you have high blood pressure as this could be raised in susceptible people. Children under the age of eight should not be given DLPA unless recommended by a practitioner, because although it is not dangerous for adults, its safety in the young has not yet been established. If you are pregnant or suffer from phenylketonuria or are taking MAOI's then DLPA must only be taken under supervision.

The effects of diuretics can be decreased by eating natural liquorice which is found in some sweets or herb teas. It contains a chemical called glycyrrhizic acid which can elevate blood pressure by causing salt and water retention.

If there is a predisposition to gout then diuretics may influence its onset. See the section on How to Help Yourself in the Pain and Inflammation chapter for more information.

CARDIOVASCULAR

CHILDREN, OVER SIXTIES AND PROLONGED USE

CHILDREN　Some of the drugs in this group are suitable for children and the dose will be adjusted accordingly.

OVER SIXTIES　As part of the ageing process the body begins to metabolize and eliminate drugs more slowly and so there may be the possibility of more frequent or severe side-effects or interactions with other medicines. With some of the drugs in this group there is an increased risk of urinary difficulty in men with prostate disorders.

The medicine may need to be adjusted during hot weather or the onset of fever, and you should contact your doctor for instructions. If you are taking diuretics which are not potassium containing or conserving you will be more prone to potassium loss.

There have been reports of these drugs affecting balance in the elderly and treatment with them is usually restricted to 2-4 weeks for the elderly or frail.

PROLONGED OR CONTINUED TREATMENT　In susceptible people some of the drugs in this group have been found to cause possible mineral imbalances when used for prolonged or continued treatment.

STOPPING THE TREATMENT　Do not discontinue or attempt to reduce the drugs without consulting your doctor as the dosage may need to be gradually reduced to prevent complications. If other drugs are being taken at the same time then their dosage may also need to be adjusted.

PERSONAL MEDICINE NOTES

CARDIOVASCULAR SYSTEM
LIPID LOWERING DRUGS

PRESCRIPTION NAMES

MEDICINES FOR HARDENING OF THE ARTERIES AND HIGH CHOLESTEROL LEVELS

The medicines in this group are used to help prevent or counteract the accumulation of excess fatty substances, such as cholesterol and triglycerides, on the walls of the arteries. They work by affecting the enzyme systems and they either prevent excess cholesterol formation or increase cholesterol breakdown and elimination. They are usually used in conjunction with dietary therapy which restricts the intake of fats and alcohol. Lipid lowering drugs may also be helpful for the treatment of skin lesions and the relief of certain types of diarrhoea.

NAMES OF PRESCRIPTION MEDICINES

The following are commonly prescribed lipid lowering drugs and are shown with the generic name first followed by the brand name. If your medicine is not listed by name you should follow the information for the generic, if you know it, as the information given will still apply to your particular medicine. If you are not sure of the generic name your pharmacist will be able to advise you. Please note that ALL the information on this fact sheet applies to lipid lowering drugs generally, not specifically to any one medicine.

Generic	Brand Name
bezafibrate	Bezalip/Mono
cholestyramine	Questran
clofibrate	Atromid-S
colestipol	Colestid
gemfibrozil	Lopid
probucol	Lurselle

WHAT TO TELL YOUR DOCTOR

It is important to make sure that your doctor or doctors are given as much information as possible. If you are aware that you are allergic to any lipid lowering drugs then do tell them so. Information on other medication is vital so if you are taking any other type of medicine, including non-prescription drugs, then they must know that too. Additionally, make sure they know if any of the following apply to you:

Breast feeding	History of jaundice
Chest pains	Liver disorders
Diabetes	Peptic ulcers
Gall bladder disorders	Pregnancy
Heart disease	Unstable heart rhythm

CARDIOVASCULAR SYSTEM
LIPID LOWERING DRUGS

SIDE-EFFECTS AND CAUTIONS

SIDE-EFFECTS It is impossible to predict how any medicine will affect a particular individual because everyone's metabolism is so very different. Sensitivity or reaction to drugs can vary greatly from one person to another and side-effects can be related to dosage. It is important to pay close attention to any changes you may notice either when starting, or during, a course of treatment.

The following are some of the side-effects reported within this group of drugs. Some of the disorders listed under Infrequent or Rare may occasionally be the symptoms of overdose and not always those of side-effects.

COMMON

Constipation	Flatulence
Diarrhoea	Vomiting or nausea

INFREQUENT OR RARE

Abdominal discomfort	Itching, skin rash, or
Appetite change	eruptions and
Blood disorders	de-pigmentation
Chest pains	Loss of hair
Dizziness	Muscle aches or pains
Drowsiness	Palpitations
Headache	Taste abnormalities
Heart rhythm disorders	Vision changes
Impotence	Weight gain

If you experience any of the listed side-effects or any other unusual symptoms, even if they seem unrelated to your medicine, you should consult your dispensing pharmacist or doctor immediately.

CAUTIONS If you are taking probucol or Lurselle it is recommended that this be withdrawn about six months before trying to become pregnant. If you suspect that you have become pregnant since beginning your treatment you must tell your doctor immediately. If you experience dizziness or drowsiness you should not drive, operate machinery or work high above the ground and if you are experiencing these side-effects then do tell your doctor. Alcohol can increase the effects of dizziness and drowsiness so should be avoided during treatment.

CARDIOVASCULAR SYSTEM
LIPID LOWERING DRUGS

INTERACTIONS

INTERACTIONS WITH OTHER MEDICINES AND SUBSTANCES

No medication works in isolation but is affected to a greater or lesser extent by many other factors such as general fitness, diet and lifestyle. When taking lipid lowering drugs it is usually advised that alcohol be severely restricted or avoided altogether.

It is also possible to unintentionally combine lipid lowering drugs with other drugs and this could be dangerous. Check with your doctor or pharmacist before taking any other medication, including non-prescription items, and if you are taking any of the drugs listed below look at the key to find out what effect they may have.

2 Contraceptives

3 Anticoagulants
3 Antidiabetic drugs and insulin

4 Digitalis drugs
4 Some antibiotics**
4 Thiazide diuretics
4 Thyroid hormones

**Often drugs within the same group differ in formulation and may or may not interact with lipid lowering drugs. Your pharmacist can tell you which specific drugs within a group do interact.

KEY

2 DECREASES the effects of lipid lowering drugs
3 LIPID LOWERING DRUGS INCREASE the effects of these medicines
4 LIPID LOWERING DRUGS DECREASE the effects of these medicines

INTERACTIONS WITH VITAMINS, MINERALS AND FOODS

Because the drugs in this group affect the way the body metabolizes fats there is the possibility of some deficiency developing in the absorption of vitamins A, D, E and K which are fat soluble.

Niacin and lecithin affect blood fat levels and could harmfully increase the effect of lipid lowering drugs.

Iron, B12 and folic acid absorption is likely to be decreased and this could especially affect the elderly and some of those who follow a vegetarian or vegan diet.

Cholesterol levels may be raised by the consumption of refined sugars and coffee, including decaffeinated coffee, and this could interfere with your treatment. Your doctor may make

CARDIOVASCULAR

certain dietary suggestions but you should certainly avoid a diet which is high in fats and refined or processed foods. For more information see the Vitamins and Minerals chapter.

CHILDREN, OVER SIXTIES AND PROLONGED USE

CHILDREN These medicines are not usually prescribed for children.

OVER SIXTIES As part of the ageing process the body begins to metabolize and eliminate drugs more slowly and so there may be the possibility of more frequent or severe side-effects or interactions with other medicines. With some of the drugs in this group there may be an increased possibility of constipation and sore or aching muscles.

With long-term use there may be more susceptibility to B12, iron and folic acid deficiency.

PROLONGED OR CONTINUED TREATMENT Unless your doctor is giving you special supplementation of vitamins A, D, E and K or has suggested ensuring your dietary intake is adequate, there is the possibility of a deficiency developing with long-term use. If taking large doses of lipid lowering drugs continuously for up to a year or more you should undergo eye examinations.

STOPPING THE TREATMENT Lipid lowering drugs should not be reduced or discontinued without your doctor's advice. If other drugs are being taken at the same time then their dosage may need to be adjusted.

PERSONAL MEDICINE NOTES

PRESCRIPTION NAMES

MEDICINES FOR HEART PAIN

Nitrite vasodilators are used to help angina pectoris; pain which results from the heart's supply of oxygen being too low for its requirements. These medicines decrease the amount of blood returning to the heart and increase the amount of blood leaving it. This reduces the amount of work the heart has to do and therefore lessens the angina pain.

NAMES OF PRESCRIPTION MEDICINES

The following are commonly prescribed nitrite vasodilators and are shown with the generic name first, followed by the brand name. If your medicine is not listed by name you should follow the information for the generic, if you know it, as the information given will still apply to your particular medicine. If you are not sure of the generic name your pharmacist will be able to advise you. Please note that ALL the information on this fact sheet applies to nitrite vasodilators generally, not specifically to any one medicine.

Generic	Brand Name
glyceryl trinitrate	Sustac, Suscard, Transiderm-Nitro 5/10, GTN, Nitrocontin, Coro-Nitro Spray, Deponit 5, Nitrolingual,
isosorbide dinitrate	Cedocard 40/Retard 40, Isoket/Retard 40, Isordil, Soni-Slo, Sorbichew, Sorbid-SA, Sorbitrate, Vascardin
isosorbide mononitrate	Monit, Elantan, Ismo, Mono-Cedocard
pentaerythritol tetra nitrate	Mycardol, Peritrate, Cardiacap

WHAT TO TELL YOUR DOCTOR

It is important to make sure that your doctor or doctors are given as much information as possible. If you are aware that you are allergic to nitrite vasodilators then do tell them so. Information on other medication is vital so if you are taking any other type of medicine, including non-prescription drugs, then they must know that too. Additionally, make sure they know if any of the following apply to you:

Breast feeding	Heart problems
Breathing disorders	Kidney disorders
Diabetes	Liver disorders
Emphysema	Low blood pressure
Glaucoma	Pregnancy
Head injury	

CARDIOVASCULAR

SIDE-EFFECTS AND CAUTIONS

SIDE-EFFECTS   It is impossible to predict how any medicine will affect a particular individual because everyone's metabolism is so very different. Sensitivity or reaction to drugs can vary greatly from one person to another and side-effects can be related to dosage. It is important to pay close attention to any changes you may notice either when starting, or during, a course of treatment.

The following are some of the side-effects reported within this group of drugs. Some of the disorders listed under Infrequent or Rare may occasionally be the symptoms of overdose and not always those of side-effects.

COMMON   Nausea or vomiting   Palpitations

INFREQUENT OR RARE
Blood disorders	Fainting
Breathing problems	Low blood pressure
Cold skin	Muscle weakness
Dizziness	Restlessness
Dry rash	Weakness

If you experience any of the listed side-effects, or any other unusual symptoms, you should consult your dispensing pharmacist or doctor immediately.

CAUTIONS   It is not advisable to put these drugs in the same container as other drugs, or to move them to a different container from the one they were dispensed in, as this will weaken their effect.

If you experience dizziness or drowsiness do not drive, operate machinery or work high above the ground. Alcohol can increase these effects and should be avoided during treatment.

INTERACTIONS

INTERACTIONS WITH OTHER MEDICINES AND SUBSTANCES   No medication works in isolation but is affected to a greater or lesser extent by many other factors such as general fitness, diet, lifestyle etc. Side-effects may be increased by alcohol. Smoking may decrease the action of nitrite vasodilators.

It is also possible to unintentionally combine nitrite vasodilators with other drugs and this could be dangerous. Check with your doctor or pharmacist before taking any other medication, including non-prescription items, and if you are taking any of the drugs listed below look at the key to find out what effect they may have.

5	Antihypertensives	5	Beta blockers
5	Antinauseants	5	Calcium antagonists

KEY   5   UNPREDICTABLE reactions

INTERACTIONS WITH VITAMINS, MINERALS AND FOODS

Niacin and nicotinic acid supplements produce a vasodilatory effect and may dangerously increase the effects of these medicines. Large supplementary doses of vitamin E also have a vasodilatory effect and should only be taken under supervision.

CHILDREN, OVER SIXTIES AND PROLONGED USE

CHILDREN

Because the safety for children has not been established, nitrite vasodilators are generally not recommended for the young.

OVER SIXTIES

As part of the ageing process the body begins to metabolize and eliminate drugs more slowly and so there may be the possibility of more frequent or severe side-effects or interactions with other medicines.

PROLONGED OR CONTINUED TREATMENT

No data found.

STOPPING THE TREATMENT

Nitrite vasodilators should not be discontinued or reduced without consulting your doctor. They may need to be gradually withdrawn, under supervision, to prevent complications.

PERSONAL MEDICINE NOTES

CARDIOVASCULAR

PRESCRIPTION NAMES

MEDICINES FOR IMPROVING BLOOD FLOW

Vasodilators increase the diameter of the blood vessels, improving blood flow and increasing its circulation throughout the body. This group is used to treat circulation disorders including arteriosclerosis, decreased circulation to the brain, head and extremities, night cramps, pain in the limbs and skin ulcers.

NAMES OF PRESCRIPTION MEDICINES

The following are commonly prescribed vasodilators and are shown with the generic name first, followed by the brand name. If your medicine is not listed by name you should follow the information for the generic, if you know it, as the information given will still apply to your particular medicine. If you are not sure of the generic name your pharmacist will be able to advise you. Please note that ALL the information on this fact sheet applies to vasodilators generally, not specifically to any one medicine.

Generic	Brand Name
cyclandelate	Cyclobral, Cyclospasmol
inositol nicotinate	Hexopal
isoxsuprine	Duvadilan, Defencin CP
naftidrofuryl	Praxilene
nicofuranose	Bradilan
nicotinyl	Ronicol
oxpentifylline	Trental
thymoxamine	Opilon

WHAT TO TELL YOUR DOCTOR

It is important to make sure that your doctor or doctors are given as much information as possible. If you are aware that you are allergic to vasodilators then do tell them so. Information on other medication is vital so if you are taking any other type of medicine, including non-prescription drugs, then they must know that too. Additionally, make sure they know if any of the following apply to you:

Blood sugar disorders	Liver disorders
Breast feeding	Low blood pressure
Diabetes	Pregnancy
Glaucoma	Stomach ulcers
Heart disorders	Stroke
Kidney disorders	Thyroid disorders

If you will be having surgery or dental treatment which requires anaesthesia it is important to tell the person in charge that you are taking vasodilators.

CARDIOVASCULAR SYSTEM
VASODILATORS

SIDE-EFFECTS AND CAUTIONS

SIDE-EFFECTS It is impossible to predict how any medicine will affect a particular individual because everyone's metabolism is so very different. Sensitivity or reaction to drugs can vary greatly from one person to another and side-effects can be related to dosage. It is important to pay close attention to any changes you may notice either when starting, or during, a course of treatment.

The following are some of the side-effects reported within this group of drugs. Some of the disorders listed under Infrequent or Rare may occasionally be the symptoms of overdose and not always those of side-effects.

INFREQUENT OR RARE

Diarrhoea	Irregular or rapid heartbeat
Digestive disorders	Low blood pressure
Dizziness	Nausea or vomiting
Fatigue	Pins and needles
Headache	Skin flushing or itching

If you experience any of the listed side-effects, or any other unusual symptoms, you should consult your dispensing pharmacist or doctor immediately.

CAUTIONS If you experience dizziness or drowsiness do not drive, operate machinery or work high above the ground. Alcohol can increase these effects and should be avoided during treatment. A sudden increase in temperature, such as going into a very warm room immediately after taking the medicine, could increase the vasodilatory effect which may not be beneficial.

INTERACTIONS

INTERACTIONS WITH OTHER MEDICINES AND SUBSTANCES No medication works in isolation but is affected to a greater or lesser extent by many other factors such as general fitness, diet, lifestyle etc. Alcohol can increase the effects of some vasodilators and smoking may decrease them.
It is also possible to unintentionally combine vasodilators with other drugs and this could be dangerous. Check with your doctor or pharmacist before taking any other medication, including non-prescription items, and if you are taking any of the drugs listed below look at the key to find out what effect they may have.

CARDIOVASCULAR SYSTEM
VASODILATORS

1 Beta blockers
1 Calcium antagonists
1 Nitrite vasodilators
1 Other vasodilators

3 Calcium antagonists
3 Insulin
3 Nitrite vasodilators
3 Other vasodilators

5 Antidepressants

KEY 1 INCREASES the effects of vasodilators
3 VASODILATORS INCREASE the effects of these drugs
5 UNPREDICTABLE reactions

INTERACTIONS WITH VITAMINS, MINERALS AND FOODS A number of these medicines are based on nicotinic acid because of its vasodilatory effects. Taking supplements of niacin or nicotinic acid with these medicines may therefore lead to an unpredictable reaction or increase in their effects. Large supplementary doses of vitamin E may have slight vasodilatory action and could increase the effects of these drugs and should only be taken under supervision.

CHILDREN, OVER SIXTIES AND PROLONGED USE

CHILDREN Vasodilators are generally not recommended for children, but where they are prescribed the dosage is adjusted accordingly.

OVER SIXTIES As part of the ageing process the body begins to metabolize and eliminate drugs more slowly and so there may be the possibility of more frequent or severe side-effects or interactions with other medicines. With some of the drugs in this group there may be an increased sensitivity to temperature changes.

PROLONGED OR CONTINUED TREATMENT No data found.

STOPPING THE TREATMENT Vasodilators should not be discontinued or the dosage reduced without your doctor's advice as they may need to be gradually withdrawn to prevent complications.

The heart is the root of life.
Nei Ching by Chinese Emperor Huang Ti

Although there are many factors which can lead to heart disease, or atherosclerosis, it seems fairly clear that stress, diet, smoking and lifestyle all play their part in determining what degree of susceptibility to cardiovascular disease you may have.

CARDIOVASCULAR

The suggestions offered here are designed to help generally with your condition, but it is very important that you do not try to treat yourself. If you suffer severely or regularly from a particular complaint, any serious disorder, or are pregnant then you should not use these remedies before discussion with a doctor. Always report any side-effects and seek medical advice before trying natural remedies and if within a period of one week there has been no improvement then you should consult your doctor.

There are only a few specific natural remedies given here for cardiovascular problems as the nature of these disorders makes it dangerous to attempt any treatment other than that given by your doctor. What can be done, however, is to work on preventive measures and in addition to the suggestions given here you may find it helpful to consult an alternative/complementary practitioner for preventive advice or assistance. Particularly useful may be an acupuncturist, herbalist, homoeopath or naturopath, or any combination of them that you may feel applicable to you. Relaxation techniques and the control of stress and tension can be useful and it may be worth looking into areas such as chiropractic, osteopathy, meditation, bio-feedback, Alexander technique, t'ai-chi, yoga, aromatherapy, massage and reflexology. For more detailed information on the individual therapies, together with how to find a practitioner in your area, please refer to the chapter on Alternative/Complementary Medicine and Therapies.

It is possible that certain remedies, supplements or foods could react dangerously with the drugs you are already using so you must check with the fact sheet relating to your medicine to avoid interactions. Please note that it is not advisable to gather your own herbs unless you are sure they are free of any chemicals or pollutants and you can positively identify the correct variety. Always make sure that supplements or natural remedies are taken two to three hours apart from any drugs.

If while reading you come across a particular word or term that is unfamiliar to you please look in The Fact Finder; information on nutrients will be found in the chapter on Vitamins and Minerals.

NATURAL REMEDIES

DIETARY SUGGESTIONS

Being overweight is the first of several negative factors you should be aware of if you suffer from heart problems because for every pound of weight gained there is a corresponding increase in blood volume, resulting in the heart having to work harder. There are many specialist books dealing solely with the diet that is recommended for those with heart problems but definitely to be avoided are saturated fats, hydrogenated fats and some vegetable oils as they can contribute to excess cholesterol in the blood and possible atherosclerosis. The consumption of refined sugars and refined carbohydrates can increase the levels of triglyceride blood fats which may also cause atherosclerosis. If alcohol is consumed in large quantities it too can increase triglycerides, as well as elevating blood pressure and causing irregular heartbeats.

Smoking can contribute to, or worsen, cardiovascular disease and angina pains because the nicotine in tobacco may accelerate hardening of the arteries. It also stimulates production of the hormone adrenalin which makes the heart beat harder and faster, putting it under more strain. The carbon monoxide in the smoke combines with the haemoglobin in the blood and reduces the amount of oxygen available to the heart and may also encourage thrombosis. Smoking also destroys vitamin C, a nutrient which is essential to cardiovascular health. Approximately 25mg is lost with each cigarette smoked and similar losses apply to cigars and loose tobacco. Requirements of vitamin A, B complex and E are also increased by smoking.

Another contributor to heart disease can be caffeine as it increases the levels of two blood proteins which are associated with high cholesterol and it also acts as a stimulant on the cardiovascular system. Sources of caffeine are listed in The Fact Finder. If it's not a sweet tooth but a savoury one that is your downfall, then please note that salt and food additives may also contribute to high blood pressure in susceptible people.

Research has been done on the soluble bran fibre found mainly in oats and in pinto beans. This fibre contains beta glucans which is what makes oatmeal or oatbran sticky. It appears that when this ferments in the intestines it may stop some of the liver's cholesterol production and help remove cholesterol from the blood.

STRENGTHENING THE CARDIOVASCULAR SYSTEM

If you want to strengthen your whole cardiovascular system and help burn up harmful fats then moderate regular exercise can help if undertaken gently at first and under supervision. If you

CARDIOVASCULAR

suffer from a severe heart condition or high blood pressure you must check with your doctor first before embarking on any new fitness regime.

IMPORTANT NUTRIENTS

The cardiovascular system must have certain nutrients to stay healthy, and you can check with the chapter on Vitamins and Minerals to see if your diet provides an adequate supply. If it does not, then try to incorporate as many into your diet as possible, but do not take vitamin supplements without checking with the data sheet for any interactions between your medicine and the supplement. You should also consult your doctor before using supplements or natural remedies.

Vitamins
Vitamin B complex for helping the body cope with stress.

B3* helps increase blood circulation, reduce high blood pressure and reduce cholesterol.

B6 helps lower cholesterol and protect the artery walls.

Vitamin C* with bioflavonoids helps strengthen the vascular system.

Vitamin E* helps prevent blood clots and high blood pressure.

Fatty acids used sparingly can help prevent atherosclerosis. IMPORTANT NOTE: *If you wish to take these nutrients in supplement form then please see the chapter on Vitamins and Minerals for important warnings about their use.

Minerals
Calcium is essential for normal heart contractions.

Magnesium has a calming influence on the nervous system and helps prevent heart disease and hypertension.

Potassium is essential for normal heartbeat and in maintaining normal blood pressure.

Selenium works with vitamin E to help prevent heart disease.

Chromium helps lower high blood pressure and cholesterol levels.

Iodine helps regulate cholesterol levels.

Others
EPA/DHA assist in strengthening the cardiovascular system.

Lecithin may help reduce or prevent the build-up of cholesterol in the arteries.

Evening primrose oil is important for a healthy cardiovascular system. It contains GLA which is required for the production of prostaglandin E1 which helps lower cholesterol levels.

Octocosonal is found in wheatgerm and is beneficial to cardiovascular health.

ANXIETY AND NERVOUSNESS

A soothing herb tea can be made by putting an eighth of a teaspoon each of sage, chamomile, catnip, lemon verbena and rosemary into a teapot and pouring boiling water over them. This should be steeped for about three minutes and drunk 2-3 times a day. It can be flavoured with lemon and a little honey if desired.

Tryptophane is an amino acid which has a calming and relaxing effect. It is important that it is taken on an empty stomach 2-3 hours after food or half an hour before eating.

High potency vitamin B complex, including B5 and B6, has been found helpful when taken two to three times per day with food. The B complex vitamins are important for healthy functioning of the nervous system and include inositol which has a calming effect on the brain similar to that of tranquillizers. Inositol is present in lecithin and if used in this form should be balanced with calcium to offset its high phosphorus content. It is generally not advisable to take B complex in the evening as it can keep some people awake. Most B complex tablets colour the urine a bright yellow, due to their B2 content, but this is a harmless reaction. Other nutrients which can be calming are the bioflavonoids including rutin and these are best taken with vitamin C.

Calcium and magnesium are also important in the proper functioning of the nervous system and have a calming effect on the body. They are often used in equal ratio doses ranging from 500-1000mg per day. Up to 30mg of zinc a day may also prove beneficial.

Homoeopathic Gelsemium 6x is often helpful for general feelings of anxiety, including visits to the dentist and stage-fright.

Many people find that the Bach flower rescue remedy helps them in situations where they experience nervousness or anxiety. The remedies can be chosen according to emotions and personality and you may find others from the Bach flower remedies which are particularly suited to you. More information on them will be found in the chapter on Alternative/Complementary Medicine and Therapies.

CARDIOVASCULAR

A very powerful relaxing herb tea can be made from a combination of no more than a sixteenth of a teaspoon each of valerian, lady's slipper, skullcap and hops mixed together and placed in a teapot. Pour boiling water over the herbs and allow them to steep for about three minutes. One cupful can be sipped throughout the day as needed, leaving a little for a bedtime drink but do not drink more than one cup of this mixture per day and avoid using it for more than a week without guidance from a herbalist. This mixture does not have a very pleasant taste or smell and honey and lemon can be added if required. If you are using this tea then valerian and hop tablets must not be taken in conjunction with it. If you prefer you can take them separately, instead of the tea, as their calming effects may be helpful.

Try to avoid alcohol, foods and beverages high in caffeine, sugar and refined or processed foods which can all rob your body of important nutrients, especially B complex vitamins and zinc.

Relaxation techniques and tapes can be very beneficial and information on Relaxation for Living can be found in the chapter on Alternative/Complementary Medicine and Therapies.

BLOOD PRESSURE Clinical studies have shown the usefulness of uncooked garlic in the lowering or normalizing of blood pressure. When you have finished your course of treatment for hypertension, you may wish to discuss this with your doctor and consult an alternative/complementary practitioner for preventive advice.

GOUT Diuretic drugs may cause gout in susceptible people, and if this happens a low purine diet is generally suggested. High purine foods can contribute to uric acid formation and should be avoided. They include offal, red meat, fish, seafoods, spinach, mushrooms, peas, asparagus and dried beans. Some items can add to gout pain such as sugar, sweetmeats, fried foods, alcohol especially port, cheeses, excess salt, refined foods, caffeine rich foods and substances such as coffee, chocolate, colas, and some cold remedies.

Cherries or unsweetened cherry juice are one of the best natural remedies for gout. Experimenting with different amounts should enable you to find how much you need to drink to obtain relief and it may take a little while before you begin to feel the benefit. Drink plenty of spring water and take supplementary vitamin C with bioflavonoids as they can help carry waste acids from the body. Foods which are high in potassium and the whole spectrum of minerals, especially calcium, magnesium, and zinc, are also important.

Orotic acid is found in whey, which is extracted from milk during the cheese making process. It helps the body excrete uric acid.

B3 competes with uric acid for excretion from the body and may worsen gout if taken in supplement form. Supplements of RNA can also worsen an attack of gout.

Homoeopathic tissue salts Nat. Phos. and Silicea are used to help gout.

PALPITATIONS OR ABNORMALLY RAPID HEARTBEAT

Palpitations may be a sign of a serious disorder and must be discussed with a doctor before any attempt is made to use natural remedies. If palpitations persist after trying a natural approach for 3-4 days then please consult your doctor.

Half a teaspoon of the herb rosemary steeped in a cup of boiled water for about three minutes makes a helpful tea which can be drunk 3-4 times a day.

The homoeopathic tissue salt Ferr. Phos. is used to help this condition.

A good dietary intake of B complex vitamins (including B6, B5, and B12) and minerals such as calcium, magnesium and especially potassium can sometimes help palpitations. It is generally not advisable to take B complex in the evening as it can keep some people awake. Most B complex tablets colour the urine a bright yellow, due to the B2 content, but this is a harmless reaction.

Plunging your face into a basin of cold water for about 15-20 seconds, although it sounds unlikely, has the temporary effect of helping palpitations, but should not be attempted if you have any type of heart disorder or before it has been discussed with a doctor.

Some items that can worsen or cause palpitations are a high salt intake, alcohol, sugar, smoking, and caffeine. Details of caffeine containing items are in The Fact Finder. Eating large quantities of natural liquorice can contribute to palpitations as it decreases potassium in the body.

DIGESTIVE SYSTEM
CONTENTS

DIGESTIVE SYSTEM

DIGESTIVE SYSTEM
INTRODUCTION

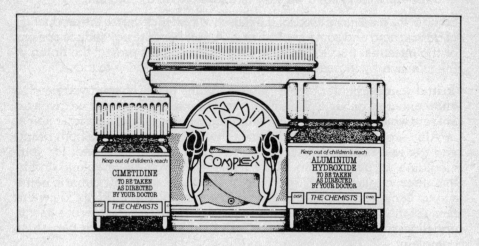

Where to find information on related disorders:
Gastro-intestinal infections — see antidiarrhoeals and antibiotics.
Ulcerative colitis — see sulphonamides.
Ulcers — see antinauseants and Domperidone.

The digestive system is a food processing factory where nutrients are broken down into a form which the body can use. This takes place without our conscious control and we are not generally aware of it unless there is some malfunction. There is a critical balance which has to be maintained between both beneficial and harmful bacteria, acidity and alkalinity, and the digestive juices. It is when this is disturbed that digestive disorders can occur.

The digestive tract begins at the mouth and includes the pharynx, oesophagus, stomach and the small and large intestine. Added to these are the secretions produced by the salivary glands, pancreas and liver, all of which are important in the digestive process. Foods and fluids are mixed in the stomach by its muscular contractions and partially digested by hydrochloric acid and pepsin which are secreted by cells in the stomach walls. The breakdown of foodstuffs and the absorption of nutrients into the bloodstream takes place in the small intestine; the matter then travels to the large intestine or colon where water is absorbed back into the body and the remaining solid wastes are excreted via the rectum.

Some of the medicines used for the digestive system decrease the production of gastric acid and some neutralize it. A number of drugs reduce spasms or the intestinal tract's muscular activity and others protect the lining of the stomach by increasing the production of protective mucus.

To find your particular prescription medicine in this chapter you need to know either its generic or brand name. For instance you may be given an antacid which is labelled either aluminium hydroxide, the generic name, or Alu-Cap which is a brand name. The index of drugs lists both brand and generic names to enable you to find the right fact sheet for your medicine. If your medicine has a name which you are unable to find in the index, contact your dispensing chemist and ask for its generic name so you can check whether it has been included. If you do not know the name of your drug, you may prefer to check in the separate index of ailments and illnesses to find the drugs that may be prescribed for your particular complaint.

At the end of this group of fact sheets you will find a section on how to help yourself with suggestions for natural remedies and therapies that may be of assistance. Information about practitioners will be found in the chapter on Alternative/Complementary Medicine and Therapies.

If you come across a particular word or term that is unfamiliar to you, please look in The Fact Finder for an explanation; information on food and nutrition will be found in the chapter on Vitamins and Minerals.

DIGESTIVE SYSTEM

PRESCRIPTION NAMES

MEDICINES FOR HEARTBURN, ACID INDIGESTION, ULCERS AND UPSET STOMACH

Antacids are alkaline and their action relieves pain by neutralizing acid in the contents of the stomach. They may be used to treat heartburn and acid indigestion and can help to relieve ulcer pain.

NAMES OF PRESCRIPTION MEDICINES

The following are commonly prescribed antacids and are shown with the generic name first, followed by the brand name. If your medicine is not listed by name you should follow the information for the generic, if you know it, as the information given will still apply to your particular medicine. If you are not sure of the generic name your pharmacist will be able to advise you. Please note that ALL the information on this fact sheet applies to aluminium hydroxide based antacids generally, not specifically to any one medicine.

Generic
aluminium hydroxide

Brand Name
Alu-Cap, APP, Diovol, Gastrocote, Gastron, Gaviscon, Gelusil, *Kolanticon, *Kolantyl, Lo-Asid, Maalox, Mucaine, Mucogel, Polyalk, Pyrogastrone, Topal

*Kolanticon and Kolantyl are aluminium hydroxide based antacids which also contain dicyclomine, an anticholinergic drug. See also the anticholinergic fact sheet.

WHAT TO TELL YOUR DOCTOR

It is important to make sure that your doctor or doctors are given as much information as possible. If you are aware that you are allergic to any antacids then do tell them so. Information on other medication is vital so if you are taking any other type of medicine, including non-prescription drugs, then they must know that too. Additionally, make sure they know if any of the following apply to you:

Acute stomach pain
Breast feeding
Colitis
Constipation
Diarrhoea
Glaucoma
Heart rhythm disorders
Hiatus hernia

Ileitis
Liver or kidney disorders
Myasthenia gravis
Pregnancy
Prostate disorders
Stomach or intestinal
  bleeding
Urine retention

SIDE-EFFECTS AND CAUTIONS

SIDE-EFFECTS It is impossible to predict how any medicine will affect a particular individual because everyone's metabolism is so very different. Sensitivity or reaction to drugs can vary greatly from one person to another and side-effects can be related to dosage. It is important to pay close attention to any changes you may notice either when starting, or during, a course of treatment.

The following are some of the side-effects reported within this group of drugs. Some of the disorders listed under Infrequent or Rare may occasionally be the symptoms of overdose and not always those of side-effects.

INFREQUENT OR RARE

Appetite loss	Gastro-intestinal upsets
Blurred vision*	Nausea or vomiting
Constipation or diarrhœa	Palpitations*
Difficulty swallowing*	Swollen ankles
Difficulty urinating*	Thirst*
Dry mouth*	Water retention
Flushing or dry skin*	Weight loss

*These particular side-effects apply only to Kolanticon and Kolantyl and are not relevant to the other drugs in this group. The other listed side-effects still apply to Kolanticon and Kolantyl.

If you experience any of the listed side-effects, or any other unusual symptoms, you should consult your dispensing pharmacist or doctor immediately.

CAUTIONS Overdose could cause fatigue, weakness or dizziness. If you experience any of these symptoms contact your doctor as soon as possible.

If you experience dizziness or drowsiness do not drive, operate machinery or work high above the ground. Alcohol can increase these effects and should be avoided during treatment.

One of the side-effects can be a dry mouth and this may contribute to the possibility of tooth decay or gum disease. If this occurs, your doctor will probably advise you to clean your teeth frequently and to use dental floss.

DIGESTIVE SYSTEM

INTERACTIONS

INTERACTIONS WITH OTHER MEDICINES AND SUBSTANCES

No medication works in isolation but is affected to a greater or lesser extent by many other factors such as general fitness, diet and lifestyle. Alcohol and smoking could decrease the effectiveness of antacids.

It is also possible to unintentionally combine antacids with other drugs and this could be dangerous. Check with your doctor or pharmacist before taking any other medication, including non-prescription items, and if you are taking anything listed below look at the key to find out what effect they may have.

3 Pseudoephedrine based decongestants
3 Quinidine antiarrhythmic drugs

4 Antibiotics and anti-infectives
4 Anticoagulants
4 Cimetidine and ranitidine
4 Digitalis drugs
4 Tranquillizers

5 Beta blockers
5 Diuretics
5 Some arthritis drugs**

**Often drugs within the same group differ in formulation and may or may not interact with antacids. Your pharmacist can tell you which specific drugs within a group do interact.

Antacids may decrease the effectiveness of the enteric coating which is found on some tablets.

KEY
3 ANTACIDS INCREASE the effects of these drugs
4 ANTACIDS DECREASE the effects of these drugs
5 UNPREDICTABLE reactions

INTERACTIONS WITH VITAMINS, MINERALS AND FOODS

Antacids can decrease the absorption of iron, vitamins A, C, some B complex, especially B1, B2, B12, B6 and folic acid. Antacids can also lead to a disturbance in phosphorus, magnesium and calcium levels, especially if used for prolonged treatment. For details of where these appear in the diet see the chapter on Vitamins and Minerals.

Food may become harder to swallow if you suffer from a dry mouth while taking these medicines, and the ability to digest starches and carbohydrates will be affected. An important element in this digestion is the enzyme ptyalin, which is present in saliva, and in order to stimulate its flow all food should be chewed extremely well before swallowing.

CHILDREN, OVER SIXTIES AND PROLONGED USE

CHILDREN Antacids are generally not recommended for the young.

OVER SIXTIES As part of the ageing process the body begins to metabolize and eliminate drugs more slowly and so there may be the possibility of more frequent or severe side-effects or interactions with other medicines. There may be an increased possibility of diarrhoea or constipation. Prolonged use of these antacids could also mean more susceptibility to weakening of the bones.

PROLONGED OR CONTINUED TREATMENT These antacids decrease the levels of phosphorus in the body, the symptoms of which include loss of appetite, tiredness and muscle weakness. This could lead to a disturbance in calcium levels and bone or joint disorders could develop. Levels of iron, vitamins A, C, and B complex, especially B1, B2, B6 and B12, are also decreased.

STOPPING THE TREATMENT Tell your doctor if your antacid has not helped your condition within seven days of treatment and follow your doctor's advice for discontinuing the medicine.

PERSONAL MEDICINE NOTES

PRESCRIPTION NAMES

MEDICINES FOR ULCERS, MUSCLE SPASMS, AND INTESTINAL CRAMPING

Anticholinergic and antispasmodic drugs are used to reduce both the stomach's acid production and the spasms which can occur in the stomach and intestines. Unlike antacids, they do not neutralize acid but instead interfere with the stimulation of cholinergic nerves which are responsible for increasing the production of gastric juices and the muscular movements of the stomach and intestines. They are used in the treatment of ulcers and cramping or spasm of the digestive or urinary systems.

NAMES OF PRESCRIPTION MEDICINES

The following are commonly prescribed anticholinergics and antispasmodics and are shown with the generic name first, followed by the brand name. If your medicine is not listed by name you should follow the information for the generic, if you know it, as the information given will still apply to your particular medicine. If you are not sure of the generic name your pharmacist will be able to advise you. Please note that ALL the information on this fact sheet applies to anticholinergics and antispasmodics generally, not specifically to any one medicine.

Generic	Brand Name
alverine	Spasmonal
dicyclomine	Merbentyl/20
glycopyrrolate	Robinul
hyoscine	Buscopan
hyoscyamine	Peptard
isopropamide	Stelabid
mebeverine	Colofac, Colven
mepenzolate	Cantil
pipenzolate	Piptal, Piptalin
piperiodlate	Dactil
pirenzipine	Gastrozepin
poldine	Nacton
propantheline	Pro-Banthine

WHAT TO TELL YOUR DOCTOR

It is important to make sure that your doctor or doctors are given as much information as possible. If you are aware that you are allergic to any anticholinergics, antispasmodics, atropine, belladonna or iodine then do tell them so. Information on other medication is vital so if you are taking any other type of medicine, including non-prescription drugs, then they must know that too. Additionally, make sure they know if any of the following apply to you:

Angina pectoris
Blood disorders

Breast feeding
Breathing difficulties

DIGESTIVE SYSTEM
ANTICHOLINERGICS AND ANTISPASMODICS

Glacucoma
Hiatus hernia
Liver or kidney disorders
Myasthenia gravis

Pregancy
Prostate disorders
Ulcerative colitis
Urinary disorders

If you will be having surgery or dental treatment which requires anaesthesia it is important to tell the person in charge that you are taking anticholinergic or antispasmodic drugs.

SIDE-EFFECTS AND CAUTIONS

SIDE-EFFECTS It is impossible to predict how any medicine will affect a particular individual because everyone's metabolism is so very different. Sensitivity or reaction to drugs can vary greatly from one person to another and side-effects can be related to dosage. It is important to pay close attention to any changes you may notice either when starting, or during, a course of treatment.

The following are some of the side-effects reported within this group of drugs. Some of the disorders listed under Infrequent or Rare may occasionally be the symptoms of overdose and not always those of side-effects.

INFREQUENT OR RARE

Bloating
Confusion
Constipation
Decreased sexual desire or
    ability
Difficulty urinating
Dry mouth
Dry skin
Flushing
Headache

Increased pulse rate
Intolerance to light
Irregular heartbeat
Loss of sense of taste
Nausea
Skin rash
Swallowing problems
Tiredness
Visual disturbances
Vomiting

If you experience any of the listed side-effects, or any other unusual symptoms, you should consult your dispensing pharmacist or doctor immediately.

CAUTIONS If you experience dizziness or drowsiness do not drive, operate machinery or work high above the ground. Alcohol can increase these effects and should be avoided during treatment.

Some of the drugs in this group can prevent you from sweating normally and could make you more sensitive to heat or heat stroke. Try not to become overheated whether from a hot atmosphere, exercise, bathing or saunas.

If you experience a dry mouth as a side-effect it can contribute to the chance of tooth decay or gum disease. Your doctor will probably advise you to clean your teeth frequently and to use dental floss.

INTERACTIONS

INTERACTIONS WITH OTHER MEDICINES AND SUBSTANCES

No medication works in isolation but is affected to a greater or lesser extent by many other factors such as general fitness, diet and lifestyle.

It is also possible to unintentionally combine anticholinergics and antispasmodics with other drugs and this could be dangerous. Check with your doctor or pharmacist before taking any other medication, including non-prescription items and if you are taking anything listed below look at the key to find out what effect they may have.

1   Antidepressants including MAOI's
1   Antihistamines
1   Antiparkinsonian drugs
1   Digitalis drugs
1   Other anticholinergics or antispasmodics
1   Tranquillizers, sedatives, sleeping tablets
1   Ulcer drugs

4   Glaucoma eye drops

Some anti-inflammatory drugs, and some tranquillizers, can cause increased pressure in the eye when taken with anticholinergic or antispasmodic medicines.

KEY

1   INCREASES the effects of anticholinergics or antispasmodics
4   ANTICHOLINERGICS AND ANTISPASMODICS DECREASE the effects of these drugs

INTERACTIONS WITH VITAMINS, MINERALS AND FOODS

If vitamin C is taken in high doses it can decrease the effects of the medicines and levels of vitamin K may be decreased during treatment. It is possible that a very large intake of alkaline foods could decrease the excretion of these drugs and increase their side-effects.

If you have a peptic ulcer you should avoid using vitamin B3 in the form of niacin or nicotinic acid because it can irritate the condition.

Food may become harder to swallow if you suffer from a dry mouth while taking these medicines, and the ability to digest starches and carbohydrates will be affected. An important element in this digestion is the enzyme ptyalin, which is present in saliva, and in order to stimulate its flow all food should be chewed extremely well before swallowing.

CHILDREN, OVER SIXTIES AND PROLONGED USE

CHILDREN These medicines may occasionally be prescribed for children and the dosage will be adjusted accordingly.

OVER SIXTIES As part of the ageing process the body begins to metabolize and eliminate drugs more slowly and so there may be the possibility of more frequent or severe side-effects or interactions with other medicines. In susceptible people there may be more chance of experiencing constipation and/or mental confusion as possible side-effects.

PROLONGED OR CONTINUED TREATMENT If you are on these drugs for a prolonged period of time chronic constipation or stool impaction could occur.

STOPPING THE TREATMENT Do not discontinue the medicine without your doctor's advice. If you experience any unusual symptoms after withdrawal of the treatment then contact your doctor.

PERSONAL MEDICINE NOTES

PRESCRIPTION NAMES

MEDICINES FOR DIARRHOEA AND SOME FORMS OF COLITIS

Certain types of acute diarrhoea and colitis can be helped by the drugs in this group because they reduce the intestinal tract's muscular activity.

NAMES OF PRESCRIPTION MEDICINES

The following are commonly prescribed antidiarrhoeals and are shown with the generic name first, followed by the brand name. If your medicine is not listed by name you should follow the information for the generic, if you know it, as the information given will still apply to your particular medicine. If you are not sure of the generic name your pharmacist will be able to advise you. Please note that ALL the information on this fact sheet applies to antidiarrhoeals generally, not specifically to any one medicine.

Generic	Brand Name
codeine phosphate	Kaodene
diphenoxylate	Lomotil
loperamide	Imodium

WHAT TO TELL YOUR DOCTOR

It is important to make sure that your doctor or doctors are given as much information as possible. If you are aware that you are allergic to any antidiarrhoeals or drugs which contain codeine then do tell them so. Information on other medication is vital so if you are taking any other type of medicine, including non-prescription drugs, then they must know that too. Additionally, make sure they know if any of the following apply to you:

Addison's disease	Intestinal obstruction
Asthma	Jaundice, or history of it
Breast feeding	Liver or kidney disorders
Colitis	Lung disorders
Diverticulitis	Pregnancy
Down's Syndrome*	Severe dehydration
Glaucoma	Thyroid disorders
Heart disorders	Urinary difficulties

*This applies to diphenoxylate drugs only, in addition to the others listed.

DIGESTIVE SYSTEM

83

SIDE-EFFECTS AND CAUTIONS

SIDE-EFFECTS It is impossible to predict how any medicine will affect a particular individual because everyone's metabolism is so very different. Sensitivity or reaction to drugs can vary greatly from one person to another and side-effects can be related to dosage. It is important to pay close attention to any changes you may notice either when starting, or during, a course of treatment.

The following are some of the side-effects reported within this group of drugs. Some of the disorders listed under Infrequent or Rare may occasionally be the symptoms of overdose and not always those of side-effects.

INFREQUENT OR RARE

Allergic skin reactions	Insomnia
Decreased urination	Loss of appetite
Depression	Nausea
Dizziness	Numbness of the extremities
Drowsiness*	Over excitability
Dry mouth	Restlessness
Fever	Swelling of the stomach
Flushing of the face	Thirst
Gum swelling	Vomiting
Headache	Weight loss

*This side-effect does not apply to loperamide drugs.

If you experience any of the listed side-effects, or any other unusual symptoms, you should consult your dispensing pharmacist or doctor immediately.

CAUTIONS With the exception of loperamide, these medicines could be habit forming.

If you experience dizziness or drowsiness do not drive, operate machinery or work high above the ground. Alcohol can increase these effects and should be avoided during treatment.

One of the side-effects can be a dry mouth which may contribute to the chance of tooth decay or gum disease. If this occurs your doctor will probably advise you to clean your teeth frequently and to use dental floss.

INTERACTIONS WITH OTHER MEDICINES AND SUBSTANCES

No medication works in isolation but is affected to a greater or lesser extent by many other factors such as general fitness, diet and lifestyle. Alcohol can have an unpredictable effect on antidiarrhoeals.

It is also possible to unintentionally combine antidiarrhoeals with other drugs and this could be dangerous. Check with your doctor or pharmacist before taking any other medication, including non-prescription items, and if you are taking anything listed below look at the key to find out what effect they may have.

1   Anticonvulsants
1   Antidepressants
1   Barbiturates
1   Sedatives and sleeping tablets

5   Antihistamines
5   Ulcer drugs

Blood pressure may be elevated drastically by some MAOI antidepressants in combination with antidiarrhoeals.

KEY

1   INCREASES the effects of antidiarrhoeals
5   UNPREDICTABLE reactions

INTERACTIONS WITH VITAMINS, MINERALS AND FOODS

As lactose can aggravate diarrhoea it is best to avoid milk and milk products during an acute attack. If vitamin C is taken in very large doses it could result in diarrhoea which will decrease the effectiveness of these medicines.

Food may become harder to swallow if you suffer from a dry mouth while taking these medicines, and the ability to digest starches and carbohydrates will be affected. An important element in this digestion is the enzyme ptyalin, which is present in saliva, and in order to stimulate its flow all food should be chewed extremely well before swallowing.

CHILDREN, OVER SIXTIES AND PROLONGED USE

CHILDREN   These medicines may be prescribed for children over the age of four and the dosage will be adjusted accordingly.

OVER SIXTIES   As part of the ageing process the body begins to metabolize and eliminate drugs more slowly and so there may be the possibility of more frequent or severe side-effects or interactions with other medicines. These medicines are not widely prescribed for the very elderly as they may cause a loss of urinary control, abdominal pain, diarrhoea, or stool impaction.

PROLONGED OR CONTINUED TREATMENT   Antidiarrhoeals can be habit forming and prolonged use may aggravate irritable bowel disorders.

STOPPING THE TREATMENT   Do not discontinue the treatment without consulting your doctor as the dosage may need to be gradually reduced. If after completing the course of treatment you experience any nausea, perspiration, shaking, stomach and muscle spasms or vomiting you should contact your doctor.

PERSONAL MEDICINE NOTES

PRESCRIPTION NAMES

MEDICINES FOR ULCERS AND EXCESS PRODUCTION OF STOMACH ACIDS

Ulcers can arise when the digestive acids attack areas of the stomach and intestines where the protective mucus lining is damaged. Of the medicines used to help ulcers, some protect the lining of the stomach from digestive acids and may increase the production of protective mucus. The drugs ranitidine and cimetidine interfere with H2 receptors in the gut which are responsible for the release of acids and work by reducing their secretions, thus allowing the ulcers to heal. The reduction in digestive acids also makes these drugs useful for the treatment of heartburn and problems associated with hiatus hernia.

NAMES OF PRESCRIPTION MEDICINES

The following are commonly prescribed ulcer medicines and are shown with the generic name first, followed by the brand name. If your medicine is not listed by name you should follow the information for the generic, if you know it, as the information given will still apply to your particular medicine. If you are not sure of the generic name your pharmacist will be able to advise you. Please note that ALL the information on this fact sheet applies to ulcer medicines generally, not specifically to any one medicine.

Generic	Brand Name
bismuth	De-Nol
carbenoxolone	Biogastrone, Duogastrone, Pyrogastrone
cimetidine	Tagamet
liquorice	Caved-S, Rabro
ranitidine	Zantac
sucralfate	Antepsin

WHAT TO TELL YOUR DOCTOR

It is important to make sure that your doctor or doctors are given as much information as possible. If you are aware that you are allergic to any ulcer medicines or H2 antagonist antihistamines then do tell them so. Information on other medication is vital so if you are taking any other type of medicine, including non-prescription drugs, then they must know that too. Additionally, make sure they know if any of the following apply to you:

Breast feeding	Liver disorders
Heart disorders	Potassium problems
High blood pressure	Pregnancy
Kidney disorders	Water retention

If you will be having surgery or dental treatment which requires anaesthesia it is important to tell the person in charge that you are taking ulcer medicines.

SIDE-EFFECTS AND CAUTIONS

SIDE-EFFECTS It is impossible to predict how any medicine will affect a particular individual because everyone's metabolism is so very different. Sensitivity or reaction to drugs can vary greatly from one person to another and side-effects can be related to dosage. It is important to pay close attention to any changes you may notice either when starting, or during, a course of treatment.

The following are some of the side-effects reported within this group of drugs. Some of the disorders listed under Infrequent or Rare may occasionally be the symptoms of overdose and not always those of side-effects.

INFREQUENT OR RARE

Allergy	Fever
Breast tenderness or swelling	Hair loss
Confusion	Headache
Dark bowel movements	Liver disorders
Darkening of the tongue	Male breast enlargement
Decreased male sex drive*	Muscle pains
Decreased sperm count*	Pancreatitis
Diarrhoea	Skin rashes
Dizziness	Sore throat
Dry mouth	Tiredness

*These particular side-effects apply only to cimetidine and are not relevant to the other drugs in this group. The other listed side-effects still apply to cimetidine.

If you experience any of the listed side-effects, or any other unusual symptoms, you should consult your dispensing pharmacist or doctor immediately.

CAUTIONS If you experience dizziness or drowsiness do not drive, operate machinery or work high above the ground. Alcohol can increase these effects and should be avoided during treatment.

One of the side-effects can be a dry mouth which may contribute to the chance of tooth decay or gum disease. If this occurs your doctor will probably advise you to clean your teeth frequently and to use dental floss.

INTERACTIONS

INTERACTIONS WITH OTHER MEDICINES AND SUBSTANCES

No medication works in isolation but is affected to a greater or lesser extent by many other factors such as general fitness, diet and lifestyle. Alcohol and smoking can cause the ulcer to worsen, or can slow down its healing.

It is possible to unintentionally combine ulcer medicines with other drugs and this could be dangerous. Check with your doctor or pharmacist before taking any other medication, including non-prescription items, and if you are taking anything listed below check the key to find out what effect they may have.

3 Anticoagulants
3 Bronchodilators
3 Nifedipine+
3 Some anticonvulsants**

4 Antibiotics and antibacterial drugs

5 Anticoagulants
5 Beta blockers
5 Diuretics
5 Sulphur drugs

+This particular interaction applies only to cimetidine and is not relevant to the other drugs in this group. Cimetidine is still affected by the other listed interactions.

**Often drugs within the same group differ in formulation and may or may not interact with ulcer medicines. Your pharmacist can tell you which specific drugs within a group do interact.

If antacids are taken with cimetidine and ranitidine then they will decrease the effectiveness of these drugs.

KEY

3 ULCER MEDICINES INCREASE the effects of these drugs
4 ULCER MEDICINES DECREASE the effects of these drugs
5 UNPREDICTABLE reactions

INTERACTIONS WITH VITAMINS, MINERALS AND FOODS

Carbenoxolone increases salt retention in the body which may lead to potassium deficiency. For details of potassium rich foods see the chapter on Vitamins and Minerals. With some of the drugs in this group there is a decreased absorption of iron, especially from vegetable sources, and iron deficiency may result.

Food may become harder to swallow if you suffer from a dry mouth while taking these medicines, and the ability to digest starches and carbohydrates will be affected. An important element in this digestion is the enzyme ptyalin, which is present in saliva, and in order to stimulate its flow all food should be chewed extremely well before swallowing.

If you have a peptic ulcer you should avoid vitamin B3 in the form of niacin or nicotinic acid because they can irritate the condition.

CHILDREN, OVER SIXTIES AND PROLONGED USE

CHILDREN Ulcer medicines are generally not recommended for the young but if they are prescribed it will be for children over eight years of age and the dosage will be adjusted accordingly.

OVER SIXTIES As part of the ageing process the body begins to metabolize and eliminate drugs more slowly and so there may be the possibility of more frequent or severe side-effects or interactions with other medicines. With some of the drugs in this group there may be an increased possibility of confusion or disorientation. These drugs are generally not suitable for the very elderly.

PROLONGED OR CONTINUED TREATMENT These drugs are usually only prescribed for short term use.

STOPPING THE TREATMENT Ulcer medicines should not be discontinued without your doctor's advice.

PERSONAL MEDICINE NOTES

I am convinced digestion is the great secret of life.
Reverend Sydney Smith

Medicines for the digestive system are widely available as over the counter
or non-prescription preparations, with laxatives and indigestion remedies

heading the list of those most frequently used. Reliance on these preparations can lead to problems, many of which could be eliminated if more care were taken with diet and natural remedies employed whenever possible.

Indigestion and acid conditions may result from many dietary causes or may be due to eating food under stress. Tension between fellow diners, meals spiced with personal worries and eating on the run can all inhibit proper digestion and if you are in the habit of taking food or liquids either very hot or very cold this too prevents the proper secretion of digestive juices. The over-use of antacids can unbalance the environment in the digestive system and can create a spiral where the body needs antacids whenever foods are eaten. It is also undesirable to have a large intake of sodium and aluminium, yet many antacids are high in both of these.

Wherever possible it is far better to treat occasional bouts of heartburn, indigestion, constipation or diarrhoea with remedies which aid the body without upsetting its delicate balance. The benefits of eating whole, unprocessed foods are that they contain enzymes and nutrients which aid in their digestion, and fibre which speeds their elimination. However, if you do plan to change your diet from processed foods to whole and raw foods you should do it slowly as your stomach has to adjust to what it may consider 'foreign' material and if this is done too rapidly it may protest.

An early advocate of sensible eating was William Shakespeare when he observed that 'things sweet to taste prove in digestion sour'. How foods are combined in any one meal can make a vital difference to how the digestive system can cope with them. To assist it as much as possible there is an important rule of food combining which may help you. The aim is to avoid eating protein with sugar, fruit, or carbohydrates. Each of these foods requires different stomach conditions to be digested properly, so when they are eaten together the result may be fermentation, acid indigestion and wind. This principle of food combining is the foundation of The Hay Diet and there are a number of books available which explain it fully.

The suggestions offered here are designed to help generally with your condition, but it is very important that you do not try to treat yourself. If you suffer severely or regularly from a particular complaint, any serious disorder, or are pregnant then you should not use these remedies before discussion with a doctor. Always report any side-effects and seek medical advice before trying natural remedies and if within a period of one week

DIGESTIVE SYSTEM

there has been no improvement then you should consult your doctor. For more individual advice on natural medicine you should consult an alternative/complementary practitioner and among those who may be able to help are a naturopath, herbalist, osteopath, chiropractor, acupuncturist or a practitioner who has had dietary training. For more detailed information on the individual therapies, together with how to find a practitioner in your area, please refer to the chapter on Alternative/Complementary Medicine and Therapies.

It is possible that certain remedies, supplements or foods could react dangerously with the drugs you are already using so you must check with the fact sheet relating to your medicine to avoid interactions. Please note that it is not advisable to gather your own herbs unless you are sure they are free of any chemicals or pollutants and you can positively identify the correct variety. Always make sure that supplements or natural remedies are taken two to three hours apart from any drugs.

If while reading you come across a particular word or term that is unfamiliar to you please look in The Fact Finder; information on nutrients will be found in the chapter on Vitamins and Minerals.

NATURAL REMEDIES

ACIDITY, ACID REFLUX AND HEARTBURN
Half a teaspoon of crushed coriander seeds made as a tea can reduce the stomach's production of hydrochloric acid, or a soothing tea can be made from any combination of the following:

Half a teaspoon of chamomile flowers
Quarter of a teaspoon of celery seeds
2-3 lemon balm leaves

Put the herbs and seeds into a small teapot and pour boiling water over them. Allow to steep for about 2-3 minutes, strain and drink slowly.

See also General Digestive Aids in this chapter.

BREATH FRESHENER AND DIGESTIVE AID
Mix an equal quantity of fennel seeds, aniseed and celery seed and store in an airtight container. Chew a pinch of the mixture well after each meal.

CONSTIPATION
See the chapter on Natural Remedies.

DIGESTIVE SYSTEM

DIARRHOEA   See the chapter on Natural Remedies.

GENERAL DIGESTIVE AIDS   The tropical melon, papaya, is a natural aid to digestion because it contains the enzyme papain and is the only fruit that defies the rules of food combining listed previously as it can be eaten with any other foods. Papaya tablets often provide relief from heartburn and a feeling of fullness in the stomach and can either be chewed after meals or during an attack of indigestion. Papaya can also help with the acid reflux which sufferers from hiatus hernia often experience, as can the juice of a potato in warm water. See Peptic Ulcers for the method of preparation.

HERBAL REMEDIES   Digestive upsets often respond very effectively to herbal remedies. This tea is very good for upset stomachs and is simple to prepare:

Half a teaspoon of chamomile flowers
Quarter of a teaspoon of crushed aniseed
Quarter of a teaspoon of crushed fennel seed
Half a teaspoon of peppermint

Put the herbs and seeds into a small teapot and pour boiling water over them. Allow to steep for about 2-3 minutes, strain and drink slowly.

The same tea can be given to children, but omit the aniseed and reduce the amount of peppermint to a quarter of a teaspoon. Allow the tea to cool and let the child sip it when it is just warm. Chamomile tea is soothing for teething or sore gums and its calming effect aids peaceful sleep.

HOMOEOPATHIC TISSUE SALTS   General digestive disorders can respond to the use of Kali. Mur. and for dyspepsia Kali. Phos. can be helpful. If you are having difficulty in digesting proteins it may be that your stomach's acid production is insufficient and taking Nat. Mur. may stimulate it. If the problem lies in the digestion of fat or fatty foods then it may be worth trying Nat. Mur., Nat. Phos. and Nat. Sulph. in combination.

NAUSEA AND VOMITING   See the chapter on Natural Remedies.

PEPTIC ULCERS   It is not advisable to attempt the following suggestions without your doctor's advice. With peptic ulcers it is very important to avoid fried, oily foods and fats because they are difficult to digest. White sugar, white flour products and alcohol should be cut out of the diet wherever possible as they rob the body of nutrients such as zinc and the B complex vitamins which it needs for healing. Raw cabbage, carrot and parsley juice are an effective team for healing ulcers so if you have a juicing machine combine and juice the following and drink immediately, twice a day for as long as you feel you need it:

1 medium potato	5 large carrots
3-4 white cabbage leaves*	2 sprigs of parsley

*If you have low thyroid function or hormone output do not use cabbage. See goitrogens in The Fact Finder.

If you do not have a juicer put the same ingredients into a blender and liquify them. Take a clean cloth that has been rinsed extremely well to rid it of any soap or detergent residue, as this can be irritating to the digestive system. It should also be one that you do not mind being permanently stained. Strain the juice through it, squeezing until the pulp is as dry as you can manage and drink the juice immediately.

Warm water and potato juice also help acid indigestion, heartburn and ulcers and can be made by either juicing a medium raw potato and adding the juice to warm water or liquefying it in a blender and straining the juice through a clean cloth into warm water. It is a very soothing drink which may be taken before breakfast or whenever it is needed.

Zinc helps healing both internally and externally and has been used successfully to help heal ulcers. Vitamins A and B complex, especially B5, and vitamin E all help ulcer healing. See the chapter on Vitamins and Minerals for more information and important warnings about vitamin E.

It is believed that stress and tension may be the cause of much peptic ulceration and techniques used to control it such as yoga, meditation and biofeedback may be of value.

STOMACH PAIN AND INABILITY TO KEEP FOOD DOWN

After illness or during times when food will not stay down, slippery elm food is an easily digested meal. It forms a protective coating and helps soothe the stomach.

WIND AND FLATULENCE

A digestive herb tea can help and instructions on how to make it are in the General Digestive Aids section. You could also try an infusion of 3-4 lemon balm leaves. Place them in a cup and pour on boiling water. Allow to steep for 2-3 minutes, strain and drink. Dill oil, if you can obtain it, may be beneficial if you add five drops to warm water and drink after meals. For more information, including remedies for acute flatulence, see the chapter on Natural Remedies.

INFECTIONS AND PARASITES
CONTENTS

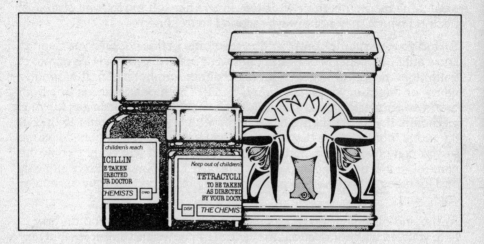

The immune system is the body's defence against invasion of harmful organisms. Its efficiency depends upon the ability of protective white cells to destroy invading foreign organisms, and the presence of antibodies which also fight infection. Antibodies are produced by exposure to substances which the body considers as foreign. A second invasion by an antigen will be attacked more vigorously because antibodies are available and the body is able to make more, faster. An example of this is childhood exposure to chickenpox and the improbability of suffering from it again despite further exposure.

Antibiotics are substances derived from micro-organisms such as bacteria or moulds and they work by killing or stopping the growth of the harmful bacteria which cause infections. This applies to all antibiotics except for a group known as the antifungals, which stop the growth of fungi and yeasts such as those which produce thrush or athlete's foot. Sulphonamides and trimethoprim act like antibiotics although technically they are known as antibacterials and are not produced from micro-organisms.

Previous civilizations, such as the ancient Egyptians, used moulds to stop wound infections but it was not until 1929 that Alexander Fleming observed that a particular mould, penicillium notatum, prevented bacteria growing

INFECTIONS & PARASITES

on a culture medium. The development of antibiotics grew rapidly after they were isolated and tested in the early 1940s and, although they are a valuable medicine, their widespread use has led to resistant strains of bacteria which may not always respond to treatment.

To find your particular prescription medicine in this chapter you need to know either its generic or brand name. For instance you may be given an antifungal medicine which is labelled either amphotericin, the generic name, or Fungilin which is a brand name. The index of drugs lists both brand and generic names to enable you to find the right fact sheet for your medicine. If your medicine has a name which you are unable to find in the index, contact your dispensing chemist and ask for its generic name so you can check whether it has been included. If you do not know the name of your drug, you may prefer to check in the separate index of ailments and illnesses to find the drugs that may be prescribed for your particular complaint.

At the end of this group of fact sheets you will find a section on how to help yourself with suggestions for natural remedies and therapies that may be of assistance. Information about practitioners will be found in the chapter on Alternative/Complementary Medicine and Therapies.

If you come across a particular word or term that is unfamiliar to you, please look in The Fact Finder for an explanation; information on food and nutrition will be found in the chapter on Vitamins and Minerals.

PRESCRIPTION NAMES

MEDICINES FOR FUNGAL INFECTIONS

Antifungal agents are used to treat a range of yeasts and yeast-type fungal infections, including thrush and candida albicans. Candida is a yeast-like fungus which is commonly part of the normal flora found in the mouth, skin, intestines, and vagina. Infection occurs when either the body's immune system is low or the bacteriological system is upset. In these situations candida multiplies in excessive amounts and the natural balance of the intestine is disturbed. This gives rise to symptoms such as abnormal vaginal discharge, athlete's foot, and severe itching. Some of the drugs in this group can also be used to treat certain types of bacteria.

NAMES OF PRESCRIPTION MEDICINES

The following are commonly prescribed antifungals and are shown with the generic name first, followed by the brand name. If your medicine is not listed by name you should follow the information for the generic, if you know it, as the information given will still apply to your particular medicine. If you are not sure of the generic name your pharmacist will be able to advise you. Please note that ALL the information on this fact sheet applies to antifungals generally, not specifically to any one medicine.

Generic	Brand Name
amphotericin	Fungilin, Fungizone
flucytosine	Alcobon
griseofulvin	Fulcin, Grisovin
ketoconazole	Nizoral
miconazole	Daktarin
natamycin	Pimafucin
nystatin	Nystan, Nystavescent, Mysteclin, Nystatin-Dome

WHAT TO TELL YOUR DOCTOR

It is important to make sure that your doctor or doctors are given as much information as possible. If you are aware that you are allergic to any antifungal drugs then do tell them so. Information on other medication is vital so if you are taking any other type of medicine, including non-prescription drugs, then they must know that too. Additionally, make sure they know if any of the following apply to you:

Blood disorders   Liver or kidney disorders
Breast feeding   Pregnancy
Digestive problems

If you will be having surgery or dental treatment which requires anaesthesia it is important to tell the person in charge that you are taking antifungal drugs.

INFECTIONS AND PARASITES
ANTIFUNGALS

SIDE-EFFECTS AND CAUTIONS

SIDE-EFFECTS It is impossible to predict how any medicine will affect a particular individual because everyone's metabolism is so very different. Sensitivity or reaction to drugs can vary greatly from one person to another and side-effects can be related to dosage. It is important to pay close attention to any changes you may notice either when starting, or during, a course of treatment.

The following are some of the side-effects reported within this group of drugs. Some of the disorders listed under Infrequent or Rare may occasionally be the symptoms of overdose and not always those of side-effects.

COMMON
Abdominal pain	Headache
Digestive disorders	Nausea or vomiting

INFREQUENT OR RARE
Bloating	Fever
Blood disorders	Irritability
Burning*	Irritation*
Confusion	Liver disorders
Dermatitis*	Loss of appetite
Diarrhoea	Ringing in the ears
Dizziness	Sensitivity to light
Dry mouth	Skin rashes*
Fatigue	Sore throat

*If you are using an antifungal cream or pessary then these are likely to be the only side-effects that may occur.

If you experience any of the listed side-effects, or any other unusual symptoms, you should consult your dispensing pharmacist or doctor immediately.

CAUTIONS If you experience dizziness or drowsiness do not drive, operate machinery or work high above the ground. Alcohol can increase these effects and should be avoided during treatment.

One of the side-effects may be a dry mouth and this can contribute to the chance of tooth decay or gum disease. If this occurs, your doctor will probably advise you to clean your teeth frequently and to use dental floss.

INTERACTIONS

INTERACTIONS WITH OTHER MEDICINES AND SUBSTANCES

No medication works in isolation but is affected to a greater or lesser extent by many other factors such as general fitness, diet, lifestyle etc. The intoxicating effects of alcohol may be increased if taken with antifungals.

It is also possible to unintentionally combine antifungals with other drugs and this could be dangerous. Check with your doctor or pharmacist before taking any other medication, including non-prescription items, and if you are taking anything listed below look at the key to find out what effect they may have.

2   Antacids
2   Anticholinergics and antispasmodics
2   Antihistamines
2   Cimetidine and ranitidine
2   Phenobarbitone
2   Rifampicin
2   Scopolamine

4   Anticonvulsants
4   Oral hypoglycaemics
4   Rifampicin

5   Anticoagulants
5   Digitalis drugs

KEY   2   DECREASES the effects of antifungals
4   ANTIFUNGALS DECREASE the effects of these drugs
5   UNPREDICTABLE reactions

INTERACTIONS WITH VITAMINS, MINERALS AND FOODS

If you have a normal amount of fat in your diet it will help in the absorption of antifungals. If you are taking amphotericin it can decrease potassium levels. This loss can be replaced through the diet, see the chapter on Vitamins and Minerals.

Food may become harder to swallow if you suffer from a dry mouth while taking these medicines, and the ability to digest starches and carbohydrates can be affected. An important element in this digestion is the enzyme ptyalin, which is present in saliva, and in order to stimulate its flow all food should be chewed thoroughly before swallowing.

CHILDREN, OVER SIXTIES AND PROLONGED USE

CHILDREN These medicines may be prescribed for children over the age of two and the dosage will be adjusted accordingly.

OVER SIXTIES As part of the ageing process the body begins to metabolize and eliminate drugs more slowly and so there may be the possibility of more frequent or severe side-effects or interactions with other medicines.

PROLONGED OR CONTINUED TREATMENT There is a possibility of the body becoming more susceptible to other infections.

STOPPING THE TREATMENT Antifungals should not be discontinued without your doctor's advice.

PERSONAL MEDICINE NOTES

PRESCRIPTION NAMES

MEDICINES FOR VIRUSES

Antivirals may be prescribed for type A influenza and disorders caused by the herpes virus such as cold sores, chickenpox, genital herpes and shingles. Amantadine may be used for Parkinsonism as well as viral infections.

NAMES OF PRESCRIPTION MEDICINES

The following are commonly prescribed antivirals and are shown with the generic name first, followed by the brand name. If your medicine is not listed by name you should follow the information for the generic, if you know it, as the information given will still apply to your particular medicine. If you are not sure of the generic name your pharmacist will be able to advise you. Please note that ALL the information on this fact sheet applies to antivirals generally, not specifically to any one medicine.

Generic	Brand Name
acyclovir	Zovirax
amantadine	Symmetrel
inosine	Imunovir

WHAT TO TELL YOUR DOCTOR

It is important to make sure that your doctor or doctors are given as much information as possible. If you are aware that you are allergic to any antivirals then do tell them so. Information on other medication is vital so if you are taking any other type of medicine, including non-prescription drugs, then they must know that too. Additionally, make sure they know if any of the following apply to you:

Breast feeding   Liver or kidney disorders
Convulsions*   Nervous system disorders
Epilepsy*   Pregnancy
Gout or high uric acid   Stomach ulcer*

*You only need to inform your doctor about these particular conditions, in addition to the others, if you are taking amantadine.

INFECTIONS AND PARASITES
ANTIVIRALS

SIDE-EFFECTS AND CAUTIONS

SIDE-EFFECTS   It is impossible to predict how any medicine will affect a particular individual because everyone's metabolism is so very different. Sensitivity or reaction to drugs can vary greatly from one person to another and side-effects can be related to dosage. It is important to pay close attention to any changes you may notice either when starting, or during, a course of treatment.

The following are some of the side-effects reported within this group of drugs. Some of the disorders listed under Infrequent or Rare may occasionally be the symptoms of overdose and not always those of side-effects.

COMMON

Digestive disturbances	Lightheadedness
Faintness	Raised uric acid levels+
Fatigue	Skin rashes*
Headache	

INFREQUENT OR RARE

Blood in urine	Hallucinations+
Blurred vision+	Insomnia+
Breathing problems	Nausea or vomiting
Convulsions+	Nervousness+
Decreased urine output	Water retention+
Dizziness+	

*This side-effect is rare with amantadine.

+These particular side-effects apply only to amantadine and are not relevant to the other drugs in this group. The other listed side-effects still apply to amantadine.

If you experience any of the listed side-effects, or any other unusual symptoms, you should consult your dispensing pharmacist or doctor immediately.

CAUTIONS   If you experience dizziness, drowsiness or blurred vision do not drive, operate machinery or work high above the ground. Alcohol can increase these effects and should be avoided during treatment.

INTERACTIONS

INTERACTIONS WITH OTHER MEDICINES AND SUBSTANCES

No medication works in isolation but is affected to a greater or lesser extent by many other factors such as general fitness, diet and lifestyle. Alcohol can increase the possibility of nervous system disorders.

It is also possible to unintentionally combine antivirals with other drugs and this could be dangerous. Check with your doctor or pharmacist before taking any other medication, including non-prescription items, and if you are taking anything listed below look at the key to find out what effect they may have.

1　Probenecid gout drugs

5　L-Dopa+
5　Anticholinergics+

+This particular interaction applies only to amantadine and is not relevant to the other drugs in this group. Amantadine is still affected by the other listed interactions.

Acyclovir if taken with some antibiotics can increase the chances of kidney problems.

KEY

1　INCREASES the effects of antivirals
5　UNPREDICTABLE effects

INTERACTIONS WITH VITAMINS, MINERALS AND FOODS

No data found.

CHILDREN, OVER SIXTIES AND PROLONGED USE

CHILDREN   Some of these medicines may be prescribed for children and the dosage will be adjusted accordingly. Symmetrel is not prescribed for children under ten years old.

OVER SIXTIES   As part of the ageing process the body begins to metabolize and eliminate drugs more slowly and so there may be the possibility of more frequent or severe side-effects or interactions with other medicines.

PROLONGED OR CONTINUED TREATMENT   No data found.

STOPPING THE TREATMENT   Antivirals should not be discontinued without your doctor's advice.

PERSONAL MEDICINE NOTES

PRESCRIPTION NAMES

MEDICINES FOR THE CONTROL OF PARASITE AND WORM INFESTATIONS

There are several types of parasitic worms which can live in the intestines, including tapeworms, roundworms, hookworms and pinworms. They can enter the body from fish and meat, the soil or if the hands are not washed properly after using the lavatory. The drugs in this group are known as anthelmintics and they are used to destroy parasitic intestinal worms. Some may also be used for abnormal vaginal discharge, dental infections and amoebic dysentery.

NAMES OF PRESCRIPTION MEDICINES

The following are commonly prescribed parasite and worm medicines and are shown with the generic name first, followed by the brand name. If your medicine is not listed by name you should follow the information for the generic, if you know it, as the information given will still apply to your particular medicine. If you are not sure of the generic name your pharmacist will be able to advise you. Please note that ALL the information on this fact sheet applies to parasite and worm medicines generally, not specifically to any one medicine.

Generic	Brand Name
bephenium	Alcopar
mebendazole	Vermox
metronidazole	Flagyl S/Compak, Metrolyl, Nidazol, Vaginyl, Zadstat
niclosamide	Yomesan
piperazine	Antepar, Ascalix, Pripsen
pyrantel	Combantrin
thiabendazole	Mintezol

WHAT TO TELL YOUR DOCTOR

It is important to make sure that your doctor or doctors are given as much information as possible. If you are aware that you are allergic to any parasite and worm medicines then do tell them so. Information on other medication is vital so if you are taking any other type of medicine, including non-prescription drugs, then they must know that too. Additionally, make sure they know if any of the following apply to you:

Breast feeding
Diabetes
Disorders of the central
  nervous system

Epilepsy
Liver or kidney disorders
Pregnancy
Vomiting

SIDE-EFFECTS AND CAUTIONS

SIDE-EFFECTS It is impossible to predict how any medicine will affect a particular individual because everyone's metabolism is so very different. Sensitivity or reaction to drugs can vary greatly from one person to another and side-effects can be related to dosage. It is important to pay close attention to any changes you may notice either when starting, or during, a course of treatment.

The following are some of the side-effects reported within this group of drugs. Some of the disorders listed under Infrequent or Rare may occasionally be the symptoms of overdose and not always those of side-effects.

COMMON

Dizziness	Nausea
Loss of appetite	Vomiting

INFREQUENT OR RARE

Abdominal bloating	Pins and needles
Chills	Rectal itching
Co-ordination problems	Ringing or buzzing
Decreased alertness	in the ears
Diarrhoea	Shaking
Drowsiness	Skin rashes or itching
Facial flushing	Sleeping disturbances
Fever	Stomach pains
Headache	Strong urine odour
High blood sugar	Vertigo
Insomnia	Vision yellow or blurred
Irritability	Yellowing of skin and eyes
Low blood pressure	

If you experience any of the listed side-effects, or any other unusual symptoms, you should consult your dispensing pharmacist or doctor immediately.

CAUTIONS If you experience dizziness or drowsiness do not drive, operate machinery or work high above the ground. Alcohol can increase these effects and should be avoided during treatment.

INTERACTIONS

INTERACTIONS WITH OTHER MEDICINES AND SUBSTANCES No medication works in isolation but is affected to a greater or lesser extent by many other factors such as general fitness, diet and lifestyle. Alcohol and smoking can decrease the effectiveness of these drugs.

It is also possible to unintentionally combine parasite or worm medicines with other drugs and this could be dangerous. Check with your doctor or pharmacist before taking any other medication, including non-prescription items, and if you are taking anything listed below look at the key to find out what effect they may have.

3   Aminophylline bronchodilators
3   Theophylline bronchodilators

KEY   3   PARASITE AND WORM INFESTATION MEDICINES INCREASE the effects of these drugs

INTERACTIONS WITH VITAMINS, MINERALS AND FOODS   No data found.

CHILDREN, OVER SIXTIES AND PROLONGED USE

CHILDREN   Children under the age of two may not be prescribed some of these medicines. Those over this age may be treated with any of the medicines in this group and the dosage will be adjusted according to the child's age or weight.

OVER SIXTIES   As part of the ageing process the body begins to metabolize and eliminate drugs more slowly and so there may be the possibility of more frequent or severe side-effects or interactions with other medicines.

PROLONGED OR CONTINUED TREATMENT   Stool examinations should be ordered by your doctor after finishing treatment.

STOPPING THE TREATMENT   Parasite and worm medicines should not be discontinued without your doctor's advice.

PERSONAL MEDICINE NOTES

INFECTIONS AND PARASITES
PENICILLINS AND RELATED ANTIBIOTICS

PRESCRIPTION NAMES

MEDICINES FOR BACTERIAL INFECTIONS

Penicillins either destroy or slow the growth of bacteria and thus allow the body's natural defences to act more effectively. Penicillin and other drugs in this group may be used for respiratory, urinary tract and gynaecological infections; skin, sinus, nose, throat and middle ear infections; prevention or treatment of endocarditis, chlamydia and a number of other infections.

NAMES OF PRESCRIPTION MEDICINES

The following are commonly prescribed drugs in this group and are shown with the generic name first, followed by the brand name. If your medicine is not listed by name you should follow the information for the generic, if you know it, as the information given will still apply to your particular medicine. If you are not sure of the generic name your pharmacist will be able to advise you. Please note that ALL the information on this fact sheet applies to these antibiotics generally, not specifically to any one medicine.

CEPHALOSPORINS AND CEPHALOMYCINS

Generic	Brand Name
cefaclor	Distaclor
cefadroxil	Baxan
cephalexin	Ceporex, Keflex/C
cephradine	Velosef

ERYTHROMYCIN AND LINCOMYCIN

Generic	Brand Name
clindamycin	Dalacin C
erythromycin	Erycen, Erythrocin, Erythromid/DS, Erythroped/A, Ilosone, Ilotycin, Erymax, Rectin, Arpimycin
lincomycin	Lincocin

PENICILLINS

Generic	Brand Name
amoxycillin	Amoxil, Augmentin, Amoxidin
ampicillin	Amfipen, Penbritin, Vidopen, Magnapen, Ampiclox, Ampilar, Britcin, Flu-Amp
bacampicillin	Ambaxin
carfecillin	Uticillin
ciclacillin	Calthor
cloxacillin	Orbenin
flucloxacillin	Floxapen, Stafoxil, Ladropen, Staphcil

penicillin V	V-Cil-K, Crystapen-V, Stabillin-VK, Apsin-VK, Distaquaine-VK, Phenoxymethylpenicillin, Econocil-VK
phenethicillin	Broxil
pivampicillin	Pondocillin, Miraxid
pivmecillinam	Selexid
talampicillin	Talpen

WHAT TO TELL YOUR DOCTOR

It is important to make sure that your doctor or doctors are given as much information as possible. If you are aware that you are allergic to any antibiotics then do tell them so. Information on other medication is vital so if you are taking any other type of medicine, including non-prescription drugs, then they must know that too. Additionally, make sure they know if any of the following apply to you:

Allergies	Jaundice
Asthma	Liver or kidney disorders
Breast feeding	Pregnancy
Diabetes	Skin rashes
Glandular fever	Ulcerative colitis
Hay fever	Yeast infections

If you will be having surgery or dental treatment which requires anaesthesia it is important to tell the person in charge that you are taking lincomycin. If you are having urine-sugar tests you should be aware that the drugs in this group can affect the results.

SIDE-EFFECTS AND CAUTIONS

SIDE-EFFECTS

It is impossible to predict how any medicine will affect a particular individual because everyone's metabolism is so very different. Sensitivity or reaction to drugs can vary greatly from one person to another and side-effects can be related to dosage. It is important to pay close attention to any changes you may notice either when starting, or during, a course of treatment.

The following are some of the side-effects reported within this group of drugs. Some of the disorders listed under Infrequent or Rare may occasionally be the symptoms of overdose and not always those of side-effects.

INFECTIONS AND PARASITES
PENICILLINS AND RELATED ANTIBIOTICS

COMMON	Diarrhoea	Nausea or vomiting
		Skin rashes or itching

INFREQUENT OR RARE

Allergies	Joint pains
Blood disorders	Liver disorders
Breathing difficulties	Phlebitis
Colitis	Sores in mouth or throat
Dark or irritated tongue	Swollen glands
Digestive disorders	Tongue inflammation
Dizziness	Vaginal discharge
Fever or chills	Vaginitis
Fungal infections	Water retention
Genital or rectal itching	
Headache	

If you experience any of the listed side-effects, or any other unusual symptoms, you should consult your dispensing pharmacist or doctor immediately.

CAUTIONS If you experience dizziness or drowsiness do not drive, operate machinery or work high above the ground. Alcohol can increase these effects and should be avoided during treatment.

INTERACTIONS

INTERACTIONS WITH OTHER MEDICINES AND SUBSTANCES

No medication works in isolation but is affected to a greater or lesser extent by many other factors such as general fitness, diet and lifestyle. Alcohol may increase stomach irritation and adds to the depletion of B complex vitamins.

It is also possible to unintentionally combine penicillins with other drugs and this could be dangerous. Check with your doctor or pharmacist before taking any other medication, including non-prescription items, and if you are taking anything listed below look at the key to find out what effect they may have.

1 Gout drugs	3 Anticoagulants
2 Antacids	4 Digitalis drugs
2 Guar gum	5 Antibiotics
2 Lipid lowering drugs	
2 Ulcer healing medicines	
5 Antidiarrhoeals	
5 Carbamazepine anticonvulsants	
5 Ergotamine migraine medicine	
5 Oral contraceptives	
5 Theophylline bronchodilators	

KEY
1 INCREASES the effects of these antibiotics
2 DECREASES the effects of these antibiotics
3 THESE ANTIBIOTICS INCREASE the effects of these drugs
4 THESE ANTIBIOTICS DECREASE the effects of these drugs
5 UNPREDICTABLE reactions

INTERACTIONS WITH VITAMINS, MINERALS AND FOODS

You will probably be instructed to take your medicine on an empty stomach as food can decrease the absorption of these antibiotics. An exception to this is the erythromycin, Ilosone, the absorption of which is actually increased by food in the stomach. Wine, carbonated beverages, fruit juice, soda, colas and other acidic drinks could affect the drug's absorption if taken at the same time as an antibiotic, or up to two hours afterwards.

Supplements of vitamin B2 taken at the same time as erythromycin can decrease its effects. Antibiotics may antagonize or decrease the absorption of certain vitamins and minerals: carotene (the form of vitamin A found in fruit and vegetables), B1, B6, B12, folic acid, biotin, vitamin C and bioflavonoids, vitamin K and potassium.

The birth control pill when taken together with antibiotics increases susceptibility to the depletion of folic acid, B6, B12 and vitamin C because the Pill already depletes these nutrients. Some vegetarians and vegans run a higher risk of B12 deficiencies and taking antibiotics will increase this susceptibility. Vitamin C can help reduce some of the side-effects of antibiotics if taken in supplementary doses of 250mg twice a day.

Regular alcohol consumption, antibiotics and smoking all increase the requirements of B complex vitamins. Smoking can also increase the need for more vitamin A, E and C, particularly C as the drugs increase its excretion. Approximately 25mg of vitamin C is used up with each cigarette smoked and similar losses apply to cigars and loose tobacco. Natural liquorice powder or extract, used in some herbal teas and liquorice confectionery, can further deplete potassium when taken with some of the drugs in this group.

Calcium and magnesium taken in the form of supplements, or in antacids containing them, and sodium bicarbonate can all decrease the effects of antibiotics and should not be taken or used within two hours of the medicine.

If you take vitamin or mineral supplements, then leave a two hour gap before or after taking the medicine; do not take them

INFECTIONS & PARASITES

at the same time. If you are taking B3 in the form of niacin or nicotinic acid you may notice an increase in the flushing sensation sometimes experienced with this nutrient, but niacinamide will not cause this reaction. It is important to ensure that your diet is well supplied with nutrients; for more details see the chapter on Vitamins and Minerals.

CHILDREN, OVER SIXTIES AND PROLONGED USE

CHILDREN These medicines may be prescribed for children and the dosage will be adjusted accordingly. Children are more susceptible to diarrhoea whilst on these antibiotics and supplemental acidophilus may prove helpful. See the How to Help Yourself section at the end of the chapter.

OVER SIXTIES As part of the ageing process the body begins to metabolize and eliminate drugs more slowly and so there may be the possibility of more frequent or severe side-effects or interactions with other medicines. There is a greater possibility of nutrient deficiencies, see Interactions with Vitamins, Minerals and Foods in this chapter, and an increased susceptibility to rectal or genital itching.

PROLONGED OR CONTINUED TREATMENT There is a risk of fungal infections such as thrush or Candida, and a possibility of susceptibility to new infections. During prolonged treatment severe diarrhoea or colitis may also occur.

STOPPING THE TREATMENT Even if your condition appears to improve early in the treatment you should complete the prescribed course of antibiotics unless your doctor gives you special instructions to the contrary. It may take a few days for the medicine to become effective, but if after five days there has been no improvement then contact your doctor for advice. Antibiotics should not be discontinued without your doctor's advice.

PERSONAL MEDICINE NOTES

PRESCRIPTION NAMES

MEDICINES FOR INFECTIONS

Sulphonamides are anti-infective drugs used for the urinary tract, respiratory system, ear, nose, and throat. They are also used in the treatment of malaria, osteomyelitis, gonorrhoea, ulcerative colitis, Crohn's disease, typhoid and other infections. Trimethoprim is not a sulphonamide but appears in this group as it has similar actions.

NAMES OF PRESCRIPTION MEDICINES

The following are commonly prescribed sulphonamides and are shown with the generic name first, followed by the brand name. If your medicine is not listed by name you should follow the information for the generic, if you know it, as the information given will still apply to your particular medicine. If you are not sure of the generic name your pharmacist will be able to advise you. Please note that ALL the information on this fact sheet applies to sulphonamides generally, not specifically to any one medicine.

Generic	Brand Name
calcium sulphaloxate	Enteromide
co-trimoxazole	Septrin, Laratrim, Bactrim, Chemotrim, Comox, Fectrim
sulfametopyrazine	Kelfizine/W
sulphadiazine	Streptotriad, Sulphatriad, Uromide
sulphadimethoxine	Madribon
sulphafurazole	Gantrisin
sulphasalazine	Salazopyrin
trimethoprim	Monotrim, Ipral, Syraprim, Trimopan, Tiempe, Trimogal

WHAT TO TELL YOUR DOCTOR

It is important to make sure that your doctor or doctors are given as much information as possible. If you are aware that you are allergic to any sulphonamides, oral anti diabetic drugs or diuretics then do tell them so. Information on other medication is vital so if you are taking any other type of medicine, including non-prescription drugs, then they must know that too. Additionally, make sure they know if any of the following apply to you:

Anaemia or blood disease	Hay fever
Breast feeding	Liver or kidney disorders
Bronchial asthma	Pregnancy

If you will be having surgery or dental treatment which requires anaesthesia it is important to tell the person in charge that you are taking sulphonamides.

INFECTIONS AND PARASITES
SULPHONAMIDES AND TRIMETHOPRIM

SIDE-EFFECTS AND CAUTIONS

SIDE-EFFECTS It is impossible to predict how any medicine will affect a particular individual because everyone's metabolism is so very different. Sensitivity or reaction to drugs can vary greatly from one person to another and side-effects can be related to dosage. It is important to pay close attention to any changes you may notice either when starting, or during, a course of treatment.

The following are some of the side-effects reported within this group of drugs. Some of the disorders listed under Infrequent or Rare may occasionally be the symptoms of overdose and not always those of side-effects.

COMMON

Fever	Nausea
Headache	Skin rash or itching
Loss of appetite	Vomiting

INFREQUENT OR RARE

Abdominal pain	Lowered sperm count*
Anaemia or blood disorders	Mental confusion
Blood in urine, or pain when urinating	Nightmares
Depression	Rectal itching
Diarrhoea	Ringing or buzzing in the ears
Difficulty swallowing	Sensitivity to sun or sunlamps
Dizziness	Sore throat
Fatigue	Swelling at the front of the neck
Gastro-intestinal problems	Weakness
Insomnia	Yellow skin and eyes
Joint or muscle aches	
Lower back pain	

*This particular side-effect applies only to sulphasalazine and co-trimoxazole and is not relevant to the other drugs in this group. The other listed side-effects still apply to these two drugs.

It is possible that whilst taking sulphonamides the urine may become orange-red in colour but this is harmless and need not be reported to your doctor.

If you experience any of the listed side-effects, or any other unusual symptoms, you should consult your dispensing pharmacist or doctor immediately.

CAUTIONS If you experience dizziness or drowsiness do not drive, operate machinery or work high above the ground. Alcohol can increase these effects and should be avoided during treatment.

If sunbathing, or using a sun-bed or lamp whilst taking these medicines, then a rash or increased tendency to burn may occur so it may be advisable to avoid exposure or to take extra precautions. You may retain this sensitivity for a few weeks or months after finishing your course of treatment.

INTERACTIONS

INTERACTIONS WITH OTHER MEDICINES AND SUBSTANCES

No medication works in isolation but is affected to a greater or lesser extent by many other factors such as general fitness, diet and lifestyle. The effects of alcohol can be increased while on sulphonamides.

It is also possible to unintentionally combine sulphonamides with other drugs and this could be dangerous. Check with your doctor or pharmacist before taking any other medication, including non-prescription items, and if you are taking anything listed below look at the key to find out what effect they may have.

1 Gout drugs

2 Aspirin
2 Pyrazinamide tuberculosis drugs

3 Anticoagulants
3 Other sulphur drugs

4 Digitalis drugs

5 Antacids and indigestion remedies
5 Anticonvulsants
5 Arthritis drugs
5 Oral diabetes drugs
5 Other antibiotics
5 Ulcer healing medicines

KEY 1 INCREASES the effects of sulphonamides
2 DECREASES the effects of sulphonamides
3 SULPHONAMIDES AND TRIMETHOPRIM INCREASE the effects of these drugs
4 SULPHONAMIDES AND TRIMETHOPRIM DECREASE the effects of these drugs
5 UNPREDICTABLE reactions

INTERACTIONS WITH VITAMINS, MINERALS AND FOODS

Sulphonamides increase the urinary excretion of vitamin C by up to three times the normal amount. However, it is important to note that if large doses of vitamin C are taken during sulphonamide treatment it may cause damage to the kidneys. Taking bicarbonate of soda can decrease the effects of sulphur drugs.

Sulphonamides and trimethoprim are powerful folic acid and PABA antagonists, in fact this is part of their mode of action, but do not take these nutrients in supplement form with these drugs as they can decrease their anti-infective effects. Iron supplements may decrease the effects of sulphonamides.

Sulphonamides may antagonize or decrease the absorption of other nutrients, vitamins and minerals, particularly B1, B3, B5, B6, B12, choline, inositol, biotin, vitamin K, magnesium and calcium.

The birth control pill when taken together with sulphonamides increases susceptibility to the depletion of folic acid, B6, B12 and vitamin C because the Pill also depletes these nutrients. Some vegetarians and vegans run a higher risk of B12 deficiencies and taking sulphonamides will increase this susceptibility.

Regular consumption of alcohol depletes magnesium and the B complex vitamins which are also depleted by sulphonamides. Tobacco can cause a considerable loss of vitamin C, because the drugs also increase its excretion. In addition to this loss, approximately 25mg of vitamin C is used up with each cigarette smoked and similar losses apply to cigars and loose tobacco. Smoking also increases the body's requirements of vitamins A, B complex and E.

Sulphonamides should be taken with plenty of water and it is important to ensure that your diet is well supplied with the nutrients mentioned, for more details see the chapter on Vitamins and Minerals.

SULPHONAMIDES AND TRIMETHOPRIM

CHILDREN, OVER SIXTIES AND PROLONGED USE

CHILDREN Over the age of four months these medicines may be prescribed for children and the dosage will be adjusted accordingly.

OVER SIXTIES As part of the ageing process the body begins to metabolize and eliminate drugs more slowly and so there may be the possibility of more frequent or severe side-effects or interactions with other medicines. There is a greater possibility of nutritional deficiencies, see Interactions with Vitamins, Minerals and Foods in this section.

PROLONGED OR CONTINUED TREATMENT While on these medicines you may be more susceptible to fungal infections such as thrush or candida, or to new infections. The thyroid gland may be affected by continued treatment with sulphonamides and this could result in a goitre developing.

STOPPING THE TREATMENT Even if your condition improves early on in the treatment you should still finish your course of sulphonamides or trimethoprim to prevent the infection recurring, unless your doctor advises otherwise. If your condition does not respond within five days you should contact your doctor. These drugs should not be discontinued without your doctor's advice.

PERSONAL MEDICINE NOTES

PRESCRIPTION NAMES

MEDICINES FOR INFECTIONS

Tetracyclines are broad spectrum antibiotics, of which minocycline is active against the widest range of bacteria. Because of the increasing resistance of bacteria to tetracyclines their usefulness is decreasing; however, they may be prescribed for patients who are allergic or sensitive to penicillins and for the following conditions: respiratory, urinary and digestive system infections, chlamydia, acne, infections of the ear, nose and throat, as a preventive measure before some types of surgery or dental procedures, other infections, burns and wounds.

NAMES OF PRESCRIPTION MEDICINES

The following are commonly prescribed tetracyclines and are shown with the generic name first, followed by the brand name. If your medicine is not listed by name you should follow the information for the generic, if you know it, as the information given will still apply to your particular medicine. If you are not sure of the generic name your pharmacist will be able to advise you. Please note that ALL the information on this fact sheet applies to tetracyclines generally, not specifically to any one medicine.

Generic	Brand Name
clomocycline	Megaclor
chlortetracycline	Aureomycin
demeclocyline	Ledermycin
doxycycline	Doxatet, Doxylar, Vibramycin/D, Nordox
lymecycline	Tetralysal
minocycline	Minocin
oxytetracycline	Terramycin, Berkmycen, Imperacin, Chemocycline, Galenomycin, Oxymycin, Unimycin
tetracycline	Achromycin, Deteclo, Sustamycin, Tetrabid, Tetrachel, Tetrex, Chymocyclar, Economycin

WHAT TO TELL YOUR DOCTOR

It is important to make sure that your doctor or doctors are given as much information as possible. If you are aware that you are allergic to any tetracyclines then do tell them so. Information on other medication is vital so if you are taking any other type of medicine, including non-prescription drugs, then they must know that too. Additionally, make sure they know if any of the following apply to you:

Allergies
Asthma
Blood disorders
Breast feeding
Breathing disorders

Diabetes
Fungal infections
Liver or kidney disorders
Myasthenia gravis
Pregnancy

If you will be having surgery or dental treatment which requires anaesthesia it is important to tell the person in charge that you are taking tetracyclines. If you are to have any blood, urine-sugar or urine tests you must tell the person in charge that you are taking tetracyclines. If you test yourself for urine-sugar you must take into account the fact that these drugs can alter the results.

SIDE-EFFECTS AND CAUTIONS

SIDE-EFFECTS It is impossible to predict how any medicine will affect a particular individual because everyone's metabolism is so very different. Sensitivity or reaction to drugs can vary greatly from one person to another and side-effects can be related to dosage. It is important to pay close attention to any changes you may notice either when starting, or during, a course of treatment.

The following are some of the side-effects reported within this group of drugs. Some of the disorders listed under Infrequent or Rare may occasionally be the symptoms of overdose and not always those of side-effects.

COMMON Sensitivity to sunlight

INFREQUENT OR RARE

Allergies
Blood disorders
Blurred vision
Darkened tongue
Dermatitis
Diarrhoea
Dizziness
Excessive thirst
Fever
Headache
Increased chance of
    other infections

Increased urination
Inflammation of the vagina
Lightheadedness
Loss of appetite
Nausea or vomiting
Rectal or genital itching
Skin rash or itching
Sore tongue or mouth
Stomach cramps or burning
Vaginal infection
Weakness or tiredness
Yellowing of eyes and skin

If you experience any of the listed side-effects, or any other

INFECTIONS AND PARASITES
TETRACYCLINES

unusual symptoms, you should consult your dispensing pharmacist or doctor immediately.

CAUTIONS It may take up to five days before the medicine starts to become fully effective. If, after this time, there has been no improvement contact your doctor for advice.

These drugs should not be used during pregnancy as they can interfere with foetal bone growth.

If you experience dizziness or drowsiness do not drive, operate machinery, or work high above the ground. Alcohol can increase these effects and should be avoided during treatment.

If sunbathing, or using a sun-bed or lamp whilst taking these medicines, then a rash or an increased tendency to burn may occur. You may retain this sensitivity for a few weeks or a number of months after finishing your course of tetracyclines.

INTERACTIONS

INTERACTIONS WITH OTHER MEDICINES AND SUBSTANCES

No medication works in isolation but is affected to a greater or lesser extent by many other factors such as general fitness, diet and lifestyle. Alcohol taken with tetracyclines can increase the chances of liver damage and smoking can increase the rate of bone calcium loss.

It is also possible to unintentionally combine tetracyclines with other drugs and this could be dangerous. Check with your doctor or pharmacist before taking any other medication, including non-prescription items, and if you are taking anything listed below look at the key to find out what effect they may have.

2 Antacids	5 Barbiturates
3 Anticoagulants	5 Digitalis drugs
	5 Laxatives
4 Oral contraceptives*	5 Lithium
4 Penicillins	5 Other antibiotics
5 Anti-inflammatories	5 Phenytoin anticonvulsants

*Mysteclin does not have this effect.

KEY 2 DECREASES the effects of tetracyclines
3 TETRACYCLINES INCREASE the effects of these drugs
4 TETRACYCLINES DECREASE the effects of these drugs
5 UNPREDICTABLE reactions

INTERACTIONS WITH VITAMINS, MINERALS AND FOODS

The following should not be consumed either two hours before or after tetracycline as they can all impair its absorption: dairy products, sardines, iron rich foods such as red meat or dark green vegetables, vitamin and mineral supplements and foods which contain calcium, magnesium, iron, or zinc. Bicarbonate of soda, or antacids which contain it, can also impair the absorption of tetracyclines.

With the exception of doxycycline and minocycline, tetracyclines should not be taken with milk products or iron-rich foods. See the chapter on Vitamins and Minerals for more details.

If you are taking a B3 niacin or nicotinic acid supplement then the skin flushing normally caused by this can become more severe, but by changing to niacinamide instead you can avoid this reaction.

The absorption of protein and fat from food is decreased, as is the absorption or effectiveness of the following vitamins and minerals: B1, B2, B5, B6. B12, folic acid, vitamin A, vitamin C and bioflavonoids, vitamin E, vitamin K, calcium, iron, magnesium, potassium, and zinc.

The birth control pill when taken together with tetracyclines increases susceptibility to the depletion of folic acid, B6, B12 and vitamin C because the Pill already depletes these nutrients. However, calcium, magnesium, zinc and iron should be taken two hours before or after the dose of medicine — never with it. Some vegetarians and vegans run a higher risk of B12 deficiencies and taking tetracyclines will increase this susceptibility.

Tetracyclines deplete magnesium and the B complex and they are further reduced by the consumption of alcohol. Tobacco can cause a considerable loss of vitamin C as the drugs increase its excretion. In addition, approximately 25mg of vitamin C is used up with each cigarette smoked, and similar losses apply to cigars and loose tobacco. Smoking also increases the body's requirements of vitamins A, B complex, and E.

CHILDREN, OVER SIXTIES AND PROLONGED USE

CHILDREN Some of the tetracyclines can cause tooth discoloration so they are not usually prescribed for children under eight years of age. They may also affect their adult teeth and normal bone growth can also be interfered with. There is a rare possibility in infants that some tetracyclines may cause an increase of pressure within the skull which will appear as a bulge. If this does occur, consult your doctor so that the medication can be stopped.

OVER SIXTIES As part of the ageing process the body begins to metabolize and eliminate drugs more slowly and so there may be the possibility of more frequent or severe side-effects or interactions with other medicines. With some of the drugs in this group there may be an increased possibility of nutrient deficiencies.

PROLONGED OR CONTINUED TREATMENT One side-effect of long-term use may be nail discoloration and there is the possibility of serious nutrient deficiencies as the intestinal production of some of the B vitamins and vitamin K is affected. Long-term use may also leave some people more susceptible to infections caused by organisms not responsive to tetracyclines, or to fungal infections such as thrush or yeast problems. In susceptible people there may be the possibility of blood disorders which may appear as unusual bruising or bleeding, painful sores in the mouth or throat or the development of fever or chills. If any of these occur they must be reported to a doctor as soon as possible.

STOPPING THE TREATMENT If your condition improves early on in the treatment you should still finish your course of antibiotics, unless your doctor specifically advises you otherwise, in order to prevent the infection recurring. If your condition does not respond within five days you should contact your doctor. Do not stop taking tetracyclines without your doctor's advice.

PERSONAL MEDICINE NOTES

PRESCRIPTION NAMES

MEDICINES FOR URINARY TRACT INFECTIONS

This group of drugs is anti-infective and they kill a number of different kinds of bacteria found in the urinary tract. As with antibiotics there is a tendency for the bacteria to become resistant to the drugs and this may limit their use. They may be prescribed for cystitis and infections of the lower urinary tract, bladder, prostate, urethra or kidney.

NAMES OF PRESCRIPTION MEDICINES

The following are commonly prescribed urinary tract infection medicines and are shown with the generic name first, followed by the brand name. If your medicine is not listed by name you should follow the information for the generic, if you know it, as the information given will still apply to your particular medicine. If you are not sure of the generic name your pharmacist will be able to advise you. Please note that ALL the information on this fact sheet applies to urinary tract infection medicines generally, not specifically to any one medicine.

Generic	Brand Name
cinoxacin	Cinobac
nalidixic acid	Mictral, Negram, Uriben
nitrofurantoin	Furadantin, Macrodantin, Urantoin

WHAT TO TELL YOUR DOCTOR

It is important to make sure that your doctor or doctors are given as much information as possible. If you are aware that you are allergic to any urinary tract infection medicines or antibiotics then do tell them so. Information on other medication is vital so if you are taking any other type of medicine, including non-prescription drugs, then they must know that too. Additionally, make sure they know if any of the following apply to you:

Allergies	Epilepsy
Blood sugar problems	Hardening of the arteries
Breast feeding	Liver or kidney disorders
Breathing difficulties	Parkinson's disease
Convulsive disorders	Pregnancy
Disorders of the central nervous system	Spinal cord damage

The drugs in this group can affect the results of urine-sugar tests so you must tell the person in charge which drug you are taking. If you are conducting the test yourself you need to be aware of this effect when analysing the result.

125

SIDE-EFFECTS AND CAUTIONS

SIDE-EFFECTS It is impossible to predict how any medicine will affect a particular individual because everyone's metabolism is so very different. Sensitivity or reaction to drugs can vary greatly from one person to another and side-effects can be related to dosage. It is important to pay close attention to any changes you may notice either when starting, or during, a course of treatment.

The following are some of the side-effects reported within this group of drugs. Some of the disorders listed under Infrequent or Rare may occasionally be the symptoms of overdose and not always those of side-effects.

COMMON Nausea   Vomiting

INFREQUENT OR RARE

Bloated stomach	Loss of appetite
Blood disorders	Muscular weakness
Blurred vision	Numbness, tingling or
Breathing difficulty	burning sensations
Constipation	Pains in the chest
Cramps	Paleness of skin
Diarrhoea	Ringing in ears
Dizziness	Sensitivity of eyes to light
Drowsiness	Skin rashes
Easy bruising and bleeding	Sleeping disturbances
Fatigue	Sore throat
Fever or chills	Stomach irritation
Headache	Tiredness or weakness
Inhibited sperm	Vision problems
production*	Yellow eyes or skin
Light coloured bowel	
movements	

*This particular side-effect applies only to nitrofurantoin and is not relevant to the other drugs in this group. The other listed side-effects may still apply to nitrofurantoin.

Nitrofurantoin may colour the urine an orange-brown but this effect is harmless.

If you experience any of the listed side-effects, or any other unusual symptoms, you should consult your dispensing pharmacist or doctor immediately.

CAUTIONS If you experience dizzines or drowsiness, do not drive, operate machinery or work high above the ground. Alcohol can increase these effects and should be avoided during treatment.

If sunbathing, or using a sun-bed or lamp whilst taking these medicines, then a rash or increased tendency to burn may occur so it may be advisable to avoid exposure or to take extra precautions.

INTERACTIONS

INTERACTIONS WITH OTHER MEDICINES AND SUBSTANCES

No medication works in isolation but is affected to a greater or lesser extent by many other factors such as general fitness, diet and lifestyle. Alcohol can cause a decrease of co-ordination and alertness.

It is also possible to unintentionally combine urinary tract medicines with other drugs and this could be dangerous. Check with your doctor or pharmacist before taking any other medication, including non-prescription items, and if you are taking anything listed below look at the key to find out what effect they may have.

2 Antacids
2 Lipid lowering drugs
2 Other urinary antibiotics
2 Ulcer healing drugs

3 Anticoagulants

5 Gout drugs

KEY

2 DECREASES the effects of urinary tract anti-infectives
3 URINARY TRACT ANTI-INFECTIVES INCREASE the effects of these drugs
5 UNPREDICTABLE reactions

INTERACTIONS WITH VITAMINS, MINERALS AND FOODS

The action of urinary tract antibiotics deplete the body's absorption of vitamins K, B1, B12, folic acid and biotin.

Iron may be depleted by nalidixic acid if there is gastric irritation, and this could lead to possible bleeding. In large doses vitamin C can increase the effect of nalidixic acid. In order to maintain normal levels, see the chapter on Vitamins and Minerals.

INFECTIONS AND PARASITES
URINARY TRACT ANTI-INFECTIVES

CHILDREN, OVER SIXTIES AND PROLONGED USE

CHILDREN These medicines may be prescribed for children over the age of 3 months and the dosage will be adjusted accordingly.

OVER SIXTIES As part of the ageing process the body begins to metabolize and eliminate drugs more slowly and so there may be the possibility of more frequent or severe side-effects or interactions with other medicines.

PROLONGED OR CONTINUED TREATMENT Some of these medicines may cause respiratory problems such as coughing and pains in the chest.

STOPPING THE TREATMENT Do not discontinue the treatment without consulting your doctor as the infection could recur. If other drugs are being taken at the same time then their dosage may need to be adjusted.

PERSONAL MEDICINE NOTES

Microbes is a vigitable, an' ivry one is like a conservatory full iv millyons iv these potted plants.
Mr Dooley's Opinions

Because many antibiotics are broad spectrum or non-selective they often destroy the vital bacteria needed both for digestion and the synthesis of vitamins. The organisms which cause diarrhoea, flatulence, constipation and yeast infections are able to multiply in these conditions and this is why some people experience intestinal troubles, thrush, exhaustion or depression after a course of antibiotics.

There is much concern over bacteria and micro-organisms becoming resistant to antibiotic treatment. Penicillins, tetracyclines, sulphonamides and other antibiotics are not effective against viral infections and the common cold and their use for these has now been stopped; however bacteria increasingly show resistance to antibiotics. Until quite recently antibiotics were given to cattle or poultry to promote growth and fight the sort of common infections which occur amongst confined animals. The use of these is now far more restricted but antibiotics are still finding their way into the meat bought by the consumer. If you have a sensitivity to antibiotics, or are a heavy meat eater, you may be ingesting antibiotics on a regular basis and this can mean that when they are needed therapeutically the bacteria have become resistant to them and the drugs do not work. Another concern is that as the bacteria become more resistant to the drugs the strains become stronger. Salmonella is an example of this.

If you are taking any antibiotic therapy the advice given for thrush and fungal infections also applies. It is necessary to counteract the loss of nutrients and important bacteria and to strengthen your immune system. Having healthy adrenal glands is important for an efficient immune system. When the adrenals are stressed by physical, emotional or environmental factors the immune system will suffer. Excessive consumption of refined carbohydrates, especially sugar, may eventually weaken the adrenal glands as they abnormally increase the secretion of adrenalin.

The suggestions offered here are designed to help generally with your condition, but it is very important that you do not try to treat yourself. If you suffer severely or regularly from a particular complaint, any serious disorder, or are pregnant then you should not use these remedies before discussion with a doctor. Always report any side-effects and seek medical advice before trying natural remedies and if within a period of one week there has been no improvement then you should consult your doctor.

If you would like to seek individual advice on strengthening your immune system and preventing recurring infections or parasitic infestations then a naturopath, homoeopath, or herbalist will be able to help you. For more detailed information on the individual therapies, together with how to find a practitioner in your area, please refer to the chapter on Alternative/Complementary Medicine and Therapies.

It is possible that certain remedies, supplements or foods could react dangerously with the drugs you are already using so you must check with the fact sheet relating to your medicine to avoid interactions. Please note that it is not advisable to gather your own herbs unless you are sure they are free of any chemicals or pollutants and you can positively identify the correct variety. Always make sure that supplements or natural remedies are taken two to three hours apart from any drugs.

If while reading you come across a particular word or term that is unfamiliar to you please look in The Fact Finder; information on nutrients will be found in the chapter on Vitamins and Minerals.

NATURAL REMEDIES

ATHLETE'S FOOT AND NAIL INFECTIONS

See the chapter on Natural Remedies.

CYSTITIS AND BLADDER INFECTIONS

If your doctor has ruled out the presence of a serious disorder causing your cystitis and the full course of your prescription medicine does not completely relieve the condition then natural remedies could be the answer. They are often effective for relieving the pain and the cause of such infections.

One of the main causes of this disorder is the transference of the bacteria, Escherichia coli, from the anal area to the bladder via the urethra. This can happen when inserting tampons, during sexual intercourse or when using the lavatory. It is important therefore to always wipe the area from front to back to prevent this transference of bacteria. To help healing and prevent further outbreaks the vaginal area should be washed frequently with warm water and a very mild, non-soap cleanser, always washing from front to back. The bladder should be emptied immediately you feel the urge and avoid any direct contact with public lavatory seats. During menstruation sanitary protection should be changed frequently. If you are experiencing external irritation around the urethra or vagina then calendula ointment or cream may help.

Vitamin C and cranberries or cranberry juice both decrease

the pH of the urine and this is protective against bacterial infection. 250mg of vitamin C with bioflavonoids can be taken every two hours during the day, up to 2500mg, until relief is obtained, then gradually reduced over the next 3-5 days. If your tongue becomes sore or if you experience diarrhoea then you should reduce the amount of vitamin C. While taking this amount of vitamin C your diet should contain plenty of vitamin B12 and calcium.

If the cystitis is severe then you may find that a predominantly liquid diet for a day or two is helpful. It is best to avoid chlorinated water, coffee, tea and citrus fruit juices as they can aggravate the condition, but you should try to drink plenty of filtered or spring water and other fluids. Drink a herb tea made from a combination of the following ingredients:

quarter of a teaspoon of marshmallow
quarter of a teaspoon of buchu
quarter of a teaspoon of uva ursi
quarter of a teaspoon of yarrow
quarter of a teaspoon of juniper

Place the herbs in a teapot and pour boiling water over them. Allow to steep for 2-3 minutes, strain and sip slowly up to four times a day.

Vitamin E, up to 400IU a day, helps prevent scar tissue forming in the bladder and foods which contain plenty of vitamin A and zinc are also important for healing. If you have rheumatic heart disease, mitral valve prolapse or are taking certain heart medicines, vitamin E should not be taken in supplement form except under supervision. If you are susceptible to high blood pressure then vitamin E can be taken in supplement form, but must be started at a very low dosage and gradually increased.

HERPES SIMPLEX   See 'cold sores' in the chapter on Natural Remedies.

HIP OR SITZ BATH   Taking a warm hip-bath can assist with relieving congestion or cramping and increasing circulation. For urinary tract infections such as cystitis it can also be very helpful. When the bathroom is comfortably warm, run enough water into the bath so that it just reaches your navel and no further. It is essential that the water is no more than blood heat, about 98°F/37°C, and if you have high blood pressure or heart disorders consult your doctor before trying this. It is best to stay in the water for about half an hour and during this time it will be necessary to continue adding hot water to maintain the right temperature. Let out a little water each time so that it remains at the height of your navel only. It may be necessary to cover the exposed parts of your body so that you do not become chilled. Hip-baths are best taken at night.

SHINGLES OR HERPES ZOSTER

This disorder is commonly known as shingles and usually affects people between the ages of forty and seventy. Its medical name comes from the Greek words herpes, 'to creep', and zoster, 'a girdle', which describes the belt-like ring the blisters sometimes form around the body. The virus is the same as chicken-pox and although it can lie dormant for years it may be re-activated by stress, illness or exposure to chicken-pox. The rash usually decreases or disappears within about fourteen days but because the roots of nerves are affected the pain may continue for many weeks or even months. There are a number of natural remedies and nutritional supplements which can help decrease its duration and pain and they should be discussed with the doctor treating your shingles before they are tried.

The homoeopathic remedy Rhus. Tox. if taken at the first signs of the disease can shorten its duration and a homoeopath can give remedies to decrease both the pain and duration of an attack. To help the skin rash and blisters that may occur the tissue salts Kali. Mur. and Kali. Phos. are often used.

Because the nerves are affected good nutritional support is essential. Vitamin B complex 50-75mg can be taken three times a day, although if taken after 4pm it may keep some people awake at night. The B complex supplement should contain niacinamide and not niacin or nicotinic acid as these two can both cause skin flushing which would irritate the sores. Taking a B supplement will colour the urine a bright yellow, but this is a harmless reaction. Vitamin B12 is also important and if supplements are used then they are best absorbed by placing them under the tongue and allowing them to dissolve. Soya lecithin is a good source of the B vitamins choline and inositol.

Vitamin A is antiviral and helps the healing of skin. Doses of up to 25,000IU a day have been used for four days, discontinued for two days, and the cycle repeated until healing is obtained. This amount of vitamin A is best taken under supervision, especially if you have any liver disorders. The mineral zinc works with vitamin A for skin health and healing and can be taken in doses up to 30mg a day.

From 500-750mg of vitamin C, in the form of calcium ascorbate, may need to be taken every 2-3 hours for up to a week and then gradually reduced to about 500mg three times a day until the sores have healed. If this amount produces diarrhoea then it should be reduced until just before diarrhoea occurs. This is known as taking the dose up to 'bowel tolerance'. Up to 1000mg of bioflavonoids a day should also be taken with vitamin C. High doses of vitamin C, such as those suggested, can decrease vitamin B12 levels. This should be taken into account when taking this much vitamin C and information on supplying adequate B12 in the diet will be found on page 304.

Vitamin E is one of the most helpful nutrients as it can be taken internally as well as being applied directly to the sores. Open up a high potency vitamin E capsule and apply the oil three times a day, but be careful to avoid the eyes as it can cause a harmless but painful burning which may last for several hours. The dosage of vitamin E may need to be as high as 1000-1400IU a day and should be started at 200IU and then gradually increased. If you have rheumatic heart disease, mitral valve prolapse or are taking certain heart medicines, vitamin E should not be taken in supplement form except under supervision. If you are susceptible to high blood pressure then vitamin E can be taken in supplement form, but must be started at a very low dosage and gradually increased.

Propolis tincture applied to the sores 3-4 times a day is helpful or apple cider vinegar can be applied undiluted every two hours. Before applying anything to the affected area you should first test it on an unaffected area of skin.

Royal jelly can help the body cope with stress as it is high in B5 and works especially well if taken with the other nutrients. Foods which are best avoided because they can decrease important nutrients include sugar, refined foods and alcohol.

THRUSH AND FUNGAL INFECTIONS

Eating certain foods can worsen fungal infections. Try to avoid sugar, refined foods, aged or 'blue' cheeses, wines, vinegar, bread, yeast, cider, tea, coffee, malt and peanuts. Increase your intake of 'live' plain yogurt, fresh fruit and vegetables — including garlic if you enjoy it.

To help your system get back to normal after taking antibiotics or cortisone treatment you may want to consider taking some additional vitamins and minerals for a few weeks. This also applies to those who are taking oral contraceptives. A good supplementary regime would include acidophilus, a yeast free high potency multi mineral tablet, a yeast free vitamin B complex and vitamin C with bioflavonoids. Virgin olive oil and raw garlic are very beneficial, but if you are not able to stomach raw garlic it can also be taken in the form of tablets or capsules.

When you start your course of antibiotics it is helpful to follow the dietary recommendations given previously so that you can help to minimize the effect of the destruction of 'good' bacteria. It is very important to note that if you do take vitamin supplements they must NOT be taken with the medicine, but at least two hours before or after it so as not to interfere with the dosage. When antibiotics are found necessary for children then the same diet and supplement regime should be followed, but scaled down to suit the child's age.

STRENGTHENING YOUR IMMUNE SYSTEM

It is essential to keep your immune system as strong as possible to be able to withstand or avoid further infections and for this you need to make sure you know what it takes to keep it healthy. The following are vital for a healthy immune system and you can see whether your diet contains adequate amounts by checking in the chapter on Vitamins and Minerals:

VITAMIN A has antiviral properties and keeps the cell membranes strong.

VITAMIN C activates interferon, a protein found in our cells which fights viral invasion and the proliferation of micro organisms such as germs. It also helps protect the white cells, the function of which is to resist viruses and bacteria, thus fighting infection.

VITAMIN B5 is essential for the manufacture of antibodies which fight infection.

CALCIUM helps protect the immune system from toxic heavy metal poisoning such as lead pollution.

CHROMIUM is lost from the body's white cells during stress. Unless this is replaced in the diet you may be more vulnerable to sickness when stressed or fatigued.

MAGNESIUM works with properdin, a blood protein, which has the ability to destroy bacteria and viruses.

MANGANESE helps vitamin C fight infections.

SELENIUM protects macrophage cells which 'eat' toxins, bacteria and viruses. It stimulates the production of co-enzymes which protect macrophages and it can protect vitamin A from oxidation or destruction in the body.

ZINC is needed to produce histamine, a component of the immune system. Histamine dilates or widens the blood vessels and increases circulation of the blood, thus taking more white cells to the site of infection or injury. Zinc also helps in the production of other infection fighting substances.

GARLIC has both antibacterial and disinfectant properties. It protects against infections if taken regularly, either raw or in tablet form. Like many herbs it has potent anthelmintic properties to destroy or expel parasitic worms.

CENTRAL NERVOUS SYSTEM
CONTENTS

NERVOUS SYSTEM

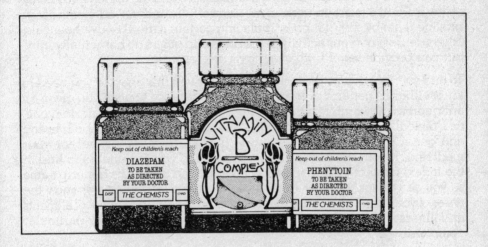

Where to find related information:

Migraine — see clonidine and beta blockers in the chapter on the Cardiovascular System, and aspirin and paracetamol in the chapter on Pain and Inflammation.

Nausea — See also antihistamines in the chapter on the Respiratory System and Allergies.

For centuries there were two schools of thought as to which was the source of intelligence, the heart or the brain. The Chinese, Hebrews and Hindus believed that it was the heart, but the Ancient Greeks held that the brain was where thought, emotion and intelligence sprang from.

In the embryo the brain starts as a simple tube but unlike the spinal cord it progresses from there into the complex and highly developed mass of nerve tissue which is divided into the forebrain, midbrain and hindbrain. The neurological system comprises the central nervous system, which is the brain and spinal cord, and the autonomic nervous system which is divided into the sympathetic and parasympathetic systems. The central nervous system controls voluntary functions, consciousness and mental activity whereas the autonomic nervous system regulates involuntary functions which include those of the glands, digestive system and heart.

CENTRAL NERVOUS SYSTEM
INTRODUCTION

It is often difficult to define some of the conditions which arise from disorders of the neurological system as a clear-cut disease and the reasons why many of the drugs in this group work are not always fully understood. Some drugs provide relief by stimulating or replacing certain natural body chemicals, others depress nervous activity in the brain and others do not actually 'cure' but can provide relief until symptoms are resolved.

To find your particular prescription medicine in this chapter you need to know either its generic or brand name. For instance you may be given an antidepressant which is labelled either amitriptyline, the generic name, or Domical which is a brand name. The index of drugs lists both brand and generic names to enable you to find the right fact sheet for your medicine. If your medicine has a name which you are unable to find in the index, contact your dispensing chemist and ask for its generic name so you can check whether it has been included. If you do not know the name of your drug, you may prefer to check in the separate index of ailments and illnesses to find the drugs that may be prescribed for your particular complaint.

At the end of this group of fact sheets you will find a section on how to help yourself with suggestions for natural remedies and therapies that may be of assistance. Information about practitioners will be found in the chapter on Alternative/Complementary Medicine and Therapies.

If you come across a particular word or term that is unfamiliar to you, please look in The Fact Finder for an explanation; information on food and nutrition will be found in the chapter on Vitamins and Minerals.

PRESCRIPTION NAMES

MEDICINES FOR EPILEPSY AND SEIZURES

Anticonvulsants are used for seizures such as petit and grand mal, as well as nerve pain, neuralgia and facial tics. Phenytoin may also be used for some forms of migraine.

NAMES OF PRESCRIPTION MEDICINES

The following are commonly prescribed anticonvulsants and are shown with the generic name first, followed by the brand name. If your medicine is not listed by name you should follow the information for the generic, if you know it, as the information given will still apply to your particular medicine. If you are not sure of the generic name your pharmacist will be able to advise you. Please note that ALL the information on this fact sheet applies to anticonvulsants generally, not specifically to any one medicine.

Generic	Brand Name
beclamide	Nydrane
carbamazepine	Tegretol
clonazepam	Rivotril
ethosuximide	Emeside, Zarontin
methylphenobarbitone	Prominal
phenobarbitone	Luminal
phenytoin	Epanutin
primidone	Mysoline
sodium valproate	Epilim

WHAT TO TELL YOUR DOCTOR

It is important to make sure that your doctor or doctors are given as much information as possible. If you are aware that you are allergic to any anticonvulsants or any of the tricyclic antidepressants then do tell them so. Information on other medication is vital so if you are taking any other type of medicine, including non-prescription drugs, then they must know that too. Additionally, make sure they know if any of the following apply to you:

Alcoholism
Asthma
Blood clots
Blood disorders
Blood sugar disorders
Bone marrow disorders
Breast feeding
Breathing disorders
Depression
Diabetes
Glaucoma

Have had a stroke
Heart disorders or disease
High blood pressure
Liver or kidney disorders
Lupus erythmatosus
Over excitability
Pregnancy
Respiratory disorders
Suicidal tendencies
Thyroid disorders
Ulcer

If you will be having surgery or dental treatment which requires anaesthesia it is important to tell the person in charge which anticonvulsant you are taking.

For blood-sugar or liver function tests tell the person testing you which anticonvulsant you are taking. If you are performing urine-sugar tests yourself you should take into account that phenytoin and other drugs in this group can produce a false positive result.

SIDE-EFFECTS AND CAUTIONS

SIDE-EFFECTS It is impossible to predict how any medicine will affect a particular individual because everyone's metabolism is so very different. Sensitivity or reaction to drugs can vary greatly from one person to another and side-effects can be related to dosage. It is important to pay close attention to any changes you may notice either when starting, or during, a course of treatment.

The following are some of the side-effects reported within this group of drugs. Some of the disorders listed under Infrequent or Rare may occasionally be the symptoms of overdose and not always those of side-effects.

COMMON

Dizziness	Nausea
Drowsiness	Vomiting

INFREQUENT OR RARE

Abdominal pains	High blood sugar
Abnormal hair growth	Insomnia
Aggressiveness	Irritability
Anaemia	Joint pains
Appetite changes	Lack of co-ordination
Bloating	Lymph gland enlargement
Blood disorders	Skin rashes or itching
Constipation	Slurred speech
Decreased memory capacity	Sore throat
Depression	Swelling of eyelids,
Digestive disorders	lips or face
Dry mouth or thirst	Tremors
Easy bruising and bleeding	Urinary frequency
Fatigue	Vision disturbances
Fever	Weakened bones
Gum disorders	Weight change
Headache	Wheeziness
Heartbeat irregularities	Yellowed skin and eyes

Phenytoin can colour the urine pink, red or brown but this effect is harmless.

If you experience any of the listed side-effects, or any other unusual symptoms, you should consult your dispensing pharmacist or doctor immediately.

CAUTIONS

If you experience dizziness or drowsiness do not drive, operate machinery or work high above the ground. Alcohol can increase these effects and should be avoided during treatment.

Check with your doctor before taking any other medicines with anticonvulsants, including non-prescription drugs.

If sunbathing, or using a sun-bed or lamp whilst taking these medicines, then a rash or increased tendency to burn may occur so it may be advisable to avoid exposure or to take extra precautions.

One of the side-effects can be a dry mouth and this may contribute to the possibility of tooth decay or gum disease. If this occurs, your doctor will probably advise you to clean your teeth frequently and to use dental floss.

INTERACTIONS

INTERACTIONS WITH OTHER MEDICINES AND SUBSTANCES

No medication works in isolation but is affected to a greater or lesser extent by many other factors such as general fitness, diet and lifestyle. Alcohol can alter the way anticonvulsants work and may also increase the severity of the drug's side-effects.

It is also possible to unintentionally combine anticonvulsants with other drugs and this could be dangerous. Check with your doctor or pharmacist before taking any other medication, including non-prescription items, and if you are taking anything listed below look at the key to find out what effect they may have.

1 Antidiabetics
1 MAOI's
1 Sulphonamides
1 Tetracyclines
1 Frusemide diuretics

2 Anxiolytics

3 Antihypertensives

4 Antifungals

NERVOUS SYSTEM

4 Anti-inflammatories
4 Beta blockers
4 Digitalis drugs
4 Diuretics

5 Antidepressants
5 Anticoagulants
5 Anticonvulsants
5 Aspirin, paracetamol
5 Barbiturates, sedatives
5 Contraceptives, oestrogens
5 Cortisone drugs
5 Tranquillizers

Antihistamines may increase the sedative effects of these drugs and anticonvulsants taken with quinidine antiarrhythmics can cause quinidine toxicity. Carbamazepine may alter the dosage requirements of warfarin anticoagulants.

KEY

1 INCREASES the effects of anticonvulsants
2 DECREASES the effects of anticonvulsants
3 ANTICONVULSANTS INCREASE the effects of these drugs
4 ANTICONVULSANTS DECREASE the effects of these drugs
5 UNPREDICTABLE reactions

INTERACTIONS WITH VITAMINS, MINERALS AND FOODS

Nutrient deficiencies may occur while taking anticonvulsants. Particularly affected are calcium, magnesium, folic acid, vitamins B12, C, D and K. Very large doses of B6 and folic acid can decrease the effectiveness of phenytoin. Vegetarians and vegans may run a higher risk of B12 deficiencies and taking anticonvulsants can increase this susceptibility.

Food may become harder to swallow if you suffer from a dry mouth while taking these medicines, and the ability to digest starches and carbohydrates will be affected. An important element in this digestion is the enzyme ptyalin, which is present in saliva, and in order to stimulate its flow all food should be chewed extremely well before swallowing. For more nutritional information see the chapter on Vitamins and Minerals.

NERVOUS SYSTEM

CHILDREN, OVER SIXTIES AND PROLONGED USE

CHILDREN These medicines may be prescribed for children and the dosage will be adjusted accordingly.

OVER SIXTIES As part of the ageing process the body begins to metabolize and eliminate drugs more slowly and so there may be the possibility of more frequent or severe side-effects or interactions with other medicines. With some of the drugs in this group there may be an increased possibility of vitamin K deficiency and there could be feelings of uneasiness and excitability.

PROLONGED OR CONTINUED TREATMENT Some of these medicines may become addictive or habit forming. If you are taking phenytoin for a prolonged period your doctor may prescribe a vitamin D supplement.

The following conditions may occur while on anticonvulsants for prolonged periods of time and if you experience any of them, or any other unusual symptoms, you should consult your doctor.

Bleeding, swelling or redness of gums
Blood disorders
Drop in body temperature
Swollen lymph glands
Thyroid enlargement
Weakened bones

STOPPING THE TREATMENT Do not discontinue the treatment without consulting your doctor as the dosage may need to be gradually reduced. If other drugs are being taken at the same time then their dosage may also need to be adjusted. Withdrawal symptoms may occur if these medicines are suddenly discontinued and if any unusual symptoms appear you should contact your doctor.

PERSONAL MEDICINE NOTES

PRESCRIPTION NAMES

MEDICINES FOR DEPRESSION

The drugs in this group are called tricyclic and tetracyclic antidepressants or mood elevators. They are used to treat depression, depression associated with lack of sleep and anxiety, agitation, alcoholism, incontinence and children's bedwetting.

NAMES OF PRESCRIPTION MEDICINES

The following are commonly prescribed tricyclic or tetracyclic antidepressants and are shown with the generic name first followed by the brand name. If your medicine is not listed by name you should follow the information for the generic, if you know it, as the information given will still apply to your particular medicine. If you are not sure of the generic name your pharmacist will be able to advise you. Please note that ALL the information on this fact sheet applies to tricyclic antidepressants generally, not specifically to any one medicine.

Generic	Brand Name
amitriptyline	Domical, Elavil, Lentizol, Limbitrol, Triptafen, Tryptizol
butriptyline	Evadyne
clomipramine	Anafranil/SR
desipramine	Pertofran
dothiepin	Prothiaden
doxepin	Sinequan
imipramine	Praminil, Tofranil
iprindole	Prondol
lofepramine	Gamanil
maprotiline	Ludiomil
mianserin	Bolvidon, Norval
nortriptyline	Allegron, Aventyl, Motival, Motipress
protriptyline	Concordin
trazodone	Molipaxin
trimipramine	Surmontil
tryptophan	Optimax/VW, Pacitron
viloxazine	Vivalan

WHAT TO TELL YOUR DOCTOR

It is important to make sure that your doctor or doctors are given as much information as possible. If you are aware that you are allergic to any tricyclic or tetracyclic antidepressants then do tell them so. Information on other medication is vital so if you are taking any other type of medicine, including non-prescription drugs, then they must know that too. Additionally, make sure they know if any of the following apply to you:

CENTRAL NERVOUS SYSTEM
ANTIDEPRESSANTS

Alcoholism
Asthma
Bladder disorders
Breast feeding
Diabetes
Epilepsy
Glaucoma
Heart disorders
High blood pressure

Intestinal disorders
Liver or kidney disorders
Pregnancy
Prostate disorders
Stomach disorders
Suicidal tendencies
Thyroid disorders
Urinary disorders

If you will be having surgery or dental treatment which requires anaesthesia it is important to tell the person in charge that you are taking tricyclic antidepressants.

SIDE-EFFECTS AND CAUTIONS

SIDE-EFFECTS It is impossible to predict how any medicine will affect a particular individual because everyone's metabolism is so very different. Sensitivity or reaction to drugs can vary greatly from one person to another and side-effects can be related to dosage. It is important to pay close attention to any changes you may notice either when starting, or during, a course of treatment.

The following are some of the side-effects reported within this group of drugs. Some of the disorders listed under Infrequent or Rare may occasionally be the symptoms of overdose and not always those of side-effects.

COMMON

Blood sugar disorders
Diarrhoea or constipation
Dizziness
Drowsiness
Dry mouth
Fatigue
Headache

Heartbeat irregularities
Low blood pressure
Nausea or vomiting
Sweating or fever
Tremors
Unpleasant taste in mouth
Vision disorders
Weight changes

INFREQUENT OR RARE

Appetite changes
Black tongue
Blood disorders
Confusion
Convulsions
Craving for sweet foods
Difficulty urinating
Digestive disorders
Disorders of sexual function

Hallucinations
Heartburn
Sensitivity of eyes and
    skin to sunlight
Skin rashes, itching
Sleeping disturbances
Sore throat
Yellowing of eyes or skin

145

If you experience any of the listed side-effects, or any other unusual symptoms, you should consult your dispensing pharmacist or doctor immediately.

CAUTIONS

It may be several weeks before antidepressants begin to help your condition so you should not expect immediate results.

If you experience dizziness or drowsiness do not drive, operate machinery or work high above the ground. Alcohol can increase these effects and should be avoided during treatment.

If sunbathing, or using a sun-bed or lamp whilst taking these medicines, then a rash or increased tendency to burn may occur so it may be advisable to avoid exposure or to take extra precautions.

One of the side-effects can be a dry mouth and this may contribute to the possibility of tooth decay or gum disease. if this occurs, your doctor will probably advise you to clean your teeth frequently and to use dental floss.

INTERACTIONS

INTERACTIONS WITH OTHER MEDICINES AND SUBSTANCES

No medication works in isolation but is affected to a greater or lesser extent by many other factors such as general fitness, diet and lifestyle. Alcohol can increase the chance and severity of some of the side-effects. Smoking can lower the effectiveness of the medicine and increase the chance of side-effects such as heartbeat irregularity or slow pulse.

It is also possible to unintentionally combine antidepressants with other drugs and this could be dangerous. Check with your doctor or pharmacist before taking any other medication, including non-prescription items, and if you are taking anything listed below look at the key to find out what effect they may have.

1 Antacids
1 Thiazide diuretics

2 Barbiturates or sleeping tablets
2 Oral contraceptives

3 Anticholinegrics or antispasmodics
3 Antidiarrhoeals
3 Antihistamines
3 Decongestants for asthma or bronchitis

4   Hydantoin anticonvulsants
4   Antihypertensives

5   Anticoagulants
5   Beta blockers
5   Narcotic analgesics
5   Other antidepressants
5   Vasodilators

MAOI's taken with antidepressants can induce convulsions and fever.

Thyroid hormones taken at the same time as antidepressants may cause irregular heartbeat.

Anticholinergics taken in conjunction with antidepressants can increase their sedative effects.

Oral contraceptives can increase the side-effects of antidepressants when taken with them.

Diuretics taken with antidepressants can dangerously lower blood pressure.

KEY

1   INCREASES the effects of tricyclic antidepressants
2   DECREASES the effects of tricyclic antidepressants
3   ANTIDEPRESSANTS INCREASE the effects of these drugs
4   ANTIDEPRESSANTS DECREASE the effects of these drugs
5   UNPREDICTABLE reactions

INTERACTIONS WITH VITAMINS, MINERALS AND FOODS

Antidepressants may decrease the effects of vitamin B2. Iron supplements should be taken at least an hour before antidepressants and alkaline foods should be avoided in excess amounts as they could increase the effects of the medicine. More details about alkaline foods are in The Fact Finder.

If you are taking amitriptyline drugs it is not advisable to have more than 8-10 drinks in a day because of possible fluid retention.

Food may become harder to swallow if you suffer from a dry mouth while taking these medicines, and the ability to digest starches and carbohydrates will be affected. An important element in this digestion is the enzyme ptyalin, which is present in saliva, and in order to stimulate its flow all food should be chewed extremely well before swallowing. For more information see the chapter on Vitamins and Minerals.

NERVOUS SYSTEM

CHILDREN, OVER SIXTIES AND PROLONGED USE

CHILDREN Some of these medicines may cause behavioural problems in children. They may be prescribed for children over the age of twelve and the dosage will be adjusted accordingly.

OVER SIXTIES As part of the ageing process the body begins to metabolize and eliminate drugs more slowly and so there may be the possibility of more frequent or severe side-effects or interactions with other medicines. With some of the drugs in this group there may be an increased possibility of fainting, dizziness, constipation, less frequent urination and feelings of agitation.

PROLONGED OR CONTINUED TREATMENT If you are taking antidepressants for a prolonged time your doctor will monitor your blood pressure and you may also require blood cell counts and liver function tests.

STOPPING THE TREATMENT Do not discontinue the treatment without consulting your doctor as the dosage may need to be gradually reduced. If other drugs are being taken at the same time then their dosage may also need to be adjusted. If these drugs are stopped abruptly then some withdrawal symptoms may occur. These can include excessive perspiration, sleeping problems, irritability, excitement, and sexual function disorders. If you experience any of them you should contact your doctor.

PERSONAL MEDICINE NOTES

NERVOUS SYSTEM

PRESCRIPTION NAMES

MEDICINES USED FOR NAUSEA

The drugs in this group consist of antihistamines, phenothiazine tranquillizers and antispasmodics. A large percentage of antinauseants are antihistamines although they are not those generally used for hay fever and allergies. Some work by affecting the brain's nerve transmitters and others decrease spasms which occur in the stomach and intestines. They are used in the treatment of motion sickness, nausea, vomiting, vertigo, anxiety, migraine, agitation, or ear and hearing disorders.

NAMES OF PRESCRIPTION MEDICINES

The following are commonly prescribed antinauseants and are shown with the generic name first, followed by the brand name. If your medicine is not listed by name you should follow the information for the generic, if you know it, as the information given will still apply to your particular medicine. If you are not sure of the generic name your pharmacist will be able to advise you. Please note that ALL the information on this fact sheet applies to antinauseants generally, not specifically to any one medicine.

Generic	Brand Name
cinnarizine	Stugeron
cyclizine	Valoid
dimenhydrinate	Dramamine
domperidone	Motilium
meclozine	Ancoloxin
metoclopramide	Maxolon, Metox, Metramid, Mygdalon, Parmid, Primperan
prochlorperazine	Stemetil, Vertigon
promethazine	Avomine

WHAT TO TELL YOUR DOCTOR

It is important to make sure that your doctor or doctors are given as much information as possible. If you are aware that you are allergic to any antinauseants, phenothiazine tranquillizers or antihistamines then do tell them so. Information on other medication is vital so if you are taking any other type of medicine, including non-prescription drugs, then they must know that too. Additionally, make sure they know if any of the following apply to you:

Anaemia	Glaucoma
Asthma	Heart disorders
Blood poisoning	Liver or kidney disorders
Breast feeding	Low blood pressure
Epilepsy*	Myasthenia gravis*

CENTRAL NERVOUS SYSTEM
ANTINAUSEANTS

Parkinson's disease*   Prostate disorders*
Peptic ulcer   Respiratory disorders
Poor circulation   Thyroid disorders
Pregnancy   Urinary tract disorders

*You only need to inform your doctor about these particular conditions, in addition to the others, if you are taking prochlorperazine.

If you will be having surgery or dental treatment which requires anaesthesia it is important to tell the person in charge that you are taking antinauseants.

SIDE-EFFECTS AND CAUTIONS

SIDE-EFFECTS It is impossible to predict how any medicine will affect a particular individual because everyone's metabolism is so very different. Sensitivity or reaction to drugs can vary greatly from one person to another and side-effects can be related to dosage. It is important to pay close attention to any changes you may notice either when starting, or during, a course of treatment.

The following are some of the side-effects reported within this group of drugs. Some of the disorders listed under Infrequent or Rare may occasionally be the symptoms of overdose and not always those of side-effects.

COMMON Confusion   Dry mouth
Drowsiness*   Dry skin

*This side-effect is rare with metoclopramide.

INFREQUENT OR RARE
Agitation   Irregular or fast heartbeat
Blood disorders   Lactation continues after
Blood pressure decrease   weaning
Blood spotting between   Loss of appetite
    periods   Menstrual cramps
Blurred vision   Muscle spasms
Breast enlargement, male   Nasal stuffiness
Constipation   Reduced perspiration
Difficulty urinating   Restlessness
Digestive disorders   Sensitivity to extreme
Dizziness   temperature changes
Fever   Sensitivity to light
Headaches   Shaking or nervousness

NERVOUS SYSTEM

Skin rash
Sleeping disturbances
Sore throat

Vision disorders
Yellow skin and eyes

If you experience any of the listed side-effects, or any other unusual symptoms, you should consult your dispensing pharmacist or doctor immediately.

CAUTIONS If you experience dizziness or drowsiness do not drive, operate machinery or work high above the ground. Alcohol can dangerously increase these effects and should be avoided during treatment.

If sunbathing, or using a sun-bed or lamp whilst taking these medicines, then a rash or increased tendency to burn may occur so it may be advisable to avoid exposure or to take extra precautions. You may retain this sensitivity for up to three months after finishing your course of treatment.

One of the side-effects can be a dry mouth and this may contribute to the possibility of tooth decay or gum disease. If this occurs, your doctor will probably advise you to clean your teeth frequently and to use dental floss.

INTERACTIONS

INTERACTIONS WITH OTHER MEDICINES AND SUBSTANCES No medication works in isolation but is affected to a greater or lesser extent by many other factors such as general fitness, diet and lifestyle. Drowsiness is one of the side-effects of this group of drugs and it may be increased by alcohol.

It is also possible to unintentionally combine antinauseants with other drugs and this could be dangerous. Check with your doctor or pharmacist before taking any other medication, including non-prescription items, and if you are taking anything listed below look at the key to find out what effect they may have.

1 Antidepressants

2 Antacids*
2 Antiparkinsonian drugs
2 Lithium

3 Anticholinergics
3 Antihistamines
3 Anxiolytics, hypnosedatives

3 Hydantoin anticonvulsants
3 Tranquillizers

4 Appetite suppressants
4 Oral hypoglycaemics
4 Levodopa

5 Barbiturates
5 Medicines for pain

*This particular interaction applies only to prochlorperazine and is not relevant to the other drugs in this group. Prochlorperazine is still affected by the other listed interactions.

Antinauseants should not be taken with cold or cough remedies.

It is possible that the normal functioning of the heart may be dangerously decreased if antiarrythmics are taken in conjunction with antinauseants.

KEY
1 INCREASES the effects of antinauseants
2 DECREASES the effects of antinauseants
3 ANTINAUSEANTS INCREASE the effects of these drugs
4 ANTINAUSEANTS DECREASE the effects of these drugs
5 UNPREDICTABLE reactions

INTERACTIONS WITH VITAMINS, MINERALS AND FOODS

It is possible that a very large intake of alkaline foods could decrease the excretion of these drugs and thus increase their side-effects. Details of alkaline foods are in The Fact Finder. Food may become harder to swallow if you suffer from a dry mouth while taking these medicines, and the ability to digest starches and carbohydrates will be affected. An important element in this digestion is the enzyme ptyalin, which is present in saliva, and in order to stimulate its flow all food should be chewed extremely well before swallowing.

NERVOUS SYSTEM

CHILDREN, OVER SIXTIES AND PROLONGED USE

CHILDREN The prochlorperazine drugs are not recommended for children but other drugs may be prescribed for those aged two and upwards. In the case of young children the dosage will be adjusted accordingly.

OVER SIXTIES As part of the ageing process the body begins to metabolize and eliminate drugs more slowly and so there may be the possibility of more frequent or severe side-effects or interactions with other medicines.

With prochlorperazine there may be a greater risk of sensitivity to extreme temperature changes and with it, and other drugs in this group, the side-effects of dizziness, drowsiness and constipation may be more pronounced.

PROLONGED OR CONTINUED TREATMENT Some of these medicines may cause constipation, or stool impaction, when used for prolonged periods.

STOPPING THE TREATMENT Antinauseants should not be discontinued without your doctor's advice.

PERSONAL MEDICINE NOTES

PRESCRIPTION NAMES

MEDICINES FOR PARKINSON'S DISEASE AND RELATED DISORDERS

The symptoms of Parkinson's disease can be the result of cholinergic excess in the body and it is believed that this occurs as a result of dopamine deficiency. These drugs work to correct that excess and may also be prescribed with levodopa, with which they work. Anticholinergic drugs are used to treat Parkinson's disease, tremors, pain due to muscle strains, and to counteract the effects of some tranquillizers. Other antiparkinsonian drugs will be found in the previous fact sheet.

NAMES OF PRESCRIPTION MEDICINES

The following are commonly prescribed antiparkinsonian anticholinergics and are shown with the generic name first, followed by the brand name. If your medicine is not listed by name you should follow the information for the generic, if you know it, as the information given will still apply to your particular medicine. If you are not sure of the generic name your pharmacist will be able to advise you. Please note that ALL the information on this fact sheet applies to antiparkinsonian anticholinergics generally, not specifically to any one medicine.

Generic	Brand Name
benzhexol	Artane, Bentex, Broflex
benztropine	Cogentin
biperiden	Akineton
methixene	Tremonil
orphenadrine	Disipal, Biorphen
procyclidine	Arpicolin, Kemadrin

WHAT TO TELL YOUR DOCTOR

It is important to make sure that your doctor or doctors are given as much information as possible. If you are aware that you are allergic to any antiparkinsonian anticholinergics then do tell them so. Information on other medication is vital so if you are taking any other type of medicine, including non-prescription drugs, then they must know that too. Additionally, make sure they know if any of the following apply to you:

Asthma, bronchitis or
  other breathing disorders
Bowel or intestinal
  obstruction
Breast feeding
Circulatory disorders
Digestive disorders
Glaucoma
Hardening of the arteries
Heart disorders

Hiatus hernia
High blood pressure
Liver or kidney disorders
Myasthenia gravis
Pregnancy
Prostate disorders
Thyroid overactivity
Ulcerative colitis
Urinary disorders

NERVOUS SYSTEM

SIDE-EFFECTS AND CAUTIONS

SIDE-EFFECTS It is impossible to predict how any medicine will affect a particular individual because everyone's metabolism is so very different. Sensitivity or reaction to drugs can vary greatly from one person to another and side-effects can be related to dosage. It is important to pay close attention to any changes you may notice either when starting, or during, a course of treatment.

The following are some of the side-effects reported within this group of drugs. Some of the disorders listed under Infrequent or Rare may occasionally be the symptoms of overdose and not always those of side-effects.

COMMON

Constipation
Diarrhoea
Difficulty urinating

Dry mouth
Nausea or vomiting
Vision disorders

INFREQUENT OR RARE

Bloating
Change in sexual desire
    and performance
Confusion
Decreased sweating
Dizziness or drowsiness
Excitement
Fatigue
Flushing

Hallucinations
Muscle cramps
Numbness of fingers
Rapid heartbeat
Sensitivity of eyes to light
Skin rash
Susceptibility to sun or
    heatstroke

If you experience any of the listed side-effects, or any other unusual symptoms, you should consult your dispensing pharmacist or doctor immediately.

CAUTIONS Some of these medicines can aggravate prostate disorders, cause nightmares, and affect normal thought processes.
If you experience dizziness or drowsiness do not drive, operate machinery or work high above the ground. Alcohol can increase these effects and should be avoided during treatment.

As some of these medicines can make you extra sensitive to heat and decrease sweating you should avoid over-exertion in the sun or hot atmospheres such as a sauna or steam bath. Your eyes may also become more sensitive to light and you may need to wear sunglasses in bright sunlight.

One of the side-effects can be a dry mouth and this may contribute to the possibility of tooth decay or gum disease. If this occurs, your doctor will probably advise you to clean your teeth frequently and to use dental floss.

NERVOUS SYSTEM

155

INTERACTIONS

INTERACTIONS WITH OTHER MEDICINES AND SUBSTANCES

No medication works in isolation but is affected to a greater or lesser extent by many other factors such as general fitness, diet and lifestyle. Alcohol can increase drowsiness, while smoking can decrease the effectiveness of these medicines.

It is also possible to unintentionally combine antiparkinsonian anticholinergics with other drugs and this could be dangerous. Check with your doctor or pharmacist before taking any other medication, including non-prescription items, and if you are taking anything listed below look at the key to find out what effect they may have.

1   Antidepressants
1   Antihistamines
1   MAOI's

2   Antacids
2   Ulcer medicines

3   Antiarrhythmics
3   Levodopa

4   Antifungals
4   Glaucoma eye drops

5   Anxiolytics and sedatives
5   Antidiarrhoeals
5   Cold and allergy medicines
5   Cardiovascular medicines
5   Other anticholinergics
5   Other antiparkinsonian medicines

Some anxiolytic, sedative or tranquillizing drugs can cause changes in behaviour, low blood sugar and extreme tiredness when taken with antiparkinsonian anticholinergics.

KEY

1   INCREASES the effects of antiparkinsonian anticholinergics
2   DECREASES the effects of antiparkinsonian anticholinergics
3   ANTIPARKINSONIAN ANTICHOLINERGICS INCREASE the effects of these drugs
4   ANTIPARKINSONIAN ANTICHOLINERGICS DECREASE the effects of these drugs
5   UNPREDICTABLE reactions

INTERACTIONS WITH VITAMINS, MINERALS AND FOODS

It is possible that a very large intake of alkaline foods could decrease the excretion of these drugs. This means they are present longer in the body and side-effects could therefore be increased. Details on alkaline foods are in The Fact Finder.

Food may become harder to swallow if you suffer from a dry mouth while taking these medicines, and the ability to digest starches and carbohydrates will be affected. An important element in this digestion is the enzyme ptyalin, which is present in saliva, and in order to stimulate its flow all food should be chewed extremely well before swallowing.

CHILDREN, OVER SIXTIES AND PROLONGED USE

CHILDREN These medicines may be prescribed for children and the dosage will be adjusted accordingly.

OVER SIXTIES As part of the ageing process the body begins to metabolize and eliminate drugs more slowly and so there may be the possibility of more frequent or severe side-effects or interactions with other medicines. With some of the drugs in this group there may be an increased possibility of prostate disorders in men who are susceptible, and confusion and nightmares are more likely to occur in this age group.

PROLONGED OR CONTINUED TREATMENT Prolonged treatment could result in glaucoma developing in susceptible people.

STOPPING THE TREATMENT Do not discontinue or decrease the drugs without consulting your doctor as the dosage may need to be gradually reduced. If other drugs are being taken at the same time then their dosage may also need to be adjusted.

PERSONAL MEDICINE NOTES

NERVOUS SYSTEM

157

CENTRAL NERVOUS SYSTEM
ANTIPARKINSONIAN DRUGS

PRESCRIPTION NAMES

MEDICINES FOR PARKINSONISM AND OTHER DISEASES

Dopamine is a natural body substance which chemically transmits nerve impulses in the central nervous system and in Parkinson's disease its supply may be subnormal. Levodopa and bromocriptine belong to a group of drugs called dopaminergics. Levodopa supplies dopa which can be converted to dopamine in the brain and bromocriptine has actions similar to those of dopamine and is used for Parkinson's disease and female disorders. Seligiline is used with levodopa to enhance its effects and to prevent dopamine breakdown in the brain. Amantadine is an antiviral drug for shingles and other viral infections and is used with levodopa to treat Parkinsonism and symptoms similar to those of Parkinson's disease. Anticholinergic antiparkinsonian drugs will be found in the next fact sheet.

NAMES OF PRESCRIPTION MEDICINES

The following are commonly prescribed antiparkinsonian dopaminergics and are shown with the generic name first, followed by the brand name. If your medicine is not listed by name you should follow the information for the generic, if you know it, as the information given will still apply to your particular medicine. If you are not sure of the generic name your pharmacist will be able to advise you. Please note that ALL the information on this fact sheet applies to antiparkinsonian drugs generally, not specifically to any one medicine.

Generic	Brand Name
amantadine	Symmetrel
bromocriptine	Parlodel
levodopa	Brocadopa, Larodopa, Madopar, Sinemet
levodopa and carbidopa	Sinemet Plus
selegiline	Eldepryl

WHAT TO TELL YOUR DOCTOR

It is important to make sure that your doctor or doctors are given as much information as possible. If you are aware that you are allergic to any antiparkinsonian drugs then do tell them so. Information on other medication is vital so if you are taking any other type of medicine, including non-prescription drugs, then they must know that too. Additionally, make sure they know if any of the following apply to you:

Breast feeding	Liver or kidney disorders
Convulsive disorders	Peptic ulcer
Diabetes	Pregnancy
Epilepsy	Respiratory disorders
Eye disorders or glaucoma	Skin cancer or melanoma
Heart disease	

NERVOUS SYSTEM

Also inform your doctor if you have any history of hallucinations, confusional states or psychotic disorders.

If you will be having surgery or dental treatment which requires anaesthesia it is important to tell the person in charge that you are taking levodopa or any of the other drugs in this group. For urine or blood tests tell the person conducting the test which drug you are taking. If you are testing yourself for urine-sugar please note that levodopa and bromocriptine can cause false results.

SIDE-EFFECTS AND CAUTIONS

SIDE-EFFECTS It is impossible to predict how any medicine will affect a particular individual because everyone's metabolism is so very different. Sensitivity or reaction to drugs can vary greatly from one person to another and side-effects can be related to dosage. It is important to pay close attention to any changes you may notice either when starting, or during, a course of treatment.

The following are some of the side-effects reported within this group of drugs. Some of the disorders listed under Infrequent or Rare may occasionally be the symptoms of overdose and not always those of side-effects.

COMMON

Loss of appetite
Nausea
Pains in the stomach
Vomiting

INFREQUENT OR RARE

Abnormal breathing
Anxiety or agitation
Bitter taste in mouth
Body odour
Bloating
Blood disorders
Confusion
Depression
Diarrhoea or constipation
Dizziness or drowsiness
Dry mouth, burning tongue
  or increased saliva
Fatigue
Flushing
Hallucinations
Headache
Heartbeat disorders
Increase in sexual drive
Insomnia
Lightheadedness
Loss of hair
Low blood pressure
Mood changes
Nervousness
Nightmares
Purpling of skin or rash
Sweating or hot flushes
Ulcers
Uncontrollable movements
  of the muscles
Vision disorders
Water retention
Weight change

NERVOUS SYSTEM

A pink or red discoloration of the urine, saliva or sweat may be caused by levodopa, but this effect is harmless.

If you experience any of the listed side-effects, or any other unusual symptoms, you should consult your dispensing pharmacist or doctor immediately.

CAUTIONS

If you experience dizziness or drowsiness do not drive, operate machinery or work high above the ground. Alcohol can increase these effects and should be avoided during treatment.

One of the side-effects can be a dry mouth and this may contribute to the possibility of tooth decay or gum disease. If this occurs, your doctor will probably advise you to clean your teeth frequently and to use dental floss.

INTERACTIONS

INTERACTIONS WITH OTHER MEDICINES AND SUBSTANCES

No medication works in isolation and is affected to a greater or lesser extent by many other factors such as general fitness, diet and lifestyle. The possibility of fainting is increased by alcohol and the body's tolerance to alcohol is decreased by bromocriptine. Smoking can decrease the effectiveness of these medicines.

It is also possible to unintentionally combine antiparkinsonian drugs with other medicines and this could be dangerous. Check with your doctor or pharmacist before taking any other medication, including non-prescription items, and if you are taking anything listed below look at the key to find out what effect they may have.

1   Anticholinergics
1   Other antiparkinsonian drugs
1   Other drugs within this group

2   Antihypertensives
2   Phenytoin
2   Tranquillizers
2   Tricyclic antidepressants

3   Antihypertensives

5   Antacids

If MAOI's are taken with antiparkinsonian medicines, or up to 14 days after their withdrawal, they can increase blood pressure to a dangerous level.

Sympathomimetics used for bronchial spasm or nasal decongestion if taken with levodopa can enhance its cardiac side-effects.

KEY

1 INCREASES the effects of antiparkinsonian drugs and dopaminergics
2 DECREASES the effects of antiparkinsonian drugs and dopaminergics
3 ANTIPARKINSONIAN DRUGS INCREASE the effects of these drugs
5 UNPREDICTABLE reactions

INTERACTIONS WITH VITAMINS, MINERALS AND FOODS

Supplements of vitamin B6 can decrease the effectiveness of levodopa drugs and should not be taken unless specifically directed. In turn, levodopa decreases the effects of B6 and B3 and it is important to ensure an adequate intake through the diet, but not from vitamin tablets.

Taking large supplemental doses of the amino acid tryptophane may detrimentally decrease levodopa's effects. Potassium, folic acid and vitamin B12 may also be depleted and some vegetarians and vegans run a higher risk of B12 deficiency. For more information see the chapter on Vitamins and Minerals.

Food may become harder to swallow if you suffer from a dry mouth while taking these medicines, and the ability to digest starches and carbohydrates will be affected. An important element in this digestion is the enzyme ptyalin, which is present in saliva, and in order to stimulate its flow all food should be chewed extremely well before swallowing.

NERVOUS SYSTEM

CENTRAL NERVOUS SYSTEM
ANTIPARKINSONIAN DRUGS

CHILDREN, OVER SIXTIES AND PROLONGED USE

CHILDREN These medicines may be prescribed for children and the dosage will be adjusted accordingly.

OVER SIXTIES As part of the ageing process the body begins to metabolize and eliminate drugs more slowly and so there may be the possibility of more frequent or severe side-effects or interactions with other medicines.

PROLONGED OR CONTINUED TREATMENT Some of these drugs when used long-term may cause involuntary movements of the body, swelling of the feet, problems with breathing, and skin eruptions. The intestinal absorption of the amino acid DLPA may be impaired during long-term treatment with levodopa; however, this should be discussed with your doctor as large supplemental doses could possibly interfere with the drug's effects.

STOPPING THE TREATMENT Antiparkinsonian drugs should not be discontinued without your doctor's advice as their dosage may need to be gradually reduced.

PERSONAL MEDICINE NOTES

NERVOUS SYSTEM

PRESCRIPTION NAMES

MEDICINES FOR NERVOUSNESS, ANXIETY AND TENSION

The drugs in this group are known as minor tranquillizers and some belong to the group known as benzodiazepines. They are used to treat nervousness, tension, restlessness, anxiety, alcohol withdrawal, convulsive disorders, itching from allergies, emotionally related asthma, insomnia, pre-menstrual syndrome and muscle spasm.

NAMES OF PRESCRIPTION MEDICINES

The following are commonly prescribed anxiolytics and hypnotics and are shown with the generic name first, followed by the brand name. If your medicine is not listed by name you should follow the information for the generic, if you know it, as the information given will still apply to your particular medicine. If you are not sure of the generic name your pharmacist will be able to advise you. Please note that ALL the information on this fact sheet applies to anxiolytics and hypnotics generally, not specifically to any one medicine.

Generic	Brand Name
alprazolam	Xanax
bromazepam	Lexotan
chloral hydrate	Noctec
chlorazepate	Tranxene
chlordiazepoxide	Librium, Tropium
chlormethiazole	Heminevrin
chlormezanone	Trancopal
clobazam	Frisium
clorazepate	Tranxene
diazepam	Alupram, Atensine, Diazemuls, Evacalm, Solis, Tensium, Valium
dichloralphenazone	Welldorm
flunitrazepam	Rohypnol
flurazepam	Dalmane, Paxane
hydroxyzine	Atarax
ketazolam	Anxon
loprazolam	Dormonoct
lorazepam	Almazine, Ativan
lormetazepam	Noctamid
medazepam	Nobrium
meprobamate	Equanil, Meptrate, Tenavoid
nitrazepam	Mogadon, Nitrados, Noctesed, Remnos, Somnite, Surem, Unisomnia
oxazepam	Oxanid
prazepam	Centrax

CENTRAL NERVOUS SYSTEM
ANXIOLYTICS AND HYPNOTICS

temazepam	Normison
triazolam	Halcion
triclofos	Triclofos elixir

WHAT TO TELL YOUR DOCTOR It is important to make sure that your doctor or doctors are given as much information as possible. If you are aware that you are allergic to any anxiolytics or hypnotics then do tell them so. Information on other medication is vital so if you are taking any other type of medicine, including non-prescription drugs, then they must know that too. Additionally, make sure they know if any of the following apply to you:

Breast feeding	Hardening of the arteries
Depression	Hyperactivity in children
Diabetes	Liver or kidney disorders
Digestive disorders	Myasthenia gravis
Drug addiction	Pregnancy
Epilepsy or seizures	Respiratory disorders
Glaucoma	Urinary system disorders
Gout	

If you will be having surgery or dental treatment which requires anaesthesia it is important to tell the person in charge that you are taking anxiolytics or hypnotics.

SIDE-EFFECTS AND CAUTIONS

SIDE-EFFECTS It is impossible to predict how any medicine will affect a particular individual because everyone's metabolism is so very different. Sensitivity or reaction to drugs can vary greatly from one person to another and side-effects can be related to dosage. It is important to pay close attention to any changes you may notice either when starting, or during, a course of treatment. The following are some of the side-effects reported within this group of drugs. Some of the disorders listed under Infrequent or Rare may occasionally be the symptoms of overdose and not always those of side-effects.

COMMON

Dizziness	Lightheadedness
Drowsiness	Vision disorders
Fatigue	

INFREQUENT OR RARE

Breathing difficulties	Constipation
Changes in sexual desire or performance	Depression
	Diarrhoea
Confusion	Difficulty sleeping

NERVOUS SYSTEM

164

Digestive disorders	Problems urinating
Dry mouth	Shakiness
Eye irritations	Skin rash or itching
Headache	Slow heartbeat
Increased appetite	Slurring of speech
Lack of muscular control	Sneezing
Low blood pressure	Sore throat or fever
Nasal congestion	Stomach cramps
Nasal irritation	Water retention
Nausea or vomiting	Weight gain
Nervousness or irritability	Yellowing of skin and eyes

If you experience any of the listed side-effects, or any other unusual symptoms, you should consult your dispensing pharmacist or doctor immediately.

CAUTIONS

Because of their addiction potential some of these drugs may only be used for 6-8 weeks at a time.

If you experience dizziness or drowsiness do not drive, operate machinery or work high above the ground. Alcohol can increase these effects and should be avoided during treatment.

One of the side-effects can be a dry mouth and this may contribute to the possibility of tooth decay or gum disease. If this occurs, your doctor will probably advise you to clean your teeth frequently and to use dental floss.

INTERACTIONS

INTERACTIONS WITH OTHER MEDICINES AND SUBSTANCES

No medication works in isolation but is affected to a greater or lesser extent by many other factors such as general fitness, diet and lifestyle. Alcohol can increase the effects of these medicines and can cause extreme drowsiness, and tobacco can decrease the effectiveness of anxiolytics or hypnotics.

It is also possible to unintentionally combine anxiolytics or hypnotics with other drugs and this could be dangerous. Check with your doctor or pharmacist before taking any other medication, including non-prescription items, and if you are taking anything listed below look at the key to find out what effect they may have.

1 Antidepressants*
1 Antihistamines*

NERVOUS SYSTEM

165

1 Antihypertensives*
1 Cimetidine*
1 Narcotic analgesics*
1 Barbiturates*
1 MAOI's*
1 Other anxiolytics or sedatives*
1 Tranquillizers*
1 Zaditen asthma and allergy drugs*

*If any of these medicines are taken with anxiolytics they could cause very serious side-effects. They can include convulsions, extreme fatigue with sedation, and overexcitability; this last effect can remain for up to two weeks after withdrawal.

2 Antacids

3 Antidiarrhoeals
3 Antihistamines
3 Anticholinergics
3 Diuretics
3 Other sedatives
3 Tranquillizers

4 Oral contraceptives

5 Anticoagulants
5 Anticonvulsants
5 Beta blockers

KEY
1 INCREASES the effects of anxiolytics or hypnotics
2 DECREASES the effects of anxiolytics or hypnotics
3 ANXIOLYTICS AND HYPNOTICS INCREASE the effects of these drugs
4 ANXIOLYTICS AND HYPNOTICS DECREASE the effects of these drugs
5 UNPREDICTABLE reactions

INTERACTIONS WITH VITAMINS, MINERALS AND FOODS

The vitamins which may be depleted by these drugs are B3, B5, B12, and D. Some vegetarians and vegans may be more susceptible to B12 deficiency. Although vitamins B3 and C have been used to increase the effectiveness of these drugs, they should not be taken in supplement form before discussion with a doctor.

Food may become harder to swallow if you suffer from a dry mouth while taking these medicines, and the ability to digest starches and carbohydrates will be affected. An important element in this digestion is the enzyme ptyalin, which is present in saliva, and in order to stimulate its flow all food should be chewed extremely well before swallowing.

NERVOUS SYSTEM

CHILDREN, OVER SIXTIES AND PROLONGED USE

CHILDREN These medicines may be prescribed for children over the age of six months and the dosage will be adjusted accordingly.

OVER SIXTIES As part of the ageing process the body begins to metabolize and eliminate drugs more slowly and so there may be the possibility of more frequent or severe side-effects or interactions with other medicines. With some of the drugs in this group there may be an increased possibility of urinary difficulties, especially in men who have prostate problems.

Feelings of agitation, and problems with balance are also more likely. Alcohol can increase the side-effects of these drugs by extending the length of time they remain in the body and this especially applies to the over sixties.

PROLONGED OR CONTINUED TREATMENT Some of the medicines in this group may become habit forming and if the body develops a tolerance to them they will then become less effective. With prolonged treatment it may be necessary to run liver function tests.

STOPPING THE TREATMENT Do not discontinue the treatment without consulting your doctor as the dosage may need to be gradually reduced. If other drugs are being taken at the same time then their dosage may also need to be adjusted. It may take some time for your body to become adjusted to the change when you stop taking some of these drugs. If after you have completed the course of treatment you experience any of the following symptoms then you must tell your doctor immediately:

a feeling of movement even when still
feelings of panic or fear
hallucinations
irritability
muscle or stomach cramps
nausea or vomiting

over sensitivity to light
seizures or convulsions
sleep disturbances
sweating
trembling
weight loss

PERSONAL MEDICINE NOTES

NERVOUS SYSTEM

PRESCRIPTION NAMES

MEDICINES FOR MIGRAINES

The drugs in this group fall into two categories, those which are used to treat migraine during an attack and those which are used preventively. Ergotamine and dihydroergotamine are isolated from ergot and are derivatives of lysergic acid (LSD). Their action affects the endings of sympathetic nerves and constricts or tightens blood vessels. They are used for migraine and vascular headaches. Some preparations contain caffeine which increases the absorption of ergotamine and its effects.

NAMES OF PRESCRIPTION MEDICINES

The following are commonly prescribed migraine and headache medicines and are shown with the generic name first, followed by the brand name. If your medicine is not listed by name you should follow the information for the generic, if you know it, as the information given will still apply to your particular medicine. If you are not sure of the generic name your pharmacist will be able to advise you. Please note that ALL the information on this fact sheet applies to migraine and headache medicines generally, not specifically to any one medicine.

Generic	Brand Name
dihydroergotamine	Dihydergot
ergotamine	Cafergot*, Lingraine, Medihaler-Ergotamine, Migril*
pizotifen	Sanomigran

*These drugs contain caffeine.

WHAT TO TELL YOUR DOCTOR

It is important to make sure that your doctor or doctors are given as much information as possible. If you are aware that you are allergic to any migraine or headache medicines then do tell them so. Information on other medication is vital so if you are taking any other type of medicine, including non-prescription drugs, then they must know that too. Additionally, make sure they know if any of the following apply to you:

Angina
Any type of infection
Blood clots or thrombosis
Blood poisoning
Breast feeding
Glaucoma*

Heart disease
High blood pressure
Liver and kidney disorders
Poor circulation
Pregnancy
Urinary retention*

*You only need to inform your doctor about these particular conditions, in addition to the others, if you are taking Sanomigran.

SIDE-EFFECTS AND CAUTIONS

SIDE-EFFECTS

It is impossible to predict how any medicine will affect a particular individual because everyone's metabolism is so very different. Sensitivity to drugs can vary greatly from one person to another and side-effects are often dose related. It is important to pay close attention to any changes you may notice either when starting, or during, a course of treatment.

The following are some of the side-effects reported within this group of drugs. Some of the disorders listed under Infrequent or Rare can be the symptoms of overdose, and not necessarily side-effects.

COMMON

Diarrhoea	Nausea or vomiting
Drowsiness	Muscle pain

INFREQUENT OR RARE

Blood pressure changes	Pins and needles
Chest pains	Severe itching
Cold skin	Stomach pains
Confusion	Thirst
Dizziness	Weak pulse
Headache	Weakness in legs
Heart rate disorders	Weight change

If you experience any of the listed side-effects, or any unusual symptoms, you should consult your dispensing pharmacist or doctor immediately.

CAUTIONS

Medicines in this group can be habit forming.

If you experience dizziness or drowsiness do not drive, operate machinery or work high above the ground. Alcohol can increase these effects and should be avoided during treatment.

INTERACTIONS

INTERACTIONS WITH OTHER MEDICINES AND SUBSTANCES

No medication works in isolation but is affected to a greater or lesser extent by many other factors such as general fitness, diet and lifestyle. Alcohol can worsen the headache, and smoking may decrease the effectiveness of the medicine as well as worsening the headache.

It is also possible to unintentionally combine migraine or headache medicines with other drugs and this could be dangerous. Check with your doctor or pharmacist before taking any other medication, including non-prescription items, and if you are taking anything listed below look at the key to find out what effect they may have.

5 Beta blockers
5 Calcium antagonists
5 Erythromycin
5 Vasodilators

Antihistamines and non-prescription remedies for colds can increase blood pressure if taken with these medicines.

KEY 5 UNPREDICTABLE reactions

INTERACTIONS WITH VITAMINS, MINERALS AND FOODS

B3 in the form of niacin or nicotinic acid has a vasodilatory effect and if taken with these drugs may decrease their effectiveness. Niacinamide and nicotinamide do not have this effect but check with your doctor if you intend using any B3 supplement.

CENTRAL NERVOUS SYSTEM
MIGRAINE AND HEADACHE MEDICINES

CHILDREN, OVER SIXTIES AND PROLONGED USE

CHILDREN   These medicines may be prescribed for children and the dosage will be adjusted accordingly.

OVER SIXTIES   As part of the ageing process the body begins to metabolize and eliminate drugs more slowly and so there may be the possibility of more frequent or severe side-effects or interactions with other medicines. There may be greater susceptibility to circulation disorders such as coldness, tingling, numbness or pins and needles of the extremeties. It is important to tell your doctor if this occurs.

PROLONGED OR CONTINUED TREATMENT   Long term use of these medicines may cause muscle soreness, cold skin, gangrene, thrombosis, angina and alteration of heart rate and blood pressure. Ergotamine medicines have a cumulative effect and if used for prolonged periods can build up in the body and may produce headaches.

STOPPING THE TREATMENT   Migraine and headache medicines should not be discontinued without your doctor's advice. Medicines containing caffeine should be gradually reduced to prevent caffeine withdrawal headaches. If you normally avoid or restrict caffeine in your diet then this effect could be particularly marked.

PERSONAL MEDICINE NOTES

When you suffer an attack of nerves you're being attacked by the nervous system. What chance has a man got against a system?
The Lion of Boaz-Jachin and Jachin-Boaz by Russell Hoban.

Disorders of the neurological system which are genetically based do not necessarily respond to natural healing, although it may be used in conjunction with other therapies to help alleviate some of the symptoms. Disorders due to chemical imbalances can respond to natural healing and a number of states such as depression, anxiety, nervousness and sleeplessness may be helped.

Diet and lifestyle are two very important points to consider in connection with emotional well-being as even marginal nutritional deficiencies may be responsible for mild to moderate disorders. Some common substances in the diet may be nutritionally worthless, and may even 'rob' the body of nutrients or impair its ability to absorb nutrients adequately. Foods and substances which do this are caffeine, sugar, tobacco, alcohol and processed foods. Exposure to pollution, chemicals, stress, environmental factors, illness, and medication also draws heavily on the body's reserves of nutrients.

The suggestions offered here are designed to help generally with your condition, but it is very important that you do not try to treat yourself. If you suffer severely or regularly from a particular complaint, any serious disorder, or are pregnant then you should not use these remedies before discussion with a doctor. Always report any side-effects and seek medical advice before trying natural remedies and if within a period of one week there has been no improvement then you should consult your doctor. For more individual advice on natural medicine you should consult an alternative/complementary practitioner and among those who may be able to help are a herbalist, naturopath, homoeopath or acupuncturist. For more detailed information on the individual therapies, together with how to find a practitioner in your area please refer to the chapter on Alternative/Complementary Medicine and Therapies.

It is possible that certain remedies, supplements or foods could react dangerously with the drugs you are already using so you must check with the fact sheet relating to your medicine to avoid interactions. Please note that it is not advisable to gather your own herbs unless you are sure they are free of any chemicals or pollutants and you can positively identify the correct variety. Always make sure that supplements or natural remedies are taken two to three hours apart from any drugs.

If while reading you come across a particular word or term that is unfamiliar to you please look in The Fact Finder; information on nutrients will be found in the chapter on Vitamins and Minerals.

NERVOUS SYSTEM

NATURAL REMEDIES

ANXIETY AND NERVOUSNESS

See the chapter on Natural Remedies.

DEPRESSION

For transitory depression see the chapter on Natural Remedies.

EPILEPSY

Epileptic seizures, petit and grand mal have responded at different levels to nutritional supplements such as zinc, magnesium and vitamin B6. In particular, manganese seems to help seizures and octocosonal found in wheat germ oil helps repair the damaged nerve transmitters in the brain which may be responsible for convulsions. Diet is also considered an important factor and if you are interested in considering a natural approach to your treatment, or as adjunctive therapy, it is important that you consult a qualified natural practitioner.

INSOMNIA

See the chapter on Natural Remedies.

MIGRAINE HEADACHES

The herb feverfew is often used for headaches or migraine and can be eaten fresh or taken in capsules or tablets. Homoeopathic tissue salts Nat. Phos., Mag. Phos., Nat. Mur., and Silicea taken together can help migraine. For more details see Headache in the chapter on Natural Remedies.

MOTION SICKNESS

Motion sickness can be helped or prevented by taking supplementary B6, which should always be taken in conjunction with the other B group vitamins.

Ginger is also very effective, especially when taken with vitamin B6, and a tea can be made from the powdered ginger root used in cooking. Put half a teaspoon of the powder in a cup and pour boiling water over it, allow to steep for 3 minutes, strain and sip slowly as it may cause a burning sensation. This tea is not suitable if you suffer from hiatus hernia; in this case ginger should only be taken in capsule form with plenty of fluid to prevent any discomfort or burning sensations.

A remedy which works for some people is to put a little cotton wool in the ears for the duration of the journey.

NERVOUS EXHAUSTION

Unusual tiredness or fatigue may be a serious side-effect of a number of medicines and must be reported to a doctor if there is no improvement within five days.

An excess of salt, sugar, refined foods, coffee, tea, colas, chocolate or alcohol can deplete numerous nutrients, especially the B complex vitamins which are important to the healthy

NERVOUS SYSTEM

function of the nervous system. Nervous exhaustion and fatigue may be helped with a good supply of B complex, either from the diet or in supplement form, but if taken late in the day it can keep some people awake. The vitamin B2 which is present in B complex tablets colours the urine a bright yellow, but this reaction is harmless.

Vitamin C is important for the healthy function of the adrenal glands and works with vitamin B5, which is also found in royal jelly. The herbal and yeast tonic Bio Strath may help to restore energy and can assist in recovery from nervous exhaustion.

Homoeopathic tissue salts Calc. Phos., Kali. Phos. and Ferr. Phos. can be used together to help fatigue and lethargy. For more details see Fatigue in the Natural Remedies chapter.

PARKINSON'S DISEASE

Parkinson's disease has responded in varying degrees during clinical trials to the amino acids DLPA and tryptophane and to B6, B5, niacinamide, lecithin, calcium, zinc and manganese. If you are interested in considering a natural approach to your treatment contact a practitioner who is trained in the use of supplements.

SCHIZOPHRENIA

It is possible for schizophrenia to be treated with varying degrees of success by nutritional and dietary therapy. If a natural approach to treatment is being considered, or as adjunctive therapy, it is important to consult a qualified practitioner after discussion with the doctor.

STRESS

T'ai-chi, biofeedback, yoga, meditation, relaxation, Alexander technique, reflexology and massage have been found helpful for relaxation and helping your body deal with stress. See also the information on anxiety which appears in the chapter on Natural Remedies as the nutrients listed there are also helpful in combating stress.

THYROID

If the thyroid gland in the neck is under-functioning or affected by stress you may find you are more susceptible to problems such as weepiness, depression, over-emotional behaviour and exhaustion. If you have had thyroid disorders or if your medicine affects this gland, discuss it with your doctor.

NERVOUS SYSTEM

PAIN AND INFLAMMATION
CONTENTS

Pain is one of the most important of our general senses and is necessary as a warning device to let us know when physical disorders arise which may require investigation. Despite considerable research, the mechanism by which pain is felt is still not completely understood. It appears that we do not have special pain receptors in the brain, but when it receives abnormal nerve impulses it may translate these as pain.

Pain is carried as stimuli along specific nerve fibres to the brain where it is perceived as a conscious sensation. The ideal treatment for pain is to remove its cause, but this may be a long or difficult process and it is often necessary to temporarily relieve the pain itself with anti-inflammatory or pain relieving drugs.

The leaves and bark of the white willow tree, and the herb meadowsweet, contain salicin and were used for hundreds of years as treatment for fever and pain. Acetyl-salicylic acid was synthesized in 1899 and became known as aspirin, the name being derived from acetyl and spirea.

Aspirin and related medicines used for pain and inflammation are known collectively as NSAI's, non steroidal anti-inflammatories. Most reduce fever and in single doses have an analgesic effect. When taken in regular dosage they have an anti-inflammatory action.

Paracetamol, although analgesic, does not have a significant anti-inflammatory effect. In 1949 it was found that corticosteroids were useful for treating inflammation and allergy, as well as other disorders. They are more popularly known as cortisone drugs and are widely used.

To find your particular prescription medicine in this chapter you need to know either its generic or brand name. For instance you may be given an oral corticosteroid which is labelled either prednisone, the generic name, or Decortisyl which is a brand name. The index of drugs lists both the brand and generic names to enable you to find the right fact sheet for your medicine. If your medicine has a name which you are unable to find in the index, contact your dispensing chemist and ask for its generic name so you can check whether it has been included. If you do not know the name of your drug, you may prefer to check in the separate index of ailments and illnesses to find the drugs that may be prescribed for your particular complaint.

At the end of this group of fact sheets you will find a section on how to help yourself with suggestions for natural remedies and therapies that may be of assistance. Information about practitioners will be found in the chapter on Alternative/Complementary Medicine and Therapies.

If you come across a particular word or term that is unfamiliar to you, please look in The Fact Finder for an explanation; information on food and nutrition will be found in the chapter on Vitamins and Minerals.

PRESCRIPTION NAMES

MEDICINES FOR PAIN, INFLAMMATION AND FEVER

Aspirin is one of the most effective and commonly used pain killers which, like some of the other analgesics, has anti-inflammatory and fever reducing capabilities. It has the ability to relieve inflammation and pain by blocking the production of prostaglandins, chemical messengers which increase the sensitivity of the nerves to pain. Aspirin is also used for disorders including headache, swelling, stiffness, joint pains, arthritis, rheumatism, and as an anti-platelet drug in the prevention of blood clots.

NAMES OF PRESCRIPTION MEDICINES

The following are commonly prescribed aspirin based drugs and are shown with the generic name first, followed by the brand name. If your medicine is not listed by name you should follow the information for the generic, if you know it, as the information given will still apply to your particular medicine. If you are not sure of the generic name your pharmacist will be able to advise you. Please note that ALL the information on this fact sheet applies to aspirin based drugs generally, not specifically to any one medicine.

Generic	Brand Name
aspirin	Caprin, Levius, Nu-Seals, Palaprin-Forte
aspirin based drugs	Robaxisal-Forte, Doloxene, Aspav, Trancoprin**, Migravess
co-codaprin*	Usually prescribed as a generic drug

*This drug contains codeine.
**This drug contains chlormezanone.

WHAT TO TELL YOUR DOCTOR

It is important to make sure that your doctor or doctors are given as much information as possible. If you are aware that you are allergic to any aspirin based drugs, salicylates, codeine or chlormezanone then do tell them so. Information on other medication is vital so if you are taking any other type of medicine, including non-prescription drugs, then they must know that too. Additionally, make sure they know if any of the following apply to you:

Anaemia
Anticoagulant therapy
Asthma
Bleeding disorders such as haemophilia

Breast feeding
Bronchial disorders
Diabetes
Epilepsy
Heart disorders

179

PAIN AND INFLAMMATION
ASPIRIN AND ASPIRIN BASED DRUGS

Hodgkin's disease | Nasal polyps
Liver or kidney disorders | Pregnancy
Myasthenia gravis | Ulcers

If you will be having surgery or dental treatment which requires anaesthesia it is important to tell the person in charge that you are taking aspirin based drugs. If you are having urine-sugar tests you should be aware that aspirin can cause inaccurate results.

SIDE-EFFECTS AND CAUTIONS

SIDE-EFFECTS It is impossible to predict how any medicine will affect a particular individual because everyone's metabolism is so very different. Sensitivity or reaction to drugs can vary greatly from one person to another and side-effects can be related to dosage. It is important to pay close attention to any changes you may notice either when starting, or during, a course of treatment.

The following are some of the side-effects reported within this group of drugs. Some of the disorders listed under Infrequent or Rare may occasionally be the symptoms of overdose and not always those of side-effects.

COMMON

Deafness* | Nausea or vomiting
Digestive upsets* | Ringing in the ears*
Heartburn* |

INFREQUENT OR RARE

Black or bloody stools | Fever*
Blood disorders* | Headache
Bloody or black vomit* | Itching
Bronchial or breathing | Kidney stones
  disorders | Skin rashes
Diarrhoea or constipation* | Stomach bleeding
Dizziness or drowsiness* | Vision disorders

*These side-effects do not apply to aspirin only drugs.
If you experience any of the listed side-effects, or any other unusual symptoms, you should consult your dispensing pharmacist or doctor immediately.

CAUTIONS If you experience dizziness or drowsiness do not drive, operate machinery or work high above the ground. Alcohol can increase these effects and should be avoided during treatment.

PAIN AND INFLAMMATION
ASPIRIN AND ASPIRIN BASED DRUGS

INTERACTIONS

INTERACTIONS WITH OTHER MEDICINES AND SUBSTANCES

No medication works in isolation but is affected to a greater or lesser extent by many other factors such as general fitness, diet and lifestyle. Alcohol, when taken with the drugs in this group, can cause inflammation and bleeding in the stomach; smoking can reduce the effectiveness of aspirin based drugs and can also deplete vitamin C.

It is also possible to unintentionally combine aspirin based drugs with other medicines and this could be dangerous. Check with your doctor or pharmacist before taking any other medication, including non-prescription items, and if you are taking anything listed below look at the key to find out what effect they may have.

1 Metoclopramide antinauseants
1 Paracetamol

2 Antacids
2 Anticonvulsants
2 Beta blockers
2 Tranquillizers
2 Corticosteroids

3 Anticoagulants
3 Hydantoin anticonvulsants
3 Antidiabetics
3 Anti-inflammatories

4 Gout drugs

If warfarin sodium and other anticoagulants are taken with aspirin it may result in dangerous bleeding. If non steroidal anti-inflammatories and other aspirin or salicylate drugs are taken with aspirin based drugs then the combination can increase the chance of ulcers and intestinal bleeding.

Some drugs have enteric coatings to help prevent stomach irritation, but the effectiveness of this coating can be reduced by the use of antacids. An example of this is Nu-seals aspirin, which is enteric coated, and should therefore not be taken with antacids.

KEY
1 INCREASES the effects of aspirin based drugs
2 DECREASES the effects of aspirin based drugs
3 ASPIRIN INCREASES the effects of these drugs
4 ASPIRIN DECREASES the effects of these drugs

INTERACTIONS WITH VITAMINS, MINERALS AND FOODS

Aspirin can deplete nutrients in the body, particularly vitamin A, some B complex vitamins, vitamin C and bioflavonoids and the minerals calcium, potassium, magnesium and phosphorus. Vitamin C and B12 can be depleted in significant amounts by each dose of aspirin but the other deficiencies are more likely with prolonged use. Those more susceptible to B12 deficiency are the elderly, some vegetarians and vegans, and women who take the birth control pill.

Because aspirin depletes vitamin C it is important to maintain an intake of up to 500mg of vitamin C, as calcium ascorbate, a day to prevent the aspirin irritating the stomach and possibly causing bleeding. Larger doses than 500mg of vitamin C may increase the amount of time that the aspirin remains in the body and this could have the action of increasing its side-effects.

Do not take bicarbonate of soda as an antacid at the same time as aspirin, or other salicylates, as they increase the rate of salicylate absorption and could increase the incidence of side-effects.

Citrus fruits and juices should be avoided when taking aspirin as they may increase stomach inflammation. Other important information can be found in How to Help Yourself at the end of this chapter, and also in the chapter on Vitamins and Minerals.

CHILDREN, OVER SIXTIES AND PROLONGED USE

CHILDREN

Aspirin and tablets which contain aspirin or are broken down into aspirin, such as Benorylate, should not be given to children under the age of twelve except under medical supervision. The Committee on Safety of Medicines has recommended this precaution because of aspirin's link with Reye's syndrome, a rare but potentially lethal childhood illness which can damage the brain and liver. Aspirin given to a child infected with chicken-pox or influenza greatly increases the risk of developing Reye's syndrome. Paracetamol is recommended by doctors as an alternative for general pain relief in children. See also How To Help Yourself for some natural remedies for pain relief.

OVER SIXTIES

As part of the ageing process the body begins to metabolize and eliminate drugs more slowly and so there may be the possibility of more frequent or severe side-effects or interactions with other medicines. With some of the drugs in this group you may experience ringing in the ears, and there could be an increased possibility of gastro-intestinal side-effects. These may include diarrhoea and intestinal bleeding which is indicated by dark bowel movements. There can also be a greater risk of vitamin B12 deficiency.

PROLONGED OR CONTINUED TREATMENT

Prolonged use can cause blood, blood-sugar and kidney disorders. If you have to take aspirin regularly for prolonged treatment it is best to avoid products which contain sodium nitrate, such as bacon or processed meat.

STOPPING THE TREATMENT

Aspirin and aspirin based prescription drugs should not be discontinued without your doctor's advice.

PERSONAL MEDICINE NOTES

PAIN AND INFLAMMATION
GOUT DRUGS

PRESCRIPTION NAMES

MEDICINES FOR GOUT

Allopurinol gout drugs are known as xanthine-oxidase inhibitors and act by reducing the formation of uric acid. The pain associated with gout is caused when uric acid is deposited around the joints. Uricosuric drugs increase the excretion of uric acid in the urine, but do not prevent uric acid formation.

The drugs in this group may be prescribed for gout, excess uric acid in the body, gouty arthritis, and the prevention of kidney stones. Uricosurics may also be used for severe infections in conjunction with some antibiotic treatments as they can increase their effectiveness.

NAMES OF PRESCRIPTION MEDICINES

The following are commonly prescribed gout medicines and are shown with the generic name first, followed by the brand name. If your medicine is not listed by name you should follow the information for the generic, if you know it, as the information given will still apply to your particular medicine. If you are not sure of the generic name your pharmacist will be able to advise you. Please note that ALL the information on this fact sheet applies to gout medicines generally, not specifically to any one medicine.

Generic	Brand Name
allopurinol	Aluline, Caplenal, Zyloric, Cosuric, Hamarin, Aloral
probenecid	Benemid
sulphinpyrazone	Anturan

WHAT TO TELL YOUR DOCTOR

It is important to make sure that your doctor or doctors are given as much information as possible. If you are aware that you are allergic to any gout drugs then do tell them so. Information on other medication is vital so if you are taking any other type of medicine, including non-prescription drugs, then they must know that too. Additionally, make sure they know if any of the following apply to you:

Acute gout attack within the last three weeks	Gastro-intestinal disorders
	Heart disease
Anaemia	Liver or kidney disorders
Blood disorders	Peptic ulcers
Breast feeding	Pregnancy
Epilepsy	Thyroid disorders

If you will be having surgery or dental treatment which requires anaesthesia it is important to tell the person in charge that you are taking gout medicines. Liver function and urine test results may be altered so it is important to tell the person in charge what drugs you are taking.

PAIN & INFLAMMATION

SIDE-EFFECTS AND CAUTIONS

SIDE-EFFECTS
It is impossible to predict how any medicine will affect a particular individual because everyone's metabolism is so very different. Sensitivity or reaction to drugs can vary greatly from one person to another and side-effects can be related to dosage. It is important to pay close attention to any changes you may notice either when starting, or during, a course of treatment.

The following are some of the side-effects reported within this group of drugs. Some of the disorders listed under Infrequent or Rare may occasionally be the symptoms of overdose and not always those of side-effects.

COMMON

Digestive disorders	Nausea
Itching or rash	Stomach pains
Loss of appetite	Vomiting*

INFREQUENT OR RARE

Bleeding or bruising easily	Heart rhythm disorders
Blood, blood fat disorders	Hepatitis
Boils	High blood pressure
Cataract formation	Kidney or urinary disorders
Change in bowel habits	Muscle co-ordination
Chest pains	disorders
Depression	Muscular weakness
Diabetes	Nocturnal emissions
Diarrhoea	Numbness or tingling of
Dizziness or drowsiness	extremities
Epilepsy	Sexual disorders
Fatigue	Skin disorders or rashes
Fever	Sore gums
Flushing	Sore throat
Gastro-intestinal bleeding+	Vision disorders
Hair discoloration	Water retention
Headache**	Yellowing of eyes or skin

*   This side-effect is infrequent with probenicid.
** This side-effect is common with probenicid.
\+ This side-effect has only been reported with Anturan.

If you experience any of the listed side-effects, or any other unusual symptoms, you should consult your dispensing pharmacist or doctor immediately.

CAUTIONS
In the early stages of treatment the drugs may actually precipitate an acute attack of gout. Your doctor will probably give you other medication to help this and may suggest a high fluid intake as it is advisable to drink plenty of water every day whilst you are taking these medicines.

185

Probenecid and sulphinpyrazone may cause uric acid stones to form. If you have blood in the urine or pains in the lower back contact your doctor.

Avoid taking aspirin, or any non-prescription remedies which contain it, at the same time as taking gout drugs.

If you experience dizziness or drowsiness do not drive, operate machinery or work high above the ground. Alcohol can increase these effects and should be avoided during treatment.

INTERACTIONS

INTERACTIONS WITH OTHER MEDICINES AND SUBSTANCES

No medication works in isolation but is affected to a greater or lesser extent by many other factors such as general fitness, diet and lifestyle. Alcohol can reduce the effects of gout drugs.

It is also possible to unintentionally combine gout drugs with other medicines and this could be dangerous. Check with your doctor or pharmacist before taking any other medication, including non-prescription items, and if you are taking anything listed below look at the key to find out what effect they may have.

2 Aspirin, salicylates and NSAI's*
2 Diuretics

3 Antibiotics
3 Anticoagulants
3 Antidiabetic drugs
3 Sulphur drugs

4 Aspirin

5 Urinary tract infection medicines

*This interaction does not apply to allopurinol.

Aspirin may cause bleeding when taken with gout drugs.
Antihistamines, antidepressants and tranquillizers taken with gout drugs can cause extreme sedation.
Oral contraceptives used at the same time as gout drugs can cause bleeding between periods.

KEY 1 INCREASES the effects of gout drugs
2 DECREASES the effects of gout drugs
3 GOUT MEDICINES INCREASE the effects of these drugs
4 GOUT MEDICINES DECREASE the effects of these drugs
5 UNPREDICTABLE reactions

PAIN AND INFLAMMATION
GOUT DRUGS

INTERACTIONS WITH VITAMINS, MINERALS AND FOODS

Caffeine may decrease the effects of gout drugs and vitamins A and B12 may not be properly absorbed.

If vitamin C in supplement form is taken with allopurinol it can increase the chances of kidney stones.

It is advisable to avoid foods which are high in sugar, refined carbohydrates and purines as they can decrease the effect of these drugs. Information on purine foods is in The Fact Finder.

CHILDREN, OVER SIXTIES AND PROLONGED USE

CHILDREN

Some of these medicines may be prescribed for children over the age of two, but because the safety for children has not been established in some of the branded gout medicines, they are generally not recommended for the very young.

OVER SIXTIES

As part of the ageing process the body begins to metabolize and eliminate drugs more slowly and so there may be the possibility of more frequent or severe side-effects or interactions with other medicines.

PROLONGED OR CONTINUED TREATMENT

Long term use of some of the drugs in this group may cause anaemia, hair loss, numbness and tingling of the extremities, possible kidney damage, unusual bleeding or bruising.

STOPPING THE TREATMENT

Do not discontinue the treatment without consulting your doctor as the dosage may need to be gradually reduced. If other drugs are being taken at the same time then their dosage may also need to be adjusted.

PERSONAL MEDICINE NOTES

PAIN AND INFLAMMATION
NON STEROIDAL ANTI-INFLAMMATORIES

PRESCRIPTION NAMES

MEDICINES FOR MILD TO MODERATE PAIN

NSAI medicines work by blocking the production of certain prostaglandins; chemical messengers which increase the sensitivity of the nerves to pain. NSAI's, as these drugs are often called, have an anti-inflammatory effect and most of them also reduce fever. They may be prescribed for gout, joint pain and stiffness, pain relief, pain from surgery or dental procedures, menstrual pains, arthritic disorders, migraine, and musculo-skeletal disorders including frozen shoulder, tendonitis, bursitis, sprains and strains.

NAMES OF PRESCRIPTION MEDICINES

The following are commonly prescribed NSAI's and are shown with the generic name first, followed by the brand name. If your medicine is not listed by name you should follow the information for the generic, if you know it, as the information given will still apply to your particular medicine. If you are not sure of the generic name your pharmacist will be able to advise you. Please note that ALL the information on this fact sheet applies to NSAI's generally, not specifically to any one medicine.

Generic	Brand Name
azapropazone	Rheumox
benorylate	Benoral
diclofenac	Voltarol/Retard
diflumisal	Dolobid
etodolac	Lodine, Ramodar
fenbufen	Lederfen/F
fenoprofen	Progesic, Fenopron
flurbiprofen	Froben
ibuprofen	Apsifen, Brufen, Ebufac, Fenbid, Motrin, Ibular, Ibumetin, Nurofen, Paxofen
indomethacin	Antracin, Imbrilon, Indocid, Indoflex, Indolar/SR, Indomod, Rheumacin-LA, Mobilan, Slo-Indo
ketoprofen	Alrheumat, Orudis, Oruvail
mefenamic acid	Ponstan
naproxen	Laraflex, Naprosyn, Synflex
nefopam	Acupan
piroxicam	Feldene, Larapam
sulindac	Clinoril
tiaprofenic acid	Surgam
tolmetin	Tolectin-DS

PAIN AND INFLAMMATION
NON STEROIDAL ANTI-INFLAMMATORIES

WHAT TO TELL YOUR DOCTOR

It is important to make sure that your doctor or doctors are given as much information as possible. If you are aware that you are allergic to any NSAI's, including aspirin, then do tell them so. Asthmatics should particularly ensure their doctor is told if they are taking anything containing ibuprofen. Information on other medication is vital so if you are taking any other type of medicine, including non-prescription drugs, then they must know that too. Additionally, make sure they know if any of the following apply to you:

Acute nasal discharge
Anaemia
Blood or bleeding disorders
Bowel disorders
Breast feeding
Digestive upset
Epilepsy
Eye disorders
Haemophilia
Heart disease

High blood pressure
Infection
Liver or kidney disorders
Pancreas disorders
Parkinson's disease
Peptic ulcers
Pregnancy
Psychological disorders
Respiratory disorders*

*It is necessary to tell your doctor if this condition is brought on by aspirin or other NSAI's.

If you will be having surgery or dental treatment which requires anaesthesia it is important to tell the person in charge that you are taking NSAI's. As some of these drugs may affect the results of urine tests you should tell the person in charge which NSAI you are taking.

SIDE-EFFECTS AND CAUTIONS

SIDE-EFFECTS

It is impossible to predict how any medicine will affect a particular individual because everyone's metabolism is so very different. Sensitivity or reaction to drugs can vary greatly from one person to another and side-effects can be related to dosage. It is important to pay close attention to any changes you may notice either when starting, or during, a course of treatment.

The following are some of the side-effects reported within this group of drugs. Some of the disorders listed under Infrequent or Rare may occasionally be the symptoms of overdose and not always those of side-effects.

189

PAIN AND INFLAMMATION
NON STEROIDAL ANTI-INFLAMMATORIES

COMMON

Diarrhoea
Digestive disorders
Gastro-intestinal bleeding

Headache
Nausea

INFREQUENT OR RARE

Bitter, metallic taste
  in the mouth
Black or bloody
  bowel movements
Bloating or flatulence
Blood disorders
Chest pain
Constipation
Depression
Difficulty concentrating
Dizziness, lightheadedness
Drowsiness
Dry mouth
Fatigue or tiredness
Fever
Hearing disorders

Heartburn
High blood pressure
Loss of appetite
Mouth soreness or ulcers
Palpitations
Respiratory disorders
Sensitivity to sun
Skin rash or itching
Sore throat
Stomach pain
Swelling of legs, hands
  and feet
Urinary, bladder disorders
Vision disorders
Vomiting
Yellowing of eyes and skin

Some of the drugs in this group may colour the urine but this is a harmless reaction.

If you experience any of the listed side-effects, or any other unusual symptoms, you should consult your dispensing pharmacist or doctor immediately.

CAUTIONS

If you experience dizziness or drowsiness do not drive, operate machinery or work high above the ground. Alcohol can increase these effects and should be avoided during treatment.

Be very careful about exposure to the sun or sunlamps as some of these medicines may make you more sensitive to burning.

It is better to avoid taking indigestion remedies and non-prescription analgesics at the same time as NSAI's.

If you are considering using a salt substitute you should discuss this with your doctor first.

INTERACTIONS

INTERACTIONS WITH
OTHER MEDICINES AND
SUBSTANCES

No medication works in isolation but is affected to a greater or lesser extent by many other factors such as general fitness, diet and lifestyle. Stomach problems, drowsiness or dizziness can occur if alcohol is taken with these drugs, and their absorption is decreased by tobacco.

It is also possible to unintentionally combine NSAI's with other drugs and this could be dangerous. Check with your doctor or pharmacist before taking any other medication, including non-prescription items, and if you are taking anything listed below look at the key to find out what effect they may have.

1 Gout drugs

2 Corticosteroids

3 Anticoagulants
3 Antihypertensives
3 Digitalis drugs
3 Lithium
3 Phenytoin

4 Beta blockers
4 Diuretics
4 Lipid lowering drugs

5 All NSAI's, including non-prescription items and other drugs in this group
5 Anticonvulsants
5 Oral antidiabetic drugs

If you have asthma and are taking any of the drugs in this group, do not take any product containing ibuprofen without first informing your doctor as the interaction could be very dangerous.

If indomethacin is taken with some other drugs in this group it may cause fatal gastric bleeding.

Other anti-inflammatories, including cortisone, can cause stomach ulcers when taken with this group of drugs and aspirin can increase the chances of stomach ulcer.

Thyroid drugs when taken with these medicines can increase blood pressure and heartbeat.

Some tranquillizers in combination with these medicines can increase pressure within the eye.

KEY
1 INCREASES the effects of NSAI's
2 DECREASES the effects of NSAI's
3 NSAI's INCREASE the effects of these drugs
4 NSAI's DECREASE the effects of these drugs
5 UNPREDICTABLE reactions

PAIN AND INFLAMMATION
NON STEROIDAL ANTI-INFLAMMATORIES

INTERACTIONS WITH VITAMINS, MINERALS AND FOODS	These drugs may deplete vitamin B1, vitamin C and iron in the diet. For more information see Vitamins, Minerals and their Food Sources.

CHILDREN, OVER SIXTIES AND PROLONGED USE

CHILDREN	These medicines may be prescribed for children over the age of 14 and the dosage will be adjusted accordingly.
OVER SIXTIES	As part of the ageing process the body begins to metabolize and eliminate drugs more slowly and so there may be the possibility of more frequent or severe side-effects or interactions with other medicines. With some of the drugs in this group, especially indomethacin, there may be an increased possibility of very severe haemorrhage if taken with warfarin sodium. Alertness and memory capacity can be reduced with some of the drugs in this group. There may be a tendency for diarrhoea to develop and an increased susceptibility to kidney disease.
PROLONGED OR CONTINUED TREATMENT	Prolonged use of these medicines may result in a number of symptoms including eye, ear and throat problems and changes in weight. Those who have rheumatoid arthritis may find it necessary to have regular eye examinations.
STOPPING THE TREATMENT	Do not discontinue the treatment without consulting your doctor as the dosage may need to be gradually reduced. If other drugs are being taken at the same time then their dosage may also need to be adjusted.

PERSONAL MEDICINE NOTES

PRESCRIPTION NAMES

MEDICINES FOR INFLAMMATION, CORTICOSTEROID INSUFFICIENCY AND ALLERGIC REACTIONS

Corticosteroid is a general term applied to the adrenal cortex hormones produced by the body and to a large number of drug preparations, better known as cortisone or steroid drugs. These drugs have similar effects to the anti-inflammatory and anti-allergic effects of the natural hormones and may be prescribed for skin disorders, bronchial asthma, Addison's disease, severe allergies, rheumatoid arthritis and related disorders.

NAMES OF PRESCRIPTION MEDICINES

The following are commonly prescribed oral corticosteroids and are shown with the generic name first, followed by the brand name. If your medicine is not listed by name you should follow the information for the generic, if you know it, as the information given will still apply to your particular medicine. If you are not sure of the generic name your pharmacist will be able to advise you. Please note that ALL the information on this fact sheet applies to oral corticosteroids generally, not specifically to any one medicine.

Generic	Brand Name
betamethasone	Betnelan, Betnesol
dexamethasone	Decadron, Oradexon
hydrocortisone	Hydrocortistab, Hydrocortone
methylprednisolone	Medrone
prednisolone	Deltacortril, Deltalone, Delta-Phoricol, Deltastab, Precortisyl/Forte, Prednesol, Sintisone
prednisone	Decortisyl, Econosone
triamcinolone	Ledercort

WHAT TO TELL YOUR DOCTOR

It is important to make sure that your doctor or doctors are given as much information as possible. If you are aware that you are allergic to any oral corticosteroids then do tell them so. Information on other medication is vital so if you are taking any other type of medicine, including non-prescription drugs, then they must know that too. Additionally, make sure they know if any of the following apply to you:

Breast feeding	Glaucoma or cataracts
Colitis	High blood pressure
Cushing's disease	Heart disorders
Diabetes	Herpes simplex
Diverticulosis	Infections
Epilepsy	Liver or kidney disorders
Fungal infection	Low thyroid function

PAIN AND INFLAMMATION
ORAL CORTICOSTEROIDS

Myasthenia gravis
Osteoporosis
Peptic ulceration
Pregnancy
Thrombosis or phlebitis*

Time spent in the tropics
Tuberculosis*
Ulcerative colitis
Unexplained diarrhoea

*Tell your doctor if there is any history of these conditions in yourself, or your family.

If you will be having surgery or dental treatment which requires anaesthesia it is important to tell the person in charge that you are taking oral corticosteroids, or if you have taken any within the last two years. If you will be having immunizations, vaccinations, skin or other medical tests tell the person in charge that you are taking corticosteroids.

SIDE-EFFECTS AND CAUTIONS

SIDE-EFFECTS It is impossible to predict how any medicine will affect a particular individual because everyone's metabolism is so very different. Sensitivity or reaction to drugs can vary greatly from one person to another and side-effects can be related to dosage. It is important to pay close attention to any changes you may notice either when starting, or during, a course of treatment.

The following are some of the side-effects reported within this group of drugs. Some of the disorders listed under Infrequent or Rare may occasionally be the symptoms of overdose and not always those of side-effects.

COMMON
Appetite increase
Change in weight
Digestive disorders

Nausea or vomiting
Sleeping disturbances

INFREQUENT OR RARE
Acne
Bloated stomach
Blood sugar disorders
Easy bruising
False sense of well-being
Fatigue
Fever
Frequent urination
High blood pressure
Impotence
Increased susceptibility
    to infections

Irregular menstruation
Mental disorders or
    mood swings
Muscle weakness
Skin rash
Slow wound healing
Sore throat
Stomach pains
Stomach ulcer bleeding
Sweating
Thirst
Unusual tiredness

Vertigo
Vision disorders

Water or salt retention

If you experience any of the listed side-effects, or any other unusual symptoms, you should consult your dispensing pharmacist or doctor immediately.

See also the section on Prolonged or Continued Treatment for information on the side-effects associated with long-term therapy.

CAUTIONS If you were given a steroid card by your doctor it is important to carry it with you at all times.

INTERACTIONS

INTERACTIONS WITH OTHER MEDICINES AND SUBSTANCES No medication works in isolation but is affected to a greater or lesser extent by many other factors such as general fitness, diet or lifestyle. Alcohol can increase the chances of developing stomach ulcers, and smoking can increase the effects of oral corticosteroids.

It is also possible to unintentionally combine corticosteroids with other drugs and this could be dangerous. Check with your doctor or pharmacist before taking any other medication, including non-prescription items, and if you are taking anything listed below look at the key to find out what effect they may have.

1 Oral contraceptives, oestrogens

2 Anticonvulsants
2 Antihistamines
2 Barbiturates
2 Beta-blockers

4 Aspirin, salicylates and NSAI's
4 Antidiabetic drugs
4 Cholinergics
4 Insulin
4 Myasthenia gravis drugs

5 Anticoagulants
5 Digitalis drugs
5 Sympathomimetics

Some diuretics, antifungals and digitalis drugs can cause potassium deficiency when taken with oral corticosteroids.

Anticholinergics and sympathomimetics when taken with oral corticosteroids may cause glaucoma.

KEY
1 INCREASES the effects of oral corticosteroids
2 DECREASES the effects of oral corticosteroids
4 ORAL CORTICOSTEROIDS DECREASE the effects of these drugs
5 UNPREDICTABLE reactions

INTERACTIONS WITH VITAMINS, MINERALS AND FOODS

Corticosteroids can decrease vitamins B6, D, C and folic acid and the minerals zinc, calcium, and phosphorus. B5 has been used therapeutically to help prevent stomach ulcers which may be a result of corticosteroid therapy.

Anyone taking steroid drugs should ensure that the diet is well supplied with calcium and potassium rich foods. Calcium supplements are recommended for those on long-term therapy to help offset the increased loss of calcium and subsequent bone and joint weakness which can occur. Calcium should be taken with magnesium and zinc, and your doctor or a natural practitioner can help you with this. Fluorine is a mineral found in a number of foods, especially goat's milk, which also helps bones and tendons remain strong.

Irregular heartbeat may be a sign of potassium deficiency and should be reported to your doctor.

It is also important to have an adequate intake of protein because corticosteroids can lead to muscle wasting when taken over a prolonged period. The exact amount in your diet should be discussed with your doctor, however, as there can also be problems associated with too much protein as well as too little.

Vitamin A is thought to help overcome the inhibiting effect of corticosteroids on wound healing. If vitamin A is taken in the form of beta carotene, or obtained mostly from vegetables and fruit, it may not be absorbed efficiently during cortisone treatment and a better source in this instance would be fish and fish oils.

Vitamin C supplements taken during cortisone treatment should not exceed 500mg taken twice per day, except under supervision.

Vitamin D should not be taken in amounts over 400IU per day, except under medical supervision. It may also be advisable to avoid fatty foods and to reduce the amount of salt and sugar in the diet and this should be discussed with your doctor.

For more information see the chapter on Vitamins and Minerals.

PAIN AND INFLAMMATION
ORAL CORTICOSTEROIDS

CHILDREN, OVER SIXTIES AND PROLONGED USE

CHILDREN These medicines may occasionally be prescribed for children and the dosage will be adjusted accordingly. They will probably not be prescribed for prolonged treatment as they may affect growth and development.

OVER SIXTIES As part of the ageing process the body begins to metabolize and eliminate drugs more slowly and so there may be the possibility of more frequent or severe side-effects or interactions with other medicines.

With long-term use some of the drugs in this group may lead to an increased possibility of osteoporosis, stomach ulcers, cataracts, diabetes, increased blood pressure, thinning of the skin and an increased susceptibility to infection. Long-term treatment may also temporarily cause loss of the ability to deal adequately with stress or stressful situations.

It is important when taking steroids that you should report any injuries of a serious nature, illness, or emotional problems to your doctor.

PROLONGED OR CONTINUED TREATMENT Dependence on some of the drugs in this group has been reported with prolonged or continued treatment. Some of the side-effects reported with long term use are:

Acne
Back pain
Blood in the stools
Depression
Diabetes and other blood
 sugar disorders
Excessive body fat
Fever or sore throat
Impotence
Irregular heartbeat
Menstrual disorders
Muscle wasting
Muscular disorders
Potassium and zinc loss
Puffiness or fullness of face

Stomach or oesophagus
 ulceration
Swelling of extremities
Swelling of legs, ankles
 or feet
Temporary inability to deal
 adequately with stress
Unusual tiredness or
 weakness
Visual disturbances,
 cataract or glaucoma
Weakening of bones, joints
 and tendons
Weight loss

STOPPING THE TREATMENT Oral corticosteroids should not be discontinued without your doctor's advice as they must be gradually reduced. If, after stopping the treatment, you experience any of the following symptoms then your doctor should be informed immediately:

Dizziness or fainting
Fever
Malaise
Muscle or joint pain

Nausea or vomiting
Shortness of breath
Unusual weight loss

PERSONAL MEDICINE NOTES

PRESCRIPTION NAMES

MEDICINES FOR PAIN AND FEVER

Paracetamol is a mild pain relieving and fever reducing drug derived from coal tar. Although it does not have the same anti-inflammatory or anti-rheumatic properties as aspirin, it may be used for some arthritic and rheumatic disorders. Paracetamol and paracetamol based drugs are often given when there is aspirin sensitivity and may be used for conditions such as moderate pain, headache, migraine, toothache, fever, neuralgia, backaches, sprains, muscular and menstrual cramps and after some injections. Distalgesic may also be used for preventing or relieving coughing.

NAMES OF PRESCRIPTION MEDICINES

The following are commonly prescribed paracetamol based drugs and are shown with the generic name first, followed by the brand name. If your medicine is not listed by name, you should follow the information for the generic, if you know it, as the information given will still apply to your particular medicine. If you are not sure of the generic name your pharmacist will be able to advise you. Please note that ALL the information on this fact sheet applies to paracetamol based medicines generally, not specifically to any one medicine.

Generic	Brand Name
co-codamol*	Usually prescribed as generic drugs
co-dydramol*	Paramol*
co-proxamol	Distalgesic, Paxalgesic
paracetamol	Calpol, Disprol, Paldesic, Panadol, Salzone
other paracetamol based drugs	Delimon, Lobak, Midrid, Migraleve, Norgesic, Paedo-sed, Pameton Panadeine,* Paramax, Solpadeine-Forte*+

*These drugs contains codeine.
+This drug contains caffeine.

WHAT TO TELL YOUR DOCTOR

It is important to make sure that your doctor or doctors are given as much information as possible. If you are aware that you are allergic to any paracetamol or phenacetin based medicines then do tell them so. Information on other medication is vital so if you are taking any other type of medicine, including non-prescription drugs, then they must know that too. Additionally, make sure they know if any of the following apply to you:

Alcoholism   Blood disorders

PAIN AND INFLAMMATION
PARACETAMOL AND PARACETAMOL BASED DRUGS

Breast feeding
Diabetes
Difficulty urinating
Glaucoma
Heart disorders
High blood pressure
Liver or kidney disorders

MAOI therapy*
Pregnancy
Prostate disorders
Psychological disorders
Respiratory disorders
Restricted salt intake
Thyroid disorders

*You only need to inform your doctor about this particular condition, in addition to the others, if you are taking Midrid.

SIDE-EFFECTS AND CAUTIONS

SIDE-EFFECTS It is impossible to predict how any medicine will affect a particular individual because everyone's metabolism is so very different. Sensitivity or reaction to drugs can vary greatly from one person to another and side-effects can be related to dosage. It is important to pay close attention to any changes you may notice either when starting, or during, a course of treatment.

The following are some of the side-effects reported within this group of drugs. Some of the disorders listed under Infrequent or Rare may occasionally be the symptoms of overdose and not always those of side-effects.

COMMON

Drowsiness
Dizziness

Nausea or vomiting
Vertigo

INFREQUENT OR RARE

Abdominal pain
Blood disorders+
Breathing disorders
Constipation
Depression or unrest
Dry mouth*
Easy bleeding or bruising
Fatigue or weakness
Fever

Headache
Itching
Lack of muscular
  co-ordination
Lightheadedness
Low blood pressure
Skin rash+
Visual disturbances
Yellowing of skin and eyes

*These side-effects apply to Lobak only.
+These side-effects, and no others, apply to paracetamol only drugs.

If you experience any of the listed side-effects, or any other unusual symptoms, you should consult your dispensing pharmacist or doctor immediately.

CAUTIONS

If you experience dizziness or drowsiness do not drive, operate machinery or work high above the ground. Alcohol can increase these effects and should be avoided during treatment.

One of the side-effects can be a dry mouth and this may contribute to the possibility of tooth decay or gum disease. If this occurs, your doctor will probably advise you to clean your teeth frequently and to use dental floss.

INTERACTIONS

INTERACTIONS WITH OTHER MEDICINES AND SUBSTANCES

No medication works in isolation but is affected to a greater or lesser extent by many other factors such as general fitness, diet and lifestyle. Alcohol can cause or increase drowsiness and possible liver damage.

It is also possible to unintentionally combine paracetamol with other drugs and this could be dangerous. Check with your doctor or pharmacist before taking any other medication, including non-prescription items, and if you are taking anything listed below look at the key to find out what effect they may have.

1 Aspirin and salicylate drugs
1 Antinauseants
1 Nifedipine+

2 Anticonvulsants*
2 Lipid lowering drugs
2 Oral contraceptives

4 Anticonvulsants*
4 Antidepressants*
4 Warfarin anticoagulants*

5 Tricyclic antidepressants
5 Barbiturates

*This interaction does not apply to paracetamol only drugs.
+Only large doses of paracetamol cause this interaction.

KEY

1 INCREASES the effects of paracetamol
2 DECREASES the effects of paracetamol
4 PARACETAMOL DECREASES the effects of these drugs
5 UNPREDICTABLE reactions

INTERACTIONS WITH VITAMINS, MINERALS AND FOODS

If paracetamol is taken with over 500mg of vitamin C per day the excretion of paracetamol from the body will be decreased, and this could lead to an increase in the drug's side-effects. See also Prolonged Use.

The amino acid methionine is found with choline and inositol in lecithin. These nutrients all affect the liver in a positive way and if methionine is taken with paracetamol it can help reduce the danger of liver damage from paracetamol overdose.

Food may become harder to swallow if you suffer from a dry mouth while taking these medicines, and the ability to digest starches and carbohydrates will be affected. An important element in this digestion is the enzyme ptyalin, which is present in saliva, and in order to stimulate its flow all food should be chewed extremely well before swallowing.

CHILDREN, OVER SIXTIES AND PROLONGED USE

CHILDREN

Children over the age of three months may be prescribed a number of these medicines, and the dosage will be adjusted accordingly. Some of the medicines in this group are not recommended for children under the age of seven.

OVER SIXTIES

As part of the ageing process the body begins to metabolize and eliminate drugs more slowly and so there may be the possibility of more frequent or severe side-effects or interactions with other medicines. The elderly or those with kidney disorders are more vulnerable to kidney, liver or pancreas problems with long term use of these drugs.

PROLONGED OR CONTINUED TREATMENT

In rare instances sodium loss and damage to the kidney, pancreas, and liver could result from long-term use of paracetamol.* Sodium loss due to kidney damage could precipitate anorexia, nausea, vomiting, and muscular weakness and if any of these symptoms occur they should be discussed immediately with a doctor. Although it is not common, there may be the chance, with a small number of drugs in this group, of physical and psychological dependence. This does not occur with paracetamol only drugs.

*Pameton contains methionine which is thought to decrease the chance of this rare side-effect.

STOPPING THE TREATMENT

After two days of treatment if there is no improvement then contact your doctor for instructions. Always take the advice of your doctor before discontinuing prescription paracetamol drugs.

I'm very brave generally . . . only today I happen to have a headache.
Alice Through The Looking Glass by Lewis Carroll.

Of all the drugs in the medicine chest painkillers must be the most familiar, and they have made life more comfortable for millions of people. It was not too long ago that herbs and other natural substances were used to help pain, inflammation and fever but the convenience and efficiency of the new non-narcotic pain killing drugs nudged the old remedies into the background. However, the convenience of using NSAI's has to be balanced against the possibility of gastric bleeding and there are also adverse effects from other medicines in this category, with the elderly being particularly vulnerable.

The suggestions offered here are designed to help generally with your condition, but it is very important that you do not try to treat yourself. If you suffer severely or regularly from a particular complaint, any serious disorder, or are pregnant then you should not use these remedies before discussion with a doctor. Always report any side-effects and seek medical advice before trying natural remedies and if within a period of one week there has been no improvement then you should consult your doctor.

For more individual advice on natural medicine you should consult an alternative/complementary practitioner and among those who may be able to help are a naturopath, homoeopath, herbalist, acupuncturist, osteopath or chiropractor. More information about these practitioners will be found in the chapter on Alternative/Complementary Medicine and Therapies.

It is possible that certain remedies, supplements or foods could react dangerously with the drugs you are already using so you must check with the fact sheet relating to your medicine to avoid interactions. Please note that it is not advisable to gather your own herbs unless you are sure they are free of any chemicals or pollutants and you can positively identify the correct variety. Always make sure that supplements or natural remedies are taken two or three hours apart from any drugs.

If while reading you come across a particular word or term that is unfamiliar to you please look in The Fact Finder; information on nutrients will be found in the chapter on Vitamins and Minerals.

NATURAL REMEDIES

ARTHRITIS AND RELATED DISORDERS Arthritic and rheumatic disorders generally require the attention of a qualified practitioner; however, some cases may respond to general dietary measures and nutritional supplements.

A chemical called solanine may be an aggravating cause in some cases of arthritis and is poisonous in large quantities. It is found in all the nightshade family of foods such as potatoes, except for sweet potatoes; all peppers such as bell, red, green, yellow, brown, tabasco, chilli, paprika and pimento; aubergines, tomatoes and tobacco. Some people who have removed these items in all forms from their diets have reported a reduction in their pain and inflammation in anywhere from one week to seven months. It is important to read labels carefully as potato starch and other nightshade derivatives are often included in convenience foods.

Some cases of arthritis respond to a gluten-free diet. Gluten is found in wheat, rye, oats, barley, and a large number of foods where sauces are used for thickening. A gluten-free trial should last for at least a month and most health food stores will stock alternative foods and gluten-free cook books.

The diet should be well supplied with whole, fresh foods and essential nutrients. Wherever possible it is best to avoid food additives, all processed and refined foods, hydrogenated and partially hydrogenated fats and oils, sugar and sugar products, foods high in salt, tea, coffee, soft drinks, and alcohol. Good alternatives include coffee substitutes, herbal teas, black cherry juice, grape juice and spring water.

Vitamin C with bioflavonoids is important for the prevention of degenerative disorders.

Vitamin E can be a helpful supplement, but if you have rheumatic heart disease, mitral valve prolapse or are taking certain heart medicines vitamin E should not be taken in supplement form except under supervision. If you are susceptible to high blood pressure then vitamin E can be taken in supplement form, but must be started at a very low dosage and gradually increased and again is best done under supervision.

Germanium is a mineral which is thought to be beneficial for a number of diseases, including arthritis and related disorders, and is found principally in garlic. There are a number of other herbal remedies or food supplements which some people have found beneficial including Bio Strath Willow Formula, evening primrose oil, the herb feverfew used either fresh or in capsule form and DLPA.

There are some cautions to be noted with DLPA. It should be used with care if you have high blood pressure as it may be increased in susceptible people. Children under the age of eight

PAIN & INFLAMMATION

should not be given DLPA unless recommended by a practitioner, because although it is not dangerous to adults, its safety in the young has not yet been established. If you are pregnant or suffer from phenylketonuria or are taking MAOI's then DLPA must only be taken under supervision.

The minerals calcium, magnesium and selenium have also been used as have vitamins A and B complex, especially B5 and B6. Other remedies to try are extract of green lipped mussel and aloe vera juice. The latter can be used externally on the affected joints and some people have also found it helpful to take 2-3 teaspoons a day internally.

It is important to watch your weight, and regular exercise is beneficial if done properly. The aim is to give slow and gentle exercise to each affected joint for a few minutes at least once a day but never reaching, or even approaching, the point of pain.

GOUT Cherries or unsweetened cherry juice are one of the best natural remedies for gout. Experimenting with different amounts should enable you to find how much you need to drink to obtain relief and it may take a while before you begin to feel the benefit.

Drink plenty of spring water and take plenty of vitamin C with bioflavonoids as they can help carry waste acids from the body. Foods which are high in potassium and the whole spectrum of minerals, especially calcium, magnesium, and zinc, are also important.

Orotic acid, B13, is found in whey, which is extracted from milk during the cheese making process. It helps the body excrete uric acid.

B3 competes with uric acid for excretion from the body and may worsen gout if taken in supplement form. Supplements of RNA can also worsen an attack of gout.

Homoeopathic tissue salts Nat. Phos. and Silicea are used for gout.

High purine foods can contribute to uric acid formation and should be avoided. They include offal, red meat, fish, seafoods, spinach, mushrooms, peas, asparagus and dried beans. Some items can add to gout pain such as sugar, sweetmeats, fried foods, alcohol especially port, cheeses, excess salt, refined foods, and caffeine. Sources of caffeine are given in The Fact Finder.

HEADACHES AND MIGRAINES See the chapter on Natural Remedies.

MENSTRUAL CRAMPS

See the How to Help Yourself in the chapter on The Female Reproductive System.

MUSCLE PAIN, CRAMPS AND MUSCLE SPASMS

See the chapter on Natural Remedies.

PAIN, FEVER AND INFLAMMATION

Bio Strath Willow Formula is based on the willow bark which contains aspirin's ancestor, salicyn. It has similar pain relieving and fever reducing qualities to synthetic aspirin, without the side-effects, but it is not as potent. If you are allergic to aspirin or salicylates then willow should not be used.

The herbs valerian and chamomile can be used for their calming and pain relieving properties, and chamomile may help with children's teething pain.

The homoeopathic tissue salt Ferr. Phos. can be used for feverish headaches in both adults and children.

DLPA is an amino acid which can help in many instances of transient pain; however, there are some cautions to be noted with its use and these are listed in the Arthritis section.

Bioflavonoids, which should be taken with vitamin C, contain quercetin which has anti-inflammatory properties and can be taken in doses up to 1000mg per day.

TOOTHACHE

Temporary relief from toothache and tooth infection can be obtained by applying oil of cloves to the painful area but you should avoid swallowing any of it. If you prefer, you can chew cloves so that the oil is released into the mouth.

Vitamin B1 taken in conjunction with the other members of the B complex, and vitamin C may help relieve post dental treatment pain. DLPA can also be used to relieve the pain, but there are cautions to be noted with its use and these are listed in this section under Arthritis.

RESPIRATORY SYSTEM AND ALLERGIES
CONTENTS

RESPIRATORY SYSTEM

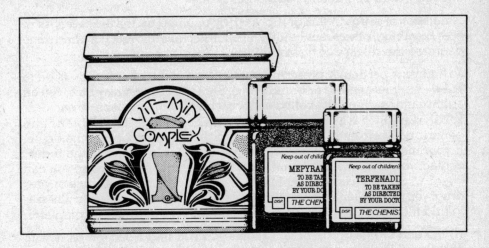

The respiratory system comprises the nose, throat, larynx, trachea and lungs. Above the trachea is the larynx or voice box containing the vocal chords which separate to let air pass on its way to the lungs. The trachea divides inside the lungs, into the right and left bronchi and then into branch-like bronchioles which end in air sacs called alveoli. When we breathe air in, oxygen travels to the alveolar sacs where it is dispersed into the bloodstream. We breathe out carbon dioxide which the blood exchanges for oxygen.

Until the seventeenth century very little was understood about the true function of the respiratory system. It was believed that the heart served to warm the blood and that respiration cooled the heart. By the seventeenth century it was realized that blood's contact with air in the lungs changed its colour from dark to bright red; that respiration was an exchange of gases and blood circulated and travelled from one side of the heart to the other via the lungs.

From the time of Hippocrates physicians listened for chest sounds by placing an ear against the patient, but in 1816 the French physician René Laënnec furthered the understanding of the respiratory system and its diseases when he invented the stethoscope. This magnified internal body sounds and enabled him to recognize heart and respiratory diseases with greater accuracy than had been possible before.

A number of drugs in this group work by opening up the air passages to ease breathing, others reduce inflammation and allergic reactions and some decrease the release of histamine.

To find your particular prescription medicine in this chapter you need to know either its generic or brand name. For instance you may be given an antihistamine which is labelled either mebhydrolin, the generic name, or Fabahistin which is a brand name. The index of drugs lists both brand and generic names to enable you to find the right fact sheet for your medicine. If your medicine has a name which you are unable to find in the index, contact your dispensing chemist and ask for its generic name so you can check whether it has been included. If you do not know the name of your drug, you may prefer to check in the separate index of ailments and illnesses to find the drugs that may be prescribed for your particular complaint.

At the end of this group of fact sheets you will find a section on how to help yourself with suggestions for natural remedies and therapies that may be of assistance. Information about practitioners will be found in the chapter on Alternative/Complementary Medicine and Therapies.

If you come across a particular word or term that is unfamiliar to you, please look in The Fact Finder for an explanation; information on food and nutrition will be found in the chapter on Vitamins and Minerals.

RESPIRATORY SYSTEM

PRESCRIPTION NAMES

MEDICINES FOR ALLERGIC SYMPTOMS AND OTHER DISORDERS

Antihistamines block the action of histamine, a natural body chemical. It is released in response to injury, irritation or allergens and can result in allergic symptoms such as hay fever or redness and swelling of the skin. Because antihistamines also affect nerve transmitters in the central nervous system they may be prescribed for nasal congestion, sleep disorders, nausea, vomiting, motion sickness and some symptoms of Parkinson's disease. Some antihistamines are also used for conjunctivitis and cramps.

NAMES OF PRESCRIPTION MEDICINES

The following are commonly prescribed antihistamines and are shown with the generic name first, followed by the brand name. If your medicine is not listed by name you should follow the information for the generic, if you know it, as the information given will still apply to your particular medicine. If you are not sure of the generic name your pharmacist will be able to advise you. Please note that ALL the information on this fact sheet applies to antihistamines generally, not specifically to any one medicine.

Generic	Brand Name
astemizole	Hismanal
azatadine	Optimine
brompheniramine	Dimotane/LA
chlorpheniramine	Alunex, Piriton
clemastine	Tavegil
cyproheptadine	Periactin
dimethindene	Fenostil Retard
diphenhydramine	Benadryl
diphenylpyraline	Histryl, Lergoban
mebhydrolin	Fabahistin
mepyramine	Anthisan
mequitazine	Primalan
oxatomide	Tinset
phenindamine	Thephorin
pheniramine	Daneral-SA
promethazine	Phenergan
terfenadine	Triludan
trimeprazine	Vallergan
triprolidine	Actidil, Pro-Actidil

WHAT TO TELL YOUR DOCTOR

It is important to make sure that your doctor or doctors are given as much information as possible. If you are aware that you are allergic to any antihistamines or phenothiazines then do tell them so. Information on other medication is vital so if you are taking any other type of medicine, including non-prescription drugs, then they must know that too. Additionally, make sure they know if any of the following apply to you:

Breast feeding
Bronchial asthma
Epilepsy
Glaucoma
High blood pressure
Liver or kidney disorders

Peptic ulcers
Pregnancy
Prostate disorders
Thyroid disorders
Urinary disorders

If you will be having surgery or dental treatment which requires anaesthesia it is important to tell the person in charge that you are taking antihistamines.

SIDE-EFFECTS AND CAUTIONS

SIDE-EFFECTS It is impossible to predict how any medicine will affect a particular individual because everyone's metabolism is so very different. Sensitivity or reaction to drugs can vary greatly from one person to another and side-effects can be related to dosage. It is important to pay close attention to any changes you may notice either when starting, or during, a course of treatment.

The following are some of the side-effects reported within this group of drugs. Some of the disorders listed under Infrequent or Rare may occasionally be the symptoms of overdose and not always those of side-effects.

COMMON

Constipation
Diarrhoea
Dizziness

Drowsiness*
Nausea
Vomiting

*This side-effect is less frequent with terfenadine and astemizole.

INFREQUENT OR RARE

Blood disorders
Breast swelling
Breathing difficulties
Change in appetite
Confusion
Convulsions
Co-ordination problems
Cough
Decreased sexual desire
Depression

Dry mouth
Fatigue
Headache
Heartbeat irregularities
Heartburn
Increased appetite
Irritability
Low blood pressure
Menstrual disorders
Nasal stuffiness

Nervousness, restlessness
or agitation
Palpitations
Ringing in the ears
Skin rashes
Sleeping disorders
Sore throat

Stomach disorders
Sweating
Urinary disorders
Vision changes
Weakness or faintness
Weight change
Yellowing of skin and eyes

If you experience any of the listed side-effects, or any other unusual symptoms, you should consult your dispensing pharmacist or doctor immediately.

CAUTIONS

If you experience dizziness or drowsiness do not drive, operate machinery or work high above the ground. Alcohol can increase these effects and should be avoided during treatment.

If sunbathing, or using a sun-bed or lamp whilst taking these medicines, then a rash or increased tendency to burn may occur so it may be advisable to avoid exposure or to take extra precautions. There may also be increased susceptibility to heat or to heat stroke.

INTERACTIONS

INTERACTIONS WITH OTHER MEDICINES AND SUBSTANCES

No medication works in isolation but is affected to a greater or lesser extent by many other factors such as general fitness, diet and lifestyle. Alcohol may increase the side-effects of drowsiness and dizziness and can induce extreme sedation.

It is also possible to unintentionally combine antihistamines with other drugs and this could be dangerous. Check with your doctor or pharmacist before taking any other medication, including non-prescription items, and if you are taking anything listed below look at the key to find out what effect they may have.

1 Antidepressants
1 Anxiolytics and hypnotics
1 Other antihistamines
1 Tranquillizers
1 Zaditen asthma and
   allergy drugs

2 Antacids

3 Anticholinergics
3 Anticonvulsants
3 Anxiolytics

3 Sedatives
3 Sympathomimetics
3 Tranquillizers

4 Anti-inflammatories
4 Antihypertensives
4 Antiparkinsonian drugs
4 Oestrogen and progestogen
4 Oral contraceptives

5 Antidiarrhoeals

RESPIRATORY SYSTEM

213

Antihistamines taken with gout drugs, tranquillizers, anticonvulsants or antidepressants may excessively increase their sedative effect.

KEY
1 INCREASES the effects of antihistamines
2 DECREASES the effects of antihistamines
3 ANTIHISTAMINES INCREASE the effects of these drugs
4 ANTIHISTAMINES DECREASE the effects of these drugs
5 UNPREDICTABLE reactions

INTERACTIONS WITH VITAMINS, MINERALS AND FOODS

These drugs may deplete vitamin C which itself has antihistamine properties. An excessive intake of alkaline foods may decrease the excretion of these drugs which may then accumulate in the body and the possibility of side-effects or overdose symptoms could be increased. For more information see the chapter on Vitamins and Minerals, and alkaline foods in The Fact Finder.

CHILDREN, OVER SIXTIES AND PROLONGED USE

CHILDREN

Some of these medicines may be prescribed for children and the dosage will be adjusted accordingly. Children may be more susceptible to restlessness and nervousness and they may experience problems with sleeping.

OVER SIXTIES

As part of the ageing process the body begins to metabolize and eliminate drugs more slowly and so there may be the possibility of more frequent or severe side-effects or interactions with other medicines. With some of the drugs in this group there may be an increased possibility of urinary problems, confusion, extreme drowsiness and decreased alertness.

PROLONGED OR CONTINUED TREATMENT

No data found.

STOPPING THE TREATMENT

Antihistamines should not be discontinued without your doctor's advice.

RESPIRATORY SYSTEM

PRESCRIPTION NAMES

MEDICINES FOR THE PREVENTION OF ASTHMA

Asthma preventives are used to decrease or stop the release of a body chemical called histamine which occurs in response to allergic reactions. They are prescribed only for the prevention of asthma.

NAMES OF PRESCRIPTION MEDICINES

The following are commonly prescribed asthma preventives and are shown with the generic name first, followed by the brand name. If your medicine is not listed by name you should follow the information for the generic, if you know it, as the information given will still apply to your particular medicine. If you are not sure of the generic name your pharmacist will be able to advise you. Please note that ALL the information on this fact sheet applies to asthma preventives generally, not specifically to any one medicine.

Generic	Brand Name
ketotifen	Zaditen
nedocromil	Tilade
sodium cromoglycate	Intal/5/Compound

WHAT TO TELL YOUR DOCTOR

It is important to make sure that your doctor or doctors are given as much information as possible. If you are aware that you are allergic to any asthma preventives then do tell them so. Information on other medication is vital so if you are taking any other type of medicine, including non-prescription drugs, then they must know that too. Additionally, make sure they know if any of the following apply to you:

Breast feeding   Liver disorders
Kidney disorders   Pregnancy

SIDE-EFFECTS AND CAUTIONS

SIDE-EFFECTS

It is impossible to predict how any medicine will affect a particular individual because everyone's metabolism is so very different. Sensitivity or reaction to drugs can vary greatly from one person to another and side-effects can be related to dosage. It is important to pay close attention to any changes you may notice either when starting, or during, a course of treatment.

The following are some of the side-effects reported within this group of drugs. Some of the disorders listed under Infrequent or Rare may occasionally be the symptoms of overdose and not always those of side-effects.

COMMON	Cough	Hoarseness
	Dry mouth or throat	Sore throat
INFREQUENT OR RARE	Bitter taste in mouth	Skin rash, itching
	Difficulty breathing	or swelling
	Dizziness or drowsiness	Urination which is
	Headache	frequent or painful
	Muscular weakness or pain	Wheezing
	Nausea or vomiting	

If you experience any of the listed side-effects, or any other unusual symptoms, you should consult your dispensing pharmacist or doctor immediately.

CAUTIONS Do not use these medicines if you are actually experiencing an asthma attack, as they can cause it to become more severe.

If you experience dizziness or drowsiness or your reactions are impaired do not drive, operate machinery or work high above the ground. Alcohol can increase these effects and should be avoided during treatment.

INTERACTIONS

INTERACTIONS WITH OTHER MEDICINES AND SUBSTANCES

No medication works in isolation but is affected to a greater or lesser extent by many other factors such as general fitness, diet and lifestyle. Alcohol's effects can be increased when consumed with asthma preventives, and smoking may worsen the asthma.

It is also possible to unintentionally combine asthma preventives with other drugs and this could be dangerous. Check with your doctor or pharmacist before taking any other medication, including non-prescription items, and if you are taking anything listed below look at the key to find out what effect they may have.

3 Antihistamines
3 Cortisone
3 Sedatives
3 Hypnotics

5 Oral antidiabetics

Anticholinergics if taken with asthma preventives may increase the side-effects of anticholinergics.

Zaditen drugs taken with oral antidiabetics may lead to a form of anaemia.

ASTHMA PREVENTIVES

KEY   3 ASTHMA PREVENTIVES INCREASE the effects of these drugs

5 UNPREDICTABLE reactions

INTERACTIONS WITH VITAMINS, MINERALS AND FOODS   No data found.

CHILDREN, OVER SIXTIES AND PROLONGED USE

CHILDREN   These medicines may be prescribed for children, and the dosage will be adjusted accordingly.

OVER SIXTIES   As part of the ageing process the body begins to metabolize and eliminate drugs more slowly and so there may be the possibility of more frequent or severe side-effects or interactions with other medicines.

PROLONGED OR CONTINUED TREATMENT   No data found.

STOPPING THE TREATMENT   Asthma preventives should not be discontinued without your doctor's advice, as their use may need to be withdrawn slowly.

PERSONAL MEDICINE NOTES

RESPIRATORY SYSTEM

PRESCRIPTION NAMES

MEDICINES USED FOR BREATHING DISORDERS

Bronchodilators ease breathing by opening up the air passages in the lungs which have become narrowed, usually by muscle spasm. Some are sympathomimetics, so called because their actions mimic some of the effects of naturally occurring body chemicals such as adrenaline or noradrenaline, others are derivatives of theophylline. Bronchodilators may be prescribed for bronchial asthma, bronchitis, emphysema and other breathing difficulties.

NAMES OF PRESCRIPTION MEDICINES

The following are commonly prescribed bronchodilators and are shown with the generic name first, followed by the brand name. If your medicine is not listed by name you should follow the information for the generic, if you know it, as the information given will still apply to your particular medicine. If you are not sure of the generic name your pharmacist will be able to advise you. Please note that ALL the information on this fact sheet applies to bronchodilators generally, not specifically to any one medicine.

Generic	Brand Name
aminophylline	Phyllocontin Continus, Theodrox
fenoterol	Berotec
pirbuterol	Exirel
reproterol	Bronchodil
rimiterol	Pulmadil/Auto
salbutamol	Asmaven, Cobutolin, Salbulin, Ventolin, Volumatic
terbutaline	Bricanyl/SA, Monovent/SA, Nebuhaler
theophyllinate	Choledyl, Sabidal-SR
theophylline	Biophylline, Lasma, Nuelin/SA, Pro-Vent, Slo-Phyllin, Theo-Dur, Theograd, Uniphyllin Continus

WHAT TO TELL YOUR DOCTOR

It is important to make sure that your doctor or doctors are given as much information as possible. If you are aware that you are allergic to any bronchodilators or sympathomimetics then do tell them so. Information on other medication is vital so if you are taking any other type of medicine, including non-prescription drugs, then they must know that too. Additionally, make sure they know if any of the following apply to you:

RESPIRATORY SYSTEM AND ALLERGIES
BRONCHODILATORS

Alcoholism
Angina
Breast feeding
Diabetes
Diverticulitis
Glaucoma
Heart disorders
Heart rhythm disorders
High blood pressure
Intestinal obstruction
Liver or kidney disorders
Peptic ulcers
Pregnancy
Steroid drugs taken
   regularly
Taking MAOI's now, or
   within the last two weeks
Thyroid disorders
Tuberculosis*
Urinary or prostate
   disorders
Viral infection

*Tell your doctor if there is any history of this condition in yourself, or your family.

SIDE-EFFECTS AND CAUTIONS

SIDE-EFFECTS It is impossible to predict how any medicine will affect a particular individual because everyone's metabolism is so very different. Sensitivity or reaction to drugs can vary greatly from one person to another and side-effects can be related to dosage. It is important to pay close attention to any changes you may notice either when starting, or during, a course of treatment.

The following are some of the side-effects reported within this group of drugs. Some of the disorders listed under Infrequent or Rare may occasionally be the symptoms of overdose and not always those of side-effects. If you are using an inhaler, rather than tablets, capsules or liquids, then the side-effects are less likely to occur.

COMMON

Headache
Irritability
Nausea
Nervousness
Restlessness
Stomach over-acidity
Stomach upsets
Vomiting

INFREQUENT OR RARE

Decreased appetite
Diarrhoea
Dizziness
Drowsiness
Flushing of the face
Fungal infection
   of the mouth
Heart rhythm disorders
Increased sweating
Lightheadedness
Muscle cramps
Palpitations
Rapid breathing
Stomach pain or cramps
Tremor
Weakness

If you experience any of the listed side-effects, or any other unusual symptoms, you should consult your dispensing pharmacist or doctor immediately.

CAUTIONS The dosage recommended by your doctor should not be exceeded. If the medicine does not seem to be helping then ask your doctor's advice.

If you experience dizziness or drowsiness do not drive, operate machinery or work high above the ground. Alcohol can increase these effects and should be avoided during treatment.

Skin rash or nettle rash usually indicates allergy to these medicines and the doctor should be contacted immediately should either of these occur.

INTERACTIONS

INTERACTIONS WITH OTHER MEDICINES AND SUBSTANCES No medication works in isolation but is affected to a greater or lesser extent by many other factors such as general fitness, diet and lifestyle. Smoking and alcohol may decrease the effects of some of these drugs.

It is also possible to unintentionally combine bronchodilators with other drugs and this could be dangerous. Check with your doctor or pharmacist before taking any other medication, including non-prescription items, and if you are taking anything listed below look at the key to find out what effect they may have.

1   Antidepressants
1   Antibiotics, especially erythromycins
1   Anxiolytics
1   Cimetidine and ranitidine ulcer medicines
1   Digitalis drugs
1   Diuretics
1   Oral contraceptives
1   Sympathomimetics

2   Anticonvulsants
2   Barbiturates
2   Beta blockers

3   Diuretics

4   Lithium

5   Gout drugs

BRONCHODILATORS

KEY
1 INCREASES the effects of bronchodilators
2 DECREASES the effects of bronchodilators
3 BRONCHODILATORS INCREASE the effects of these drugs
4 BRONCHODILATORS DECREASE the effects of these drugs
5 UNPREDICTABLE reactions

INTERACTIONS WITH VITAMINS, MINERALS AND FOODS

Nervousness, irritability, and sleeping problems can be increased by a high intake of tea, coffee, colas, cocoa, and any caffeine drinks and so they should be avoided wherever possible. Large quantities of carbohydrate-rich foods and sugary food or drinks are not recommended with these drugs.

Potassium levels may be temporarily decreased by some of these medicines and plenty of potassium rich foods should be included in the diet. See the chapter on Vitamins and Minerals for further information.

CHILDREN, OVER SIXTIES AND PROLONGED USE

CHILDREN

Children over six years old may be prescribed some of these medicines, generally in syrup or elixir form, and the dosage will be adjusted accordingly. Certain inhalers may be prescribed to be used with adult supervision.

OVER SIXTIES

As part of the ageing process the body begins to metabolize and eliminate drugs more slowly and so there may be the possibility of more frequent or severe side-effects or interactions with other medicines.

PROLONGED OR CONTINUED TREATMENT

Long term use of some of these medicines may cause stomach disorders.

STOPPING THE TREATMENT

Bronchodilators should not be discontinued without your doctor's advice.

RESPIRATORY SYSTEM

PRESCRIPTION NAMES

MEDICINES FOR THE PREVENTION OF ASTHMA

Corticosteroids reduce allergic reactions, swelling and inflammation. The medicines in this group act only on the lungs and have very little effect on the rest of the body. They are used by inhalation and are prescribed for the prevention and treatment of asthma, hay fever and bronchospasm.

NAMES OF PRESCRIPTION MEDICINES

The following are commonly prescribed corticosteroid inhalers and are shown with the generic name first, followed by the brand name. If your medicine is not listed by name you should follow the information for the generic, if you know it, as the information given will still apply to your particular medicine. If you are not sure of the generic name your pharmacist will be able to advise you. Please note that ALL the information on this fact sheet applies to corticosteroid inhalers generally, not specifically to any one medicine.

Generic	Brand Name
beclomethasone	Becloforte, Becotide, Volumatic, Ventide
betamethasone	Bextasol
budesonide	Nebuhaler, Pulmicort/LS, Rhinocort

WHAT TO TELL YOUR DOCTOR

It is important to make sure that your doctor or doctors are given as much information as possible. If you are aware that you are allergic to any corticosteroids then do tell them so. Information on other medication is vital so if you are taking any other type of medicine, including non-prescription drugs, then they must know that too. Additionally, make sure they know if any of the following apply to you:

Breast feeding	Pregnancy
Liver or kidney disorders	Tuberculosis*
Oral corticosteroid treatment taken long-term within the past year	Viral or fungal infection of the respiratory tract

*Tell your doctor if there is any history of this condition in yourself, or your family.

If you will be having surgery or dental treatment which requires anaesthesia tell the person in charge if you are, or have been, taking corticosteroids.

RESPIRATORY SYSTEM AND ALLERGIES
CORTICOSTEROID INHALERS

SIDE-EFFECTS AND CAUTIONS

SIDE-EFFECTS It is impossible to predict how any medicine will affect a particular individual because everyone's metabolism is so very different. Sensitivity or reaction to drugs can vary greatly from one person to another and side-effects can be related to dosage. It is important to pay close attention to any changes you may notice either when starting, or during, a course of treatment.

The following are some of the side-effects reported within this group of drugs. Some of the disorders listed under Infrequent or Rare may occasionally be the symptoms of overdose and not always those of side-effects.

INFREQUENT OR RARE

Dry or sore throat	Hoarseness
Fungus infection of throat or mouth+	Sneezing attacks after using inhaler

+ Rinsing the mouth out with water after using the inhaler may decrease the chance of oral fungal infections.

If you experience any of the listed side-effects, or any other unusual symptoms, you should consult your dispensing pharmacist or doctor immediately.

CAUTIONS If you were receiving long term oral corticosteroid therapy recently, or up to a year before using corticosteroid inhalers, you should contact your doctor if you experience periods of stress, infections or worsened asthma.

If the relief obtained from an inhaler lasts 4 hours or less contact your doctor of pharmacist for advice.

If you were given a steroid card by your doctor it is important to carry it with you at all times.

INTERACTIONS

INTERACTIONS WITH OTHER MEDICINES AND SUBSTANCES No medication works in isolation but is affected to a greater or lesser extent by many other factors such as general fitness, diet, lifestyle etc.

It is also possible to unintentionally combine corticosteroid inhalers with other drugs and this could be dangerous. Check with your doctor or pharmacist before taking any other medication, including non-prescription items, and if you are taking anything listed below look at the key to find out what effect they may have.

1 Anti-inflammatories
1 Bronchodilators
1 Combined oral contraceptives
1 Oestrogens
1 Sympathomimetics

4 Insulin

5 Antihistamines

KEY   1 INCREASES the effects of corticosteroid inhalers
4 CORTICOSTEROID INHALERS DECREASE the effects of these drugs
5 UNPREDICTABLE reactions

INTERACTIONS WITH VITAMINS, MINERALS AND FOODS   No data found.

CHILDREN, OVER SIXTIES AND PROLONGED USE

CHILDREN   Some of these medicines may be prescribed for children and the dosage will be adjusted accordingly.

OVER SIXTIES   As part of the ageing process the body begins to metabolize and eliminate drugs more slowly and so there may be the possibility of more frequent or severe side-effects or interactions with other medicines.

PROLONGED OR CONTINUED TREATMENT   If the inhalers are used in very large doses over a prolonged period of time your doctor may find it necessary to occasionally prescribe oral corticosteroids on a temporary basis.

STOPPING THE TREATMENT   Corticosteroid inhalers should not be discontinued without your doctor's advice as their use may need to be slowly withdrawn.

RESPIRATORY SYSTEM AND ALLERGIES
HOW TO HELP YOURSELF

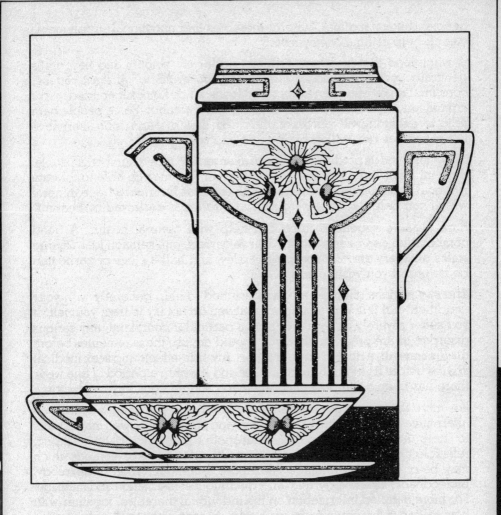

Among the Haida Indians of the Pacific Northwest, the verb for 'making poetry' is the same as the verb 'to breathe'.
Another Roadside Attraction by Tom Robbins.

Many asthma and allergy sufferers have to rely on medicines to relieve their suffering, but for some people these can produce unwanted side-effects.

Special dietary regimes, natural therapies and nutritional supplements can all help asthma or hay fever.

A wholefood diet free from artificial additives, colours and flavours is generally recommended. It is far better to avoid, or at least reduce, consumption of refined and processed foods, white flour, sugar, fried foods, animal fats, chocolate, cocoa, tea, coffee and alcohol. Some people gain relief by excluding all sources of wheat from their diet and using alternative flours such as rye, millet, buckwheat and soya.

Cow's milk and its products may be an allergen for quite a number of people. Soya milk is often used as an alternative or you may be able to tolerate raw goat or sheep milk. Raw goat milk contains fluorine, a trace mineral which can help decrease catarrh, but fluorine is destroyed by heating.

Raw, organic vegetable juice can help with general health. A good combination can be made from 3 large carrots, one spinach leaf, 2 large stalks of celery and 2-3 sprigs of parsley, and half a clove of garlic can be helpful if you wish to add it.

The suggestions offered here are designed to help generally with your condition, but it is very important that you do not try to treat yourself. If you suffer severely or regularly from a particular complaint, any serious disorder, or are pregnant then you should not use these remedies before discussion with a doctor. Always report any side-effects and seek medical advice before trying natural remedies and if within a period of one week there has been no improvement then you should consult your doctor.

For more individual advice on natural medicine you should consult an alternative/complementary practitioner and among those who may be able to help are a homoeopath, naturopath, acupuncturist, herbalist, reflexologist, osteopath or chiropractor. Other therapies or methods which may be of assistance include Alexander technique, yoga, reflexology, biofeedback, kinesiology, relaxation techniques, meditation and massage. For more detailed information on the individual therapies, together with how to find a practitioner in your area, please refer to the chapter on Alternative/Complementary Medicine and Therapies.

It is possible that certain remedies, supplements or foods could react dangerously with the drugs you are already using so you must check with the fact sheet relating to your medicine to avoid interactions. Please note that it is not advisable to gather your own herbs unless you are sure they are free of any chemicals or pollutants and you can positively identify the correct variety. Always make sure that supplements or natural remedies are taken two to three hours apart from any drugs.

If while reading you come across a particular word or term that is unfamiliar to you please look in The Fact Finder; information on nutrients will be found in the chapter on Vitamins and Minerals.

NATURAL REMEDIES

ASTHMA AND RELATED BREATHING DIFFICULTIES

If you suffer from asthma or other related breathing difficulties, please do not try to treat yourself without the consent of your doctor.

The diet should contain plenty of wholefoods and fresh fruit and vegetables, but dairy products should be avoided as they can increase mucus. Good alternatives to try are goat or soya milk.

It is thought that some asthmatics produce less hydrochloric acid than they need to digest and assimilate food and nutrients properly. The homoeopathic remedy Nat. Mur. can help the body produce normal amounts of hydrochloric acid (HC1), or tablets of HC1 with pepsin can be swallowed after main or heavy meals to help digestion. Those with peptic ulcers, or children and teenagers should avoid HC1 with pepsin tablets, and take Nat. Mur. or papaya or bromelain tablets instead to help with digestion.

There is growing evidence to suggest that asthmatics may need more B6. Supplementation of up to 25mg twice a day taken with a B complex supplement may help to reduce some types of wheezing and should take effect within about a week. Other important nutrients include vitamins A, E, C and bioflavonoids, and the minerals magnesium, zinc and selenium.

Herbal remedies include garlic, which has anti-infective qualities and helps relieve mucus. A clove can be taken raw in salad, or it may be more convenient to take it in capsule form instead. Propolis also has anti-infective qualities and assists with healing.

A helpful tea can be made by mixing equal amounts of sage, thyme, lavender, aniseed and nettle and using a teaspoonful to a cup. Add boiling water and allow to steep for 3 minutes,

RESPIRATORY SYSTEM

227

strain and drink up to 2-3 times a day. A little honey and lemon can be added if required.

Homoeopathic remedies to help breathing difficulties include Ipecacuanha for 'rattling' mucus in inflamed bronchial tubes; Bryonia for breathing difficulties accompanied by a dry throat and chesty cough, and Arsen. Alb. for when, in order to draw breath, it helps to sit up or bend forward.

The homoeopathic tissue salt Calc. Phos. is a good general remedy for asthmatics. For asthma accompanied by fever, inflammation or congestion the tissue salt Ferr. Phos. can be used.

Thick white catarrh may be treated with Kali. Mur. alternating with Kali. Phos. Yellow, watery or green catarrh may be treated with Kali. Sulph. and thick yellow catarrh, with Silicea. Asthma and bronchial spasm due to nervousness can be treated with Mag. Phos. alternating with Kali. Phos.

Coltsfoot, pine and honey balsam is very helpful for catarrhal conditions. It is made by Allens of Anglesey and is available in some health food stores.

Ionizers can be useful in areas like offices where indoor pollution from dust, smoke, air conditioning or central heating may be a major contributor to some types of asthma. Using an ionizer at night in the bedroom may also help.

Gentle exercise such as walking or t'ai-chi may be helpful and yoga breathing techniques may help with lung capacity and breath control.

See also nervousness and anxiety in the chapter on Natural Remedies.

HAY FEVER

If your hay fever becomes active around early spring then you are likely to be allergic to tree pollen. If active around the end of June through July and August grass pollens are probably the culprit. Shrub pollens and seasonal moulds or spores may be responsible if hay fever appears in late summer or early autumn. Drugless hay fever control may take a long time to work and often needs to be started in winter or at least three months before the hay fever usually begins. Overall lifestyle changes need to be made and general dietary suggestions are listed in the main introduction. One day a week it is a good idea to eat only fruit or vegetables in order to help cleanse the body. A natural practitioner is recommended to guide you through individual desensitization and detoxification of the body.

Allergies may be worsened when food is not digested properly and as with asthmatics hydrochloric acid may be decreased so that food is not completely broken down in the stomach. The homoeopathic remedy Nat. Mur. can help the body produce normal amounts of hydrochloric acid (HC1), or tablets of HC1 with pepsin can be swallowed after main or heavy meals to help digestion. Those with peptic ulcers, or children and teenagers should avoid HC1 with pepsin tablets, and take Nat. Mur. or papaya or bromelain tablets instead to help with digestion.

Important nutrients include vitamin A, B complex, B12 taken under the tongue, vitamin E and minerals such as calcium, magnesium, chromium, selenium, potassium and manganese. If you have rheumatic heart disease, mitral valve prolapse or are taking certain heart medicines vitamin E should not be taken in supplement form except under supervision. If you are susceptible to high blood pressure then vitamin E can be taken in supplement form, but must be started at a very low dosage and gradually increased and again is best done under supervision.

Vitamin C is a natural antihistamine. It helps to decrease toxins in the bloodstream and is necessary for the adrenal glands which produce allergy and inflammation counteracting hormones. When hay fever is active 250-500mg of vitamin C, in the form of calcium ascorbate, can be taken every 2 hours or up to the point just before the bowels become loose. As the hay fever begins to improve, gradually decrease the dose and at the end of the season it should also be decreased slowly. Calcium ascorbate is recommended as calcium is also antihistamine and this form of vitamin C is generally tolerated by people with peptic ulcers. If large amounts of vitamin C in other forms are taken then calcium is decreased. Vitamin B12 can be decreased by amounts of vitamin C over 750mg daily. For more information about B12 please see the chapter on Vitamins and Minerals.

Some of the bioflavonoids can decrease the release of histamine. When hay fever is active bioflavonoids can be taken up to 500mg three times a day.

B5 is important for the function of the adrenal glands and decreases histamine production. 50-100mg can be taken every three hours. Royal jelly is one of the highest natural sources of B5 and can be used advantageously with the other supplements.

New Era's Combination H tissue salts are for general hay fever symptoms. Nat. Mur. is used for watery discharges, Ferr. Phos.

can help congestion and catarrh and Kali. Mur. is for advanced stages of hay fever where it is very catarrhal. Homoeopathic remedies include Sabadilla for streaming nose and eyes and Allium Cepa for itching eyes and streaming sore nose. Homoeopathically potentized mixed pollen is used for de-sensitization.

Herbs such as ginseng may be useful to counteract the stress of hay fever. Garlic can be taken either raw or in capsules to help mucus conditions. A helpful herb tea can be made from an equal mixture of fenugreek, stinging nettle, aniseed and horehound. Place a teaspoonful in a cup and pour boiling water over it. Allow to steep for three minutes, strain and drink slowly 2-3 times a day.

A chamomile splash can be used as often as necessary to help itchy eyes. Place 3 heaped teaspoons of chamomile in a measuring jug and pour boiling water over it. Allow to steep for five minutes, strain and then transfer to a large bowl or saucepan. Add cooler water until it can be used as a facial dip or splash. If you are able to open your eyes with your face submerged, the itching is helped much faster. Chamomile or ordinary teabags which have been used then cooled are soothing when placed over each eye for up to ten minutes.

A soothing eyewash can be made from goldenseal, rosemary and eyebright. Place an eighth of a teaspoon of each herb in a cup which has been sterilized with boiling water. Pour boiling water over them and allow to steep for three minutes, then strain through a clean filter and leave to cool to blood heat. Use as often as needed in a sterilized eye bath.

Breathing steam for up to four minutes often helps congestion. Pour boiling water into a large bowl or saucepan and add 2-3 eucalyptus leaves or a few drops of Olbas oil. Place a large towel over the head and breathe in the steam from a height of at least a foot above the water. Close the towel gradually round the bowl, being careful not to be burned by the hot steam.

On windy or bright days wearing dark glasses helps protect the eyes and prevent itching. An ionizer often helps during the hay fever season, see the section on asthma for more details.

Exercise releases endorphins which are believed to be involved in decreasing allergy symptoms and this may account for the fact that many hay fever sufferers feel better when they jog or engage in exercise.

RESPIRATORY SYSTEM

PERSONAL MEDICINE NOTES

FEMALE REPRODUCTIVE SYSTEM AND ENDOCRINE GLANDS

REPRODUCTIVE SYSTEM

FEMALE REPRODUCTIVE SYSTEM AND ENDOCRINE GLANDS

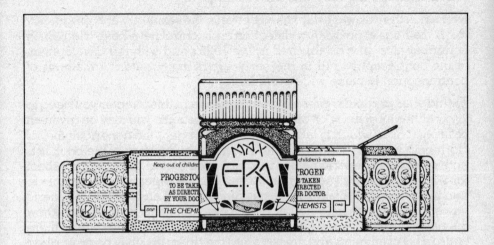

Where to find information on related disorders:

Prostate gland — there are no specific medicines used commonly for prostate disorders. Antibiotics may be prescribed, see the chapter on Infections and Parasites and the index for more information.

The therapeutic use of natural and synthetically produced hormones has made it possible to control and assist many body processes. The glands produce and secrete hormones and other substances which act elsewhere in the body and include the pituitary, pineal, ovaries, testes, thyroid, parathyroids, thymus, pancreas, and adrenals.

Insulin is a hormone produced in the pancreas and secreted into the bloodstream which maintains blood sugar metabolism and blood sugar levels. Insulin dependent diabetics need supplementary insulin which can only be utilized by the body when injected. Other forms of diabetes, where the pancreas still produces some insulin, are treated first with diet and then, if necessary, with antidiabetic drugs.

The thyroid gland produces and secretes hormones which affect metabolism. Too little results in hypothyroidism which may be treated with thyroid hormones. Excessive production and secretion of thyroid hormones

FEMALE REPRODUCTIVE SYSTEM AND ENDOCRINE GLANDS

is known as hyperthyroidism and may be controlled with anti-thyroid drugs which decrease the hormone production.

Ever since the link was established between the sexual act and pregnancy many methods of pregnancy detection and control have been tried. Birth control clinics were established in the 1920's and with the development of the contraceptive pill in the early 1960's many different methods of contraception became widely available.

To find your particular prescription medicine in this chapter you need to know either its generic or brand name. For instance you may be given an oestrogen drug which is labelled either oestrogen, the generic name, or Hormonin which is a brand name. The index at the back of the book lists both brand and generic names to enable you to find the right fact sheet for your medicine. If your medicine has a name which you are unable to find in the index, contact your dispensing chemist and ask for its generic name so you can check whether it has been included. If you do not know the name of your drug, you may prefer to check in the index where there is also a list of ailments and illnesses and the drugs that may be prescribed for these.

At the end of this group of fact sheets you will find a section on how to help yourself with suggestions for natural remedies and therapies that may be of assistance. Information about practitioners will be found in the chapter on Alternative/Complementary Medicine and Therapies.

If you come across a particular word or term that is unfamiliar to you, please look in The Fact Finder for an explanation; information on food and nutrition will be found in the chapter on Vitamins and Minerals.

ENDOCRINE GLANDS
ANTITHYROID DRUGS

PRESCRIPTION NAMES

MEDICINES FOR OVERACTIVE THYROID GLAND

When the thyroid gland produces too much of the hormone thyroxine, the result is hyperthyroidism and carbimazole is used to treat this condition. It interferes with the thyroid's use of iodine and reduces its production of thyroid hormones. Carbimazole may also be used before thyroidectomy surgery for goitre.

NAMES OF PRESCRIPTION MEDICINES

The following is a commonly prescribed antithyroid drug and is shown with the generic name first, followed by the brand name. If your medicine is not listed by name you should follow the information for the generic, if you know it, as the information given will still apply to your particular medicine.

Generic	Brand Name
carbimazole	Neo-Mercazde 20

WHAT TO TELL YOUR DOCTOR

It is important to make sure that your doctor or doctors are given as much information as possible. If you are aware that you are allergic to any antithyroid drugs then do tell them so. Information on other medication is vital so if you are taking any other type of medicine, including non-prescription drugs, then they must know that too. Additionally, make sure they know if any of the following apply to you:

Blood disorders
Breast feeding
Infection
Liver or kidney disorders
Obstruction in the windpipe
Pregnancy
Recent iodine intake

If you will be having surgery or dental treatment which requires anaesthesia it is important to tell the person in charge that you are taking antithyroid drugs.

SIDE-EFFECTS AND CAUTIONS

SIDE-EFFECTS

It is impossible to predict how any medicine will affect a particular individual because everyone's metabolism is so very different. Sensitivity or reaction to drugs can vary greatly from one person to another and side-effects can be related to dosage. It is important to pay close attention to any changes you may notice either when starting, or during, a course of treatment.

The following are some of the side-effects reported within this group of drugs. Some of the disorders listed under Infrequent or Rare may occasionally be the symptoms of overdose and not always those of side-effects.

ENDOCRINE GLANDS
ANTITHYROID DRUGS

COMMON Gastro-intestinal disorders   Nausea
Headache   Rashes
Joint pain

INFREQUENT OR RARE Bleeding gums   Irregular heartbeat
Blood disorders   Loss of sense of taste
Diarrhoea   Sore throat
Dizziness   Swelling of the front of
Drowsiness   the neck, feet or legs
Fever   Unusual or easy bruising
Hair loss   or bleeding
Hepatitis   Yellow skin or eyes

If you experience any of the listed side-effects, or any other unusual symptoms, you should consult your dispensing pharmacist or doctor immediately.

CAUTIONS Tell your doctor if you have an injury, illness or infection while you are taking this medicine.

INTERACTIONS

INTERACTIONS WITH OTHER MEDICINES AND SUBSTANCES No medication works in isolation but is affected to a greater or lesser extent by many other factors such as general fitness, diet and lifestyle. Alcohol may increase the chance of liver disorders, and tobacco may cause rapid heartbeat.

It is also possible to unintentionally combine carbimazole with other drugs which could be dangerous. Check with your doctor or pharmacist before taking any other medication, including non-prescription medicines, and if you are taking anything listed below look at the key to find out what effect they may have:

3 Anticoagulants

KEY 3 ANTITHYROID DRUGS INCREASE the effects of these drugs

INTERACTIONS WITH VITAMINS, MINERALS AND FOODS These drugs may affect calcium and phosphorus levels in the body so an adequate intake should come from the diet.

ENDOCRINE GLANDS
ANTITHYROID DRUGS

CHILDREN, OVER SIXTIES AND PROLONGED USE

CHILDREN These medicines may be prescribed for children and the dosage will be adjusted accordingly.

OVER SIXTIES As part of the ageing process the body begins to metabolize and eliminate drugs more slowly and so there may be the possibility of more frequent or severe side-effects or interactions with other medicines.

PROLONGED OR CONTINUED TREATMENT No data found.

STOPPING THE TREATMENT Do not discontinue the treatment without consulting your doctor as the dosage may need to be gradually reduced. If other drugs are being taken at the same time then their dosage may also need to be adjusted.

PERSONAL MEDICINE NOTES

FEMALE REPRODUCTIVE SYSTEM
OESTROGENS AND PROGESTOGENS

PRESCRIPTION NAMES

MEDICINES FOR THE MENOPAUSE, REPLACEMENT THERAPY AND FEMALE DISORDERS

The oestrogens and progestogens in this group are prescribed for menopausal symptoms such as hot flushes, sweating, irritability, anxiety and depression. Post-menopausal use includes certain types of incontinence, sleep difficulties, osteoporosis, irritability and depression. They may also be used for vaginal and cervical disorders, inhibition or prevention of lactation, dysfunctional uterine bleeding, dysmenorrhoea, other female disorders and replacement therapy. They are not used for contraception although the data is very similar to contraceptives in other respects.

NAMES OF PRESCRIPTION MEDICINES

The following are commonly prescribed oestrogens or oestrogens and progestogens. Brand names only are given as generics are not usually prescribed. Please note that ALL the information on this fact sheet applies to oestrogens or oestrogens and progestogens generally, not specifically to any one brand name medicine.

Oestrogen only

Estrovis	Ovestin
Ethinyloestradiol	Pentovis
Harmogen	Premarin
Hormonin	Progynova

Oestrogens and Progestogens

Controvlar	Prempak
Cyclo-progynova	Trisequens
Menophase	

Mixogen is a mixture of oestrogen and androgen but the data for this group applies to it.

WHAT TO TELL YOUR DOCTOR

It is important to make sure that your doctor or doctors are given as much information as possible. If you are aware that you are allergic to any oestrogens or oestrogens and progestogens then do tell them so. Information on other medication is vital so if you are taking any other type of medicine, including non-prescription drugs, then they must know that too. Additionally, make sure they know if any of the following apply to you:

Abnormal vaginal bleeding	Cancer of the reproductive system
Arteriosclerosis	
Asthma or breathing disorders	Candida albicans
Breast cysts or cancer	Cardiovascular disease
Breast soreness	Cholesterol disorders
	Contact lens wearer

FEMALE REPRODUCTIVE SYSTEM
OESTROGENS AND PROGESTOGENS

Depression*
Diabetes
Dubin Johnson syndrome
Endometriosis
Epilepsy
Eye disorders
Gall bladder disorders
Gall stones
Heart disorders or disease
Herpes or shingles*
High blood pressure*
Jaundice
Liver or kidney disorders
Migraine or headaches
Multiple sclerosis
Ovarian cysts
Overweight
Porphyria
Pregnancy or breast feeding**
Rotor syndrome
Sickle cell anaemia
Thrombosis*
Use of tobacco or cigarettes
Uterine fibroids
Uterus displacement
Varicose veins
Water retention

*Tell your doctor if there is any history of these conditions in yourself, or your family.

**Your doctor should also be informed if you have any history of worsening of deafness, toxaemia, severe itching, skin discoloration or pigmentation during pregnancy.

Oestrogens or oestrogens and progestogens must be withdrawn at least six weeks before surgery so it is important to discuss this with your doctor. Laboratory tests can be affected so you should tell the person in charge which hormone drugs you are taking.

SIDE-EFFECTS AND CAUTIONS

SIDE-EFFECTS   It is impossible to predict how any medicine will affect a particular individual because everyone's metabolism is so very different. Sensitivity or reaction to drugs can vary greatly from one person to another and side-effects can be related to dosage. It is important to pay close attention to any changes you may notice either when starting, or during, a course of treatment. If you experience any of the listed side-effects or any other unusual symptoms, even if they seem unrelated to your medicine, you should consult your dispensing pharmacist or doctor immediately. Although this list may seem frightening, most of the side-effects are very rare and as most of these medicines are low dosage it is unlikely that you will experience any side-effects that are not common. The following are some of the side-effects reported within this groups of drugs.

FEMALE REPRODUCTIVE SYSTEM
OESTROGENS AND PROGESTOGENS

COMMON — Nausea

INFREQUENT OR RARE —

Abdominal bloating
Acne
Backache
Breast lumps, tenderness, enlargement or secretion
Breathing disorders
Candida albicans
Change in weight
Changes in sexual desire or libido
Cough
Dark skin patches
Decreased glucose tolerance
Depression
Diarrhoea
Fatigue
Gastro-intestinal upsets
Headaches
Increased blood pressure
Increased growth of body hair
Increased triglyceride or cholesterol levels
Muscular or joint pains
Nervousness
Pains or swelling in upper leg
Scalp hair loss
Sensitivity to light
Severe stomach pains
Skin rash
Spotting or abnormal vaginal bleeding
Thrombosis*
Vaginal discharges or itch
Vomiting
Water and salt retention

*Tell your doctor if there is any history of this condition in yourself, or your family.

OESTROGENS OR OESTROGENS AND PROGESTERONES SHOULD BE STOPPED IMMEDIATELY AND THE DOCTOR INFORMED IF ANY OF THE FOLLOWING OCCUR:

Blood in the urine
Dizziness or nosebleeds
Eyes or skin become yellow
Fainting, collapse or sudden weakness
Migraine or any unusually severe headaches
Numbness or tingling
Part of the body becomes cold or blue
Pregnancy
Severe or prolonged injury or illness where you will be confined to bed
Severe stomach pains or tenderness
Severe or sudden pain in the side of the chest
Spitting blood
Sudden or extreme increase in blood pressure which may be characterized by unusually severe headache
Vision disturbances

If squeezing or heavy pressure in the chest occurs, possibly accompanied by pain in the shoulder, neck, arm and fingers of the left hand, nausea, sweating and shortness of breath then a doctor or hospital must be called IMMEDIATELY. These are symptoms of a heart attack and delay could be dangerous or even fatal.

CAUTIONS

It is essential to consult with your doctor so that you can be taken off oestrogens and progestogens 6-8 weeks in advance of any surgery.

It is important to make regular visits to the doctor for routine health checks and monthly self-examination of the breasts should be carried out. Your doctor or pharmacist should be able to give you a leaflet showing how to carry this out.

Excessive exposure to sunlight or sunlamps should be avoided as you may be more susceptible to sunburn or skin rashes.

INTERACTIONS

INTERACTIONS WITH OTHER MEDICINES AND SUBSTANCES

No medication works in isolation but is affected to a greater or lesser extent by many other factors such as general fitness, diet and lifestyle. Smoking can increase the risk of a stroke, heart attack and blood clots, especially in women who smoke and are over the age of 35.

It is also possible to unintentionally combine oestrogen and progestogens with other drugs and this could be dangerous. Check with your doctor or pharmacist before taking any other medication, including non-prescription items, and if you are taking anything listed below look at the key to find out what effect they may have.

2 Antibiotics	2 Phenytoin anticonvulsants
2 Anticoagulants	4 Anticoagulants
2 Anticonvulsants	4 Antidepressants, tricyclic
2 Antihistamines	4 Antidiabetics
2 Anti-inflammatories and NSAI's	4 Antihypertensives
2 Anxiolytics	4 Danazol
2 Barbiturates	4 Insulin
2 Laxatives	4 Lipid lowering drugs
2 Liquid paraffin	4 Thyroid hormones

Oestrogens or oestrogens and progestogens taken with tricyclic antidepressants can increase the antidepressant side-effects.

FEMALE REPRODUCTIVE SYSTEM
OESTROGENS AND PROGESTOGENS

KEY	2	DECREASES the effects of oestrogens or oestrogens and progestogens
	4	OESTROGENS AND PROGESTOGENS DECREASE the effects of these drugs

INTERACTIONS WITH VITAMINS, MINERALS AND FOODS

Oestrogen or oestrogen and progestogen can change the way the body metabolizes vitamins, minerals and amino acids. For important information about the interactions with nutritional supplements and foods see Oral Contraceptives in the How to Help Yourself section at the end of this chapter.

CHILDREN, OVER SIXTIES AND PROLONGED USE

CHILDREN

Not used.

OVER SIXTIES

As part of the ageing process the body begins to metabolize and eliminate drugs more slowly and so there may be the possibility of more frequent or severe side-effects or interactions with other medicines.

PROLONGED OR CONTINUED TREATMENT

With some of these medicines there is a possibility of a gradual increase in blood pressure or of gall stones developing. Oestrogens taken without progestogens for prolonged periods increase the chance of the occurrence of fibroid tumours in the breast or reproductive system. It is important to have regular health check-ups, including smear tests.

STOPPING THE TREATMENT

If you wish to discontinue your treatment you should seek your doctor's advice.

PERSONAL MEDICINE NOTES

PRESCRIPTION NAMES

MEDICINES FOR DIABETES

It is thought that these drugs work by stimulating the body's production and release of insulin in order to lower blood sugar levels. They are used only where the pancreas is still capable of producing insulin and when dietary measures alone have not been successful. They are sulphonamide derivatives but do not have the antibacterial activity of sulphonamide antibiotics.

NAMES OF PRESCRIPTION MEDICINES

The following are commonly prescribed antidiabetics and are shown with the generic name first, followed by the brand name. If your medicine is not listed by name you should follow the information for the generic, if you know it, as the information given will still apply to your particular medicine. If you are not sure of the generic name your pharmacist will be able to advise you. Please note that ALL the information on this fact sheet applies to antidiabetics generally, not specifically to any one medicine.

Generic	Brand Name
acetohexamide	Dimelor
chlorpropamide	Diabinese, Glymese
glibenclamide	Daonil, Semi Daonil, Euglucon, Libanil, Malix
glibornuride	Glutril
gliclazide	Diamicron
glipizide	Glibenese, Minodiab
gliquidone	Glurenorm
glymidine	Gondafon
tolazamide	Tolanase
tolbutamide	Glyconon, Pramidex, Rastinon

WHAT TO TELL YOUR DOCTOR

It is important to make sure that your doctor or doctors are given as much information as possible. If you are aware that you are allergic to any antidiabetic drugs then do tell them so. Information on other medication is vital so if you are taking any other type of medicine, including non-prescription drugs, then they must know that too. Additionally, make sure they know if any of the following apply to you:

Adrenal, thyroid or pituitary gland disorders
Breast feeding
Heart disorders
History of diabetic coma
Hormone disorders
Insulin dependent diabetes
Juvenile or growth onset diabetes
Liver or kidney disorders
Pregnancy
Recent trauma
Severe infection
Unstable 'brittle' diabetes with ketosis and acidosis

ENDOCRINE GLANDS
ORAL ANTIDIABETICS

If you will be having surgery or dental treatment which requires anaesthesia it is important to tell the person in charge that you are taking antidiabetics.

SIDE-EFFECTS AND CAUTIONS

SIDE-EFFECTS It is impossible to predict how any medicine will affect a particular individual because everyone's metabolism is so very different. Sensitivity or reaction to drugs can vary greatly from one person to another and side-effects can be related to dosage. It is important to pay close attention to any changes you may notice either when starting, or during, a course of treatment.

The following are some of the side-effects reported within this group of drugs. Some of the disorders listed under Infrequent or Rare may occasionally be the symptoms of overdose and not always those of side-effects.

COMMON
Appetite loss	General digestive upsets
Diarrhoea	Nausea or vomiting

INFREQUENT OR RARE
Blood disorders	Numbing of lips,
Constipation	fingers or nose
Dark urine	Ringing in the ears
Dizziness	Seizures
Drowsiness	Sensitivity of skin or
Excessively low blood sugar	eyes to light
Extreme fatigue or lethargy	Skin allergies, rashes
Facial flushing	or itching
Fever	Sore throat
Headache	Sweating or nervousness
Heartburn	Swelling or puffiness of
Insomnia	face, legs or ankles
Light coloured stools	Unusual bleeding or
Low blood pressure	bruising
Muscle cramps	Weight changes
	Yellowing of eyes and skin

If you experience any of the listed side-effects, or any other unusual symptoms, you should consult your dispensing pharmacist or doctor immediately.

CAUTIONS If you experience dizziness or drowsiness do not drive, operate machinery or work high above the ground. Alcohol can increase these effects and should be avoided during treatment.

SYMPTOMS OF LOW BLOOD SUGAR (HYPOGLYCAEMIA)

It is important to be able to recognize the symptoms of low blood sugar. These are nervousness, excessive drowsiness, impaired concentration, sweating, feeling of warmth, headache, and numbness of the fingers, lips and nose. If any of these symptoms occur contact your doctor immediately, and do not take another dose of medicine. If you feel as if you will faint it is important to call your doctor or a hospital without delay.

Fever, trauma, burns or infection must also be reported to a doctor and regular testing of urine and/or blood sugar is important.

A good diet is essential and it is important not to skip meals. Gentle daily exercise is also beneficial, but strenuous or prolonged exercise may cause low blood sugar and if this happens contact your doctor immediately.

INTERACTIONS

INTERACTIONS WITH OTHER MEDICINES AND SUBSTANCES

No medication works in isolation but is affected to a greater or lesser extent by many other factors such as general fitness, diet and lifestyle. Alcohol taken in conjunction with these medicines can cause low blood sugar, facial flushing, nausea, vomiting, drowsiness, low blood pressure and headache. The symptoms of low blood sugar are listed under Cautions.

It is also possible to unintentionally combine antidiabetics with other drugs and this could be dangerous. Check with your doctor or pharmacist before taking any other medication, including non-prescription items, and if you are taking anything listed below look at the key to find out what effect they may have.

1   Anticoagulants
1   Antidepressants
1   Aspirin, NSAI's, salicylates
1   Beta blockers
1   Chloramphenicol antibiotics
1   Drugs within this group
1   Lipid lowering drugs
1   MAOI's
1   Probenecid gout drugs
1   Sulphonamide antibiotics
1   Tetracycline antibiotics

2   Adrenaline drugs

ENDOCRINE GLANDS
ORAL ANTIDIABETICS

2 Calcium antagonists
2 Corticosteroids
2 Diuretics
2 Isoniazid antituberculosis drugs
2 Laxatives in large quantities
2 Nasal sprays, bronchodilators
2 Oestrogens
2 Oral contraceptives which contain oestrogens
2 Phenothiazine anxiolytics, antinauseants
2 Phenytoin anticonvulsants
2 Thyroid hormones

3 Anticoagulants
3 Barbiturates

5 Ketotifen asthma preventives
5 Zaditen asthma preventives

KEY
1 INCREASES the effects of antidiabetic drugs
2 DECREASES the effects of antidiabetic drugs
3 ORAL ANTIDIABETIC DRUGS INCREASE the effects of these drugs
5 UNPREDICTABLE reactions

INTERACTIONS WITH VITAMINS, MINERALS AND FOODS

Sulphonylurea antidiabetics may affect iodine levels so the diet should contain plenty of iodine rich food.

Niacin or nicotinic acid, which are forms of vitamin B3, may decrease the effectiveness of these drugs when taken in large supplementary doses. Normal dietary intake will not affect antidiabetic treatment.

CHILDREN, OVER SIXTIES AND PROLONGED USE

CHILDREN

These antidiabetics are generally not recommended for the young.

OVER SIXTIES

As part of the ageing process the body begins to metabolize and eliminate drugs more slowly and so there may be the possibility of more frequent or severe side-effects or interactions with other medicines. With some of the drugs in this group there may be an increased possibility of low blood sugar and hypoglycaemia, the symptoms of which are listed in the Cautions section. If you miss a meal do not take your medicine and contact your pharmacist for instructions.

PROLONGED OR CONTINUED TREATMENT

With some of the drugs in this group it is thought that glucose tolerance may improve with prolonged use.

STOPPING THE TREATMENT

Do not discontinue the treatment without consulting your doctor as the dosage may need to be gradually reduced. If other drugs are being taken at the same time then their dosage may also need to be adjusted.

PERSONAL MEDICINE NOTES

FEMALE REPRODUCTIVE SYSTEM
ORAL CONTRACEPTIVES

PRESCRIPTION NAMES

MEDICINES FOR CONTRACEPTION

The balance of oestrogen and progesterone in the body is an important factor in fertility and oral contraceptives contain either both of these hormones or progestogen only. They work by interfering with this delicate balance, 'imitating' pregnancy so that ovulation is inhibited and the mucus at the entrance of the cervix becomes impenetrable to sperm. The lining of the uterus is also affected so that implantation of a fertilized egg is made very difficult and pregnancy is prevented. They may also be used for dysfunctional uterine bleeding and dysmenorrhoea.

NAMES OF PRESCRIPTION MEDICINES

The following are commonly prescribed oral contraceptives, the brand names only are given as it is not usual to prescribe generics. Please note that ALL the information on this fact sheet applies to oral contraceptives generally, not specifically to any one brand name medicine.

Oestrogen and Progestogen combined

Anovlar-21	Minovlar/ED
BiNovum	Neocon-1/35
Brevinor	Norimin
Conova-30	Norinyl-1
Eugynon-30/50	Ortho-Novin-1/50
Gynovlar-21	Ovran/30
Loestrin-20/30	Ovranette
Logynon/ED	Ovysmen
Marvelon	Synphase
Microgynon	Trinordiol
Minilyn	TriNovum

Progestogen only

Femulen	Neogest
Micronor	Norgeston
Microval	Noriday

WHAT TO TELL YOUR DOCTOR

It is important to make sure that your doctor or doctors are given as much information as possible. If you are aware that you are allergic to any oral contraceptives then do tell them so. Information on other medication is vital so if you are taking any other type of medicine, including non-prescription drugs, then they must know that too. Additionally, make sure they know if any of the following apply to you:

Abnormal vaginal bleeding	Breast feeding
Atherosclerosis	Breast soreness or cysts
Asthma or other breathing	Cancer
disorders	Candida albicans

ORAL CONTRACEPTIVES

Cardiovascular disease
Cholesterol disorders
Contact lens wearer
Depression*
Diabetes
Dubin Johnson syndrome
Endometriosis
Epilepsy
Eye disorders
Fibroids or ovarian cysts
Gall bladder disorder
Gall stones
Given birth or miscarried
  within the last month
Heart disorders*

Herpes or shingles*
High blood pressure*
Jaundice
Liver or kidney disorders
Migraines, headaches
Multiple sclerosis
Overweight
Porphyria
Rotor syndrome
Sickle cell anaemia
Thrombosis*
Use of tobacco, cigarettes
Uterus displacement
Varicose veins
Water retention

*Tell your doctor if there is any history of these conditions in yourself, or your family.

Your doctor should also be informed if you have any history of worsening of deafness, toxaemia, severe itching, skin discoloration or pigmentation during pregnancy.

Oral contraceptives must be withdrawn at least six weeks before surgery so it is important to discuss this with your doctor.

The results of laboratory tests, including glucose tolerance, can be affected so you should tell the person in charge that you are taking oral contraceptives.

SIDE-EFFECTS AND CAUTIONS

SIDE-EFFECTS It is impossible to predict how any medicine will affect a particular individual because everyone's metabolism is so very different. Sensitivity or reaction to drugs can vary greatly from one person to another and side-effects can be related to dosage. It is important to pay close attention to any changes you may notice either when starting, or during, a course of treatment.

If you experience any of the listed side-effects, or any other unusual symptoms, you should consult your dispensing pharmacist or doctor immediately. Although this list may seem rather frightening, most of the side-effects are very rare and it is unlikely that you will experience those which are not common. It seems that a number of the common side-effects are like those of the first three months of pregnancy and often disappear within this time. However, if your doctor decides that the Pill you are taking is not suitable then there are many others that may be tried. The following are some of the side-effects reported within this group of drugs:

COMMON

Bloating
Breast tenderness, enlargement or secretion
Candida albicans*
Change in menstrual flow
Change in weight
Changes in sexual desire or libido
Dark patches on the skin
Decreased or missed menstruation
Gastro-intestinal upset
Increased blood pressure
Nausea or vomiting
Spotting or bleeding between periods
Vaginal discharges*
Vaginal itching*
Water retention

*Oral contraceptives change vaginal acidity which increases susceptibility to vaginal candidiasis, other vaginal infections and gonorrhoea.

INFREQUENT OR RARE

Backache
Breast lumps
Breathing disorders
Cough
Decreased glucose tolerance
Depression
Diarrhoea
Fatigue
Headaches
Increased growth of body hair
Increased triglyceride or cholesterol levels
Muscular or joint pains
Nervousness
Pains or swelling in upper leg
Scalp hair loss
Sensitivity to light
Severe stomach pains
Skin rash
Thrombosis, stroke or blood clots*
Yellowing of eyes and skin

*You are very unlikely to experience this side-effect unless there is any history of this condition in yourself, or your family.

THE PILL SHOULD BE STOPPED IMMEDIATELY AND THE DOCTOR INFORMED IF ANY OF THE FOLLOWING OCCUR:

Blood in the urine
Dizziness or nosebleeds
Eyes or skin become yellow
Fainting, collapse or sudden weakness
Migraine or any unusually severe headaches
Numbness or tingling

Part of the body becomes cold or blue

Pregnancy

Severe or prolonged injury or illness where you will be confined to bed

Severe or sudden pain in the side of the chest

Severe stomach pains or tenderness

Spitting blood

Sudden or extreme increase in blood pressure which may be characterized by unusually severe headaches

Vision disturbances

If squeezing or heavy pressure in the chest occurs which may possibly be accompanied by pain in the shoulder, neck, arm and fingers of the left hand, nausea, sweating and shortness of breath then a doctor or hospital must be called IMMEDIATELY. These are symptoms of a heart attack and delay could be dangerous or even fatal.

CAUTIONS
Whilst taking oral contraceptives regular visits to the doctor are important so that routine health checks can be made. Monthly self breast examination is important and leaflets explaining the procedure should be available from family planning clinics or your doctor.

The contraceptive's effectiveness is decreased if you miss a dose at a regular time, have diarrhoea or an attack of vomiting. If this occurs you should contact your pharmacist for instructions.

It is essential to consult with your doctor so that you can be taken off contraceptives 6-8 weeks in advance of any surgery.

Avoid excessive exposure to sunlight and sunlamps while on oral contraceptives as you will be more susceptible to sunburn or skin rashes.

INTERACTIONS

INTERACTIONS WITH OTHER MEDICINES AND SUBSTANCES
No medication works in isolation but is affected to a greater or lesser extent by many other factors such as general fitness, diet and lifestyle. Smoking can increase the risk of a stroke, heart attack and blood clots, especially in women over the age of 35.

It is also possible to unintentionally combine oral contraceptives with other drugs and this could be dangerous. Check with your doctor or pharmacist before taking any other medication,

REPRODUCTIVE SYSTEM

including non-prescription items, and if you are taking anything listed below look at the key to find out what effect they may have.

2	Antibiotics	3	Hydantoin anticonvulsants
2	Anticoagulants	3	Oral corticosteroids
2	Antihistamines		
2	Anxiolytics	4	Anticoagulants
2	Barbiturates	4	Antidepressants, tricyclic
2	Laxatives	4	Antidiabetics
2	Liquid paraffin	4	Antihistamines
2	NSAI's	4	Antihypertensives
2	Phenytoin	4	Danazol
2	Tranquillizers	4	Insulin
		4	Lipid lowering drugs
3	Bronchodilators	4	Thyroid hormones

Medicines which decrease the effects of oral contraceptives increase the incidence of breakthrough bleeding and therefore the chance of pregnancy. Oral contraceptives taken with tricyclic antidepressants can increase antidepressant side-effects. If antibiotics are taken with oral contraceptives they can further increase the possibility of candida or thrush infection.

KEY

2 DECREASES the effects of oral contraceptives
3 ORAL CONTRACEPTIVES INCREASE the effects of these drugs
4 ORAL CONTRACEPTIVES DECREASE the effects of these drugs

INTERACTIONS WITH VITAMINS, MINERALS AND FOODS

Oral contraceptives change the way the body metabolizes vitamins, minerals and amino acids. Very large supplementary doses of vitamins E, C, B6, and B5 can stimulate the body's production of oestrogens and they should therefore be used with caution. For important information about oral contraceptives' interaction with vitamins and minerals see How to Help Yourself at the end of this chapter.

The herbs sarsaparilla, liquorice, and elder contain oestrogens and should be avoided when taking oestrogen containing drugs as they may increase their side-effects in sensitive people.

The herb agnus castus should be avoided when taking drugs containing progesterone.

CHILDREN, OVER SIXTIES AND PROLONGED USE

CHILDREN Not used.

OVER SIXTIES Not used.

PROLONGED OR CONTINUED TREATMENT With some of these medicines there is a possibility of gradual blood pressure increase, gall stones, and difficulty in becoming pregnant in the future. If the combined pill has been taken for eight years or more there may be a rare risk of liver cancer. Regular smear tests and health check-ups should be given.

STOPPING THE PILL It is very common for the first natural period to be delayed for six weeks to six months after stopping the combined pill. The rhythm method of birth control will be particularly unreliable until the periods become regular and other methods of contraception should be discussed with a doctor.

It is quite common for women to suffer from symptoms resembling PMS after discontinuing the combined pill. Information on PMS is in the How To Help Yourself section at the end of this chapter.

It is advisable not to conceive for approximately six months after stopping the Pill. This is because the Pill can alter the body's nutritional balance and the result of this may be a slight possibility of birth defects if conception takes place before this balance is restored.

PERSONAL MEDICINE NOTES

FEMALE REPRODUCTIVE SYSTEM
OTHER MEDICINES FOR WOMEN

PRESCRIPTION NAMES

MEDICINES FOR MENSTRUAL AND OTHER DISORDERS

Danazol partially prevents the output of the pituitary gonadotrophins which has the effect of reducing oestrogen production in the body. Danazol may be prescribed for endometriosis, infertility, benign breast disease, menstrual disorders, PMS, accelerated puberty or abnormally enlarged breasts.

NAMES OF PRESCRIPTION MEDICINES

The following is a commonly prescribed medicine for menstrual and other disorders and is shown with the generic name first, followed by the brand name. If your medicine is not listed by name you should follow the information for the generic, if you know it, as the information given will still apply to your particular medicine

Generic	Brand Name
danazol	Danol

WHAT TO TELL YOUR DOCTOR

It is important to make sure that your doctor or doctors are given as much information as possible. If you are aware that you are allergic to any danazol then do tell them so. Information on other medication is vital so if you are taking any other type of medicine, including non-prescription drugs, then they must know that too. Additionally, make sure they know if any of the following apply to you:

Absence of periods
Breast feeding
Diabetes
Epilepsy
Heart disorders
History of blood clots or
    thrombosis

Liver or kidney disorders
Migraine
Porphyria
Pregnancy
Taking oral contraceptives

If you will be having liver or thyroid tests, tell the person in charge that you are taking danazol or Danol.

SIDE-EFFECTS AND CAUTIONS

SIDE-EFFECTS

It is impossible to predict how any medicine will affect a particular individual because everyone's metabolism is so very different. Sensitivity to drugs can vary greatly from one person to another and side-effects are often dose related. It is important to pay close attention to any changes you may notice either when starting, or during, a course of treatment.

FEMALE REPRODUCTIVE SYSTEM
OTHER MEDICINES FOR WOMEN

The following are some of the side-effects reported within this group of drugs. Some of the disorders listed under Infrequent or Rare may occasionally be the symptoms of overdose and not always those of side-effects.

INFREQUENT OR RARE

Abnormal growth of
   body hair
Acne
Backache
Bleeding gums
Bloating
Change in sexual drive
Change in weight
Changeable emotions
Decrease in breast size
Decreased glucose
   tolerance
Dizziness
Enlargement of the clitoris

Flushing
Hoarseness
Loss of scalp hair
Muscular cramps
Nausea
Oily skin
Rashes
Slight weight gain
Unusual or easy bleeding
   or bruising
Vaginal itch or burning
Voice changes
Water retention
Yellowing of eyes or skin

If you experience any of the listed side-effects, or any other unusual symptoms, you should consult your dispensing pharmacist or doctor immediately.

CAUTIONS   No data found.

INTERACTIONS

INTERACTIONS WITH OTHER MEDICINES AND SUBSTANCES

No medication works in isolation but is affected to a greater or lesser extent by many other factors such as general fitness, diet and lifestyle. Alcohol in combination with danazol can increase existing depression and smoking may cause irregular and rapid heartbeat.

It is also possible to unintentionally combine danazol with other drugs and this could be dangerous. Check with your doctor or pharmacist before taking any other medication, including non-prescription items, and if you are taking anything listed below look at the key to find out what effect they may have.

2   Oral contraceptives, oestrogens and progestogens

3   Anticoagulants

5   Anticonvulsants

FEMALE REPRODUCTIVE SYSTEM
OTHER MEDICINES FOR WOMEN

KEY   3   DANAZOL AND DANOL INCREASE the effects of these drugs

5   UNPREDICTABLE reactions

INTERACTIONS WITH VITAMINS, MINERALS AND FOODS   It is best to avoid excessive salt in the diet. For more information see sodium in the chapter on Vitamins and Minerals.

CHILDREN, OVER SIXTIES AND PROLONGED USE

CHILDREN   These medicines may be prescribed for accelerated puberty and the dosage will be adjusted accordingly.

OVER SIXTIES   As part of the ageing process the body begins to metabolize and eliminate drugs more slowly and so there may be the possibility of more frequent or severe side-effects or interactions with other medicines.

PROLONGED OR CONTINUED TREATMENT   These drugs should not be taken for prolonged periods of time.

STOPPING THE TREATMENT   Do not discontinue the treatment without consulting your doctor as the dosage may need to be gradually reduced. If other drugs are being taken at the same time then their dosage may also need to be adjusted.

PERSONAL MEDICINE NOTES

PRESCRIPTION NAMES

MEDICINES FOR FEMALE DISORDERS AND PROGESTERONE DEFICIENCIES

Progestogens are prescribed where there is progesterone deficiency, infertility, irregular menstrual periods, pre-menstrual syndrome, excessive bleeding or pain during periods, habitual or threatened miscarriage or in conjunction with oestrogens in hormone replacement therapy. They are also used for dysfunctional uterine bleeding and dysmenorrhoea.

NAMES OF PRESCRIPTION MEDICINES

The following are commonly prescribed progestogens and brand names only are given as it is not usual to prescribe generics. Please note that ALL the information on this fact sheet applies to progestogens generally, not specifically to any one brand name medicine.

Duphaston	Provera
Primolut N	Utovlan

WHAT TO TELL YOUR DOCTOR

It is important to make sure that your doctor or doctors are given as much information as possible. If you are aware that you are allergic to any progestogens then do tell them so. Information on other medication is vital so if you are taking any other type of medicine, including non-prescription drugs, then they must know that too. Additionally, make sure they know if any of the following apply to you:

Asthma	Pregnancy, or suspected
Breast feeding	pregnancy**
Breast or genital cancer	Rotor syndrome
Dubin-Johnson syndrome	Smoker
Epilepsy	Thrombosis*
Liver or kidney disorders	Uterine or vaginal
Migraine*	bleeding that is irregular
Over 35 years of age	or abnormal

*Tell your doctor if there is any history of this condition in yourself, or your family.

**Your doctor should also be informed if you have any history of severe itching, jaundice or herpes during pregnancy.

FEMALE REPRODUCTIVE SYSTEM
PROGESTOGENS

SIDE-EFFECTS AND CAUTIONS

SIDE-EFFECTS It is impossible to predict how any medicine will affect a particular individual because everyone's metabolism is so very different. Sensitivity or reaction to drugs can vary greatly from one person to another and side-effects can be related to dosage. It is important to pay close attention to any changes you may notice either when starting, or during, a course of treatment.

The following are some of the side-effects reported within this group of drugs.

COMMON Gastro-intestinal upsets

INFREQUENT OR RARE

Acne	Nausea or vomiting
Breakthrough bleeding	Severe itching
Breast tenderness	Water retention
Change in sex drive	Weight change
Irregular menstrual cycles	Yellow eyes or skin

Precipitation of existing epilepsy, migraine or asthma may occur.

If you experience any of the listed side-effects, or any other unusual symptoms, you should consult your dispensing pharmacist or doctor immediately.

CAUTIONS No data found.

INTERACTIONS

INTERACTIONS WITH OTHER MEDICINES AND SUBSTANCES No medication works in isolation but is affected to a greater or lesser extent by many other factors such as general fitness, diet and lifestyle. Smoking increases the very rare risk of heart attack in women over the age of 35.

It is also possible to unintentionally combine progestogen drugs with other medicines and this could be dangerous. Check with your doctor or pharmacist before taking any other medication, including non-prescription items, and if you are taking anything listed below look at the key to find out what effect they may have.

4 Danol and danazol

KEY 4 PROGESTOGENS DECREASE the effects of these drugs.

INTERACTIONS WITH VITAMINS, MINERALS AND FOODS	You should avoid using the herb agnus castus while taking progestogen medicines.

CHILDREN, OVER SIXTIES AND PROLONGED USE

CHILDREN	Not used pre-puberty.
OVER SIXTIES	No data found.
PROLONGED OR CONTINUED TREATMENT	Cholesterol levels may be affected if progestogens are taken in large or prolonged dosage.
STOPPING THE TREATMENT	With progestogen medicines it is normal for menstrual type bleeding to occur 2-3 days after they have been stopped. If you find this does not occur you should tell your doctor. Progestogens should not be discontinued without your doctor's advice.

PERSONAL MEDICINE NOTES

ENDOCRINE GLANDS
THYROID HORMONES

PRESCRIPTION NAMES

MEDICINES FOR THYROID HORMONE DEFICIENCIES

Thyroxine is a hormone produced by the thyroid gland which assists in the regulation of metabolism. When too little is produced disorders such as lack of energy, weight gain, hair loss, dry skin, sensitivity to cold and poor growth in children may occur. Thyroid hormones may be prescribed to help correct and reverse these symptoms.

NAMES OF PRESCRIPTION MEDICINES

The following are commonly prescribed thyroid hormones and are shown with the generic name first, followed by the brand name. If your medicine is not listed by name you should follow the information for the generic, if you know it, as the information given will still apply to your particular medicine. If you are not sure of the generic name your pharmacist will be able to advise you. Please note that ALL the information on this fact sheet applies to thyroid hormones generally, not specifically to any one medicine.

Generic	Brand Name
liothyronine	Tertroxin
thyroxine	Eltroxin-50/100

WHAT TO TELL YOUR DOCTOR

It is important to make sure that your doctor or doctors are given as much information as possible. If you are aware that you are allergic to thyroid hormones then do tell them so. Information on other medication is vital so if you are taking any other type of medicine, including non-prescription drugs, then they must know that too. Additionally, make sure they know if any of the following apply to you:

Adrenal or pituitary gland disorders
Angina
Breast feeding
Diabetes
Hardening of the arteries

Heart disorders
High blood pressure
History of overactive thyroid
Liver or kidney disorders
Pregnancy

If you will be having surgery or dental treatment which requires anaesthesia it is important to tell the person in charge that you are taking thyroid hormones.

SIDE-EFFECTS AND CAUTIONS

SIDE-EFFECTS   It is impossible to predict how any medicine will affect a particular individual because everyone's metabolism is so very different. Sensitivity or reaction to drugs can vary greatly from one person to another and side-effects can be related to dosage. It is important to pay close attention to any changes you may notice either when starting, or during, a course of treatment.

The following are some of the side-effects reported within this group of drugs. Some of the disorders listed under Infrequent or Rare may occasionally be the symptoms of overdose and not always those of side-effects.

COMMON

Appetite change	Menstrual irregularities
Diarrhoea	Muscle cramps
Headache	Sweating
Heat sensitivity	Temperature rise
Irritability	Weight loss

INFREQUENT OR RARE

Anxiety	Shaking or tremor
Chest pains	Skin rash
Excitability	Thirst
Flushing	Trouble sleeping
Irregular or rapid heartbeat	Vomiting
Restlessness	Weakness

If you experience any of the listed side-effects, or any other unusual symptoms, you should consult your dispensing pharmacist or doctor immediately.

CAUTIONS   Thyroid hormones may take several weeks before they seem to work. If the existing symptoms of your condition do not improve after several weeks of treatment, then contact your doctor as the dosage may need to be adjusted.

INTERACTIONS

INTERACTIONS WITH OTHER MEDICINES AND SUBSTANCES   No medication works in isolation but is affected to a greater or lesser extent by many other factors such as general fitness, diet and lifestyle.

It is also possible to unintentionally combine thyroid hormones with other drugs and this could be dangerous. Check with your doctor or pharmacist before taking any other medication,

REPRODUCTIVE SYSTEM

including non-prescription items, and if you are taking anything listed below look at the key to find out what effect they may have.

1   Phenytoin anticonvulsants

2   Lipid lowering drugs
2   Oral contraceptives

3   Anticoagulants
3   Antidepressants
3   Antidiabetics
3   Digitalis drugs
3   Sympathomimetics

4   Barbiturates

5   Corticosteroids

Antidepressants taken with thyroid hormones may increase the chance of experiencing irregular heartbeat.

NSAI's taken with thyroid hormones may increase both blood pressure and heartbeat.

KEY   1   INCREASES the effects of thyroid hormones
       2   DECREASES the effects of thyroid hormones
       3   THYROID HORMONES INCREASE the effects of these drugs
       4   THYROID HORMONES DECREASE the effects of these drugs
       5   UNPREDICTABLE reactions

INTERACTIONS WITH VITAMINS, MINERALS AND FOODS   These drugs can decrease magnesium levels so an adequate intake should be ensured through the diet. It is best to avoid eating large quantities of foods containing goitrogens; these include cabbage, spinach, cauliflower, kale, turnips, soyabeans, carrots, brussels sprouts, peaches, and beans. See The Fact Finder for more information.

ENDOCRINE GLANDS
THYROID HORMONES

CHILDREN, OVER SIXTIES AND PROLONGED USE

CHILDREN These medicines may be prescribed for children and the dosage will be adjusted accordingly.

OVER SIXTIES As part of the ageing process the body begins to metabolize and eliminate drugs more slowly and so there may be the possibility of more frequent or severe side-effects or interactions with other medicines.

PROLONGED OR CONTINUED TREATMENT If you experience shaking, muscular cramps or diarrhoea the dosage of your medicine may need to be adjusted.

STOPPING THE TREATMENT Do not discontinue the treatment without consulting your doctor as the dosage may need to be gradually reduced. If other drugs are being taken at the same time then their dosage may also need to be adjusted.

PERSONAL MEDICINE NOTES

263

FEMALE REPRODUCTIVE SYSTEM
HOW TO HELP YOURSELF

What we say is sexual reproduction is an improvement
over binary fission and conjugation.
Sex in Human Loving by Eric Berne.

A proper hormone balance is crucial for controlling many of the body's
functions. The reproductive system is very sensitive to any fluctuations,

and imbalances can result in disorders such as pre-menstrual syndrome, menstrual irregularities, menopausal symptoms and difficulty in conceiving.

Diabetes mellitus is a disorder which results from the shortage or absence of the hormone, insulin, which is produced by the pancreas. Of the types of diabetes juvenile-onset can be controlled by insulin injections and diet, and maturity-onset diabetes is treated with diet and antidiabetic drugs.

A number of disorders may be linked with diet or could be a sign that the body is not getting the proper nutrition it needs. It is important to have a varied diet which includes whole grains, seeds such as pumpkin, sesame and sunflower, fresh fruit, vegetables and protein. Essential nutrients can be depleted by sugar, refined foods, large amounts of coffee, tea, alcohol and smoking.

The suggestions offered here are designed to help generally with your condition, but it is very important that you do not try to treat yourself. If you suffer severely or regularly from a particular complaint, any serious disorder, or are pregnant then you should not use these remedies before discussion with a doctor. Always report any side-effects and seek medical advice before trying natural remedies and if within a period of one week there has been no improvement then you should consult your doctor. Thyroid disorders which require drugs or medical treatment must not be treated with natural remedies except with medical consent and by a qualified natural practitioner.

For more individual advice on natural medicine you should consult an alternative/complementary practitioner and among those who may be able to help are a homoeopath, naturopath, herbalist, osteopath, chiropractor, or an acupuncturist. Other therapies or systems to try include reflexology, relaxation therapy, t'ai-chi, yoga, meditation, biofeedback, shiatsu, aromatherapy or massage.

It is possible that certain remedies, supplements or foods could react dangerously with the drugs you are already using so you must check with the fact sheet relating to your medicine to avoid interactions. Please note that it is not advisable to gather your own herbs unless you are sure they are free of any chemicals or pollutants and you can positively identify the correct variety. Always make sure that supplements or natural remedies are taken two to three hours apart from any drugs.

FEMALE REPRODUCTIVE SYSTEM
HOW TO HELP YOURSELF

If while reading you come across a particular word or term that is unfamiliar to you please look in The Fact Finder; information on nutrients will be found in the chapter on Vitamins, Minerals and their Food Sources and information about practitioners is in the chapter on Alternative/Complementary Medicine and Therapies.

NATURAL REMEDIES

BREAST TENDERNESS

Any suspicion of breast tenderness must be reported to a doctor and if the condition does not require medical treatment then some of the following suggestions can be tried.

Evening primrose oil, vitamin F, B complex, B6 and selenium are all considered useful for this condition.

Vitamin E is especially helpful, but if you have rheumatic heart disease, mitral valve prolapse or are taking certain heart medicines vitamin E should not be taken in supplement form except under supervision. If you are susceptible to high blood pressure then vitamin E can be taken in supplement form, but must be started at a very low dosage and gradually increased and again is best done under supervision.

A relatively large intake of PABA and folic acid may contribute to breast tenderness. If taken in supplement form this amounts to over 30mg a day for PABA and over 200mcg a day for folic acid.

See the general introduction for dietary suggestions.

CANDIDA AND THRUSH

See How to Help Yourself in the Infections and Parasites chapter.

CYSTITIS

See How to Help Yourself in the Infections and Parasites chapter.

DIABETES

Natural practitioners may be able to help some cases of diabetes. Certain types of glucose intolerance, which are not drug or insulin dependent, may be helped by the addition of the mineral chromium. Vitamin B complex is also useful because it helps the body to use carbohydrates more efficiently. There may also be a requirement for extra vitamin C in the diet.

Diabetics who require drugs or insulin should not take vitamins B1, B3, E or chromium in supplement form without medical supervision. In particular diabetics need and use greater amounts of vitamin E as it improves insulin's action; however it should only be taken under supervision as the dosage of insulin will need to be adjusted according to the amount of vitamin E taken.

See under Breast Tenderness for important warnings on the use of vitamin E.

Supplements of the amino acid cysteine should be used with great caution by diabetics as it can interfere with insulin's action.

MENOPAUSE

Menopausal symptoms, or the lack of them, are often related to how strong the adrenal glands are. Vitamins C and B5 are two nutrients which the adrenal glands need to stay healthy and can help some women experience an easier menopause.

Nutritional supplements which can help include lecithin, kelp, vitamins E and C, high potency vitamin B complex, zinc, calcium and magnesium orotate. Whey powder, a natural by-product of cheese making, contains orotic acid and calcium. It makes a soothing bedtime drink when 1-2 teaspoons are mixed with boiled water. Gentle exercise and fresh air will help the body to utilize calcium properly.

Hot flushes are a common symptom which may accompany the menopause. They can be helped with vitamins E, C and bioflavonoids, up to 200mcg of selenium a day, and the homoeopathic cell salt Ferr. Phos. You can make a useful tea by breaking open one ginseng capsule and placing the powder in a cup with half a teaspoon of yarrow and boiling water. Allow to steep for 2-3 minutes, strain off the yarrow and drink. It can be taken up to three times a day, one hour before or after vitamin C supplements.

Help for other symptoms such as depression, anxiety and nervousness may be found in the chapter on Natural Remedies.

MENSTRUAL DISORDERS

If your doctor has ruled out the possibility of a serious disorder causing your menstrual problems then it may be helpful to try the following natural remedies:

MENSTRUAL CRAMPS AND PAINFUL MENSTRUATION

Calcium levels can drop sharply both before and during menstruation so taking a supplement for up to ten days before the period starts and during the first few days may be enough to prevent cramps. At least 1000mg of calcium with 500-1000mg of magnesium should be taken before going to bed. If cramping does occur then two or three times a day calcium and magnesium can also be taken with 250mg of vitamin C and up to 500mg of bioflavonoids. The homoeopathic tissue salt, Mag. Phos. can also be helpful.

Menstrual cramps can be helped by pouring boiling water over a quarter of a teaspoon each of thyme and raspberry leaf in a cup. Allow to steep for three minutes, strain and drink once or twice a day until the cramping stops.

A fiery but effective tea can be made from powdered or fresh ginger root, or ordinary baking ginger. Pour boiling water over an eighth to a quarter of a teaspoon placed in a cup. Allow to cool a little and sip slowly, leaving the sediment. 1-2 cups per day can be taken. If you have a hiatus hernia, ginger should only be taken in capsule form, with plenty of water, to prevent burning of sensitive tissue.

The amino acid DLPA can often help pain and cramping but there are some cautions to be noted. It should be used with care if you have high blood pressure as it may be increased in susceptible people. If you are pregnant or suffer from phenylketonuria or are taking MAOI's then DLPA must only be taken under supervision.

A hip or sitz bath can also help menstrual cramping and instructions on how to prepare this are listed under cystitis in the How to Help Yourself section of the chapter on Infections and Parasites.

HEAVY MENSTRUATION

If this condition continues or has been occurring regularly for some time, there is the danger of anaemia developing and it should be discussed with a doctor before natural remedies are tried.

A quarter of a teaspoon of the herb, shepherd's purse, can be made into tea by pouring boiling water over it in a cup. Allow to steep for three minutes, strain and drink, up to two cups a day.

Bioflavonoids up to 500mg three times a day with 500-1000mg of vitamin C often helps control heavy bleeding. Iron and zinc rich foods are important to replace their loss and for details see the chapter on Vitamins and Minerals. A liquid herbal and fruit iron supplement called Floradix is available from health food stores.

Excessive, painful menstrual flow can be helped by the homoeopathic tissue salt, Ferr. Phos.

MISSED, LATE OR SCANTY MENSTRUATION

Late or scanty menstruation accompanied by stress, exhaustion or depression may be helped by the homoeopathic tissue salts Kali. Phos. or Kali. Sulph.

A multiple vitamin and mineral supplement may also help and

extra vitamin E and vitamin C with bioflavonoids can be taken with it. For important warnings on the use of vitamin E, please see under Breast Tenderness in this section.

ORAL CONTRACEPTIVES The Pill and other prescribed hormones can affect both the availability and the way in which the body uses a number of nutrients. It is important to know which nutrients are involved and exactly what their effect is in order to avoid some of the more common side-effects experienced with these drugs. The following table summarizes the main nutrients and their effects in conjunction with oral contraceptives. If you wish to take supplements while on the Pill, please discuss this with your doctor.

Nutrient	Effect	Notes
Vitamin A		Supplements of vitamin A should not be taken as the Pill may cause excessive blood levels of this vitamin. However, vitamin A should be plentiful in the diet.
Vitamin B2*	Decreased	Up to 50mg a day may be needed.
Vitamin B3*	Decreased	Up to 50mg a day may be needed in the form of niacinamide or nicotinamide.
Vitamin B6*	Decreased	Up to 100-150mg a day may be needed.
Vitamin B12*	Decreased	Up to 1000mcg a day may be needed.
Vitamin C*	Decreased	Up to 250mg twice a day may be needed. If more vitamin C is taken it can have the effect of increasing a low dose pill to a high dose pill which can lead to an increase in side-effects.
Bioflavonoids	Decreased	Up to 100mg twice a day may be needed.
Folic acid*	Decreased	Up to 1000mcg a day may be needed.
Inositol*	Decreased	Up to 250mg a day may be needed.

PABA*	Decreased	Up to 50mg a day may be needed.
Vitamin E		Up to 400IU a day may be needed. Please see important warnings about vitamin E under Breast Tenderness in this section.
Vitamin K		Increases the risk of blood clots if taken in supplement form.
Copper	Raised	Increases the risk of blood clots, hair loss and zinc depletion. Do not take in supplement form and avoid large amounts of foods high in copper.
Zinc	Decreased	Up to 30mg a day may be needed.
Calcium	Raised	Levels may be raised due to improved absorption.
Iron		Less iron is lost while on the Pill because of less menstrual bleeding.
Magnesium		Up to 500mg may be needed daily during long term oral contraceptive use.
Manganese	Decreased	May need up to 9mg a day as it can be decreased by the increase in copper levels while on the Pill.

*Extremely large supplemental doses of these vitamins can increase the activity of oestrogen and therefore may increase the side-effects of the Pill.

A number of side-effects such as lethargy, insomnia, restless sleep and depression can be due to nutritional deficiencies which arise particularly through a lack of B complex vitamins and especially B6. When B6 is lacking the amino acid, tryptophane, is decreased and both B6 and tryptophane are important in preventing sleep disorders and depression. When taking the Pill it is best to take a B complex supplement rather than individual B vitamins, but extra B6 can be taken with the complex, subject to the comments in the nutrients table.

All users of oral contraceptives, especially some of those on a vegetarian or vegan diet, are prone to B12 deficiency and should ensure that the intake from food and/or supplements is adequate. As protein metabolism is affected it is important to ensure that proteins such as fish, eggs, cheese, nuts, seeds and dairy products are eaten. Vegetarians need to watch their diet carefully to ensure that foods are combined to make complete proteins.

The Pill can make fingernails brittle and zinc and sulphur rich foods and protein foods may help counteract this.

OSTEOPOROSIS PREVENTION

It is very important to ensure that the body absorbs calcium properly so that it gets into the bones and does not stay in the soft tissues of the body where it can aggravate arthritic disorders, or in the arteries where it can contribute to hardening of the arteries. Vitamin D from foods, or that produced in the body from the action of sunlight on the skin, is important in the absorption of calcium. If calcium supplements are taken then they must contain magnesium for best absorption. In the diet, dairy products are a good source of calcium but not magnesium so if they are your main source of calcium then it is important to ensure that plenty of foods which contain magnesium are also eaten with them.

Manganese is another important mineral which must be supplied in significant amounts in the diet. It is found abundantly in ordinary tea but the tannin content prevents it from being used by the body. Sources of manganese are given in the chapter on Vitamins and Minerals.

Hydrochloric acid is important for the absorption of minerals but as we get older the stomach produces less of it so it is best to take minerals in orotate form as they are more readily absorbed. Large quantities of phosphorus will interfere with calcium metabolism so it is best to avoid colas and a number of other carbonated drinks which are a major source.

PRE-MENSTRUAL SYNDROME, PRE-MENSTRUAL TENSION

Large numbers of women suffer from a disorder called PMS, pre-menstrual syndrome. The name pre-menstrual syndrome was first coined in the 1930s and is an umbrella term for a group of symptoms, including pre-menstrual tension, which can appear with the menstrual cycle.

The symptoms are varied and can include tension, headache, bloating, irritability, anxiety, craving for sweet foods, aggression, breast tenderness, depression, weepiness, skin eruptions, lack of self-esteem, a feeling of helplessness, insomnia, change in sex drive, water retention, palpitations, back pain, sinus problems, cold symptoms and herpes outbreaks. What characterizes this collection of seemingly unrelated symptoms is that they appear with the monthly cycle, maybe ten to seven days beforehand, and disappear when the period begins.

If your doctor has ruled out any actual disease which could be causing the symptoms then you may find relief by altering your diet and perhaps taking some supplementary nutrients. Although it is only one of a number of self-help or medical treatments available for PMS, dietary therapy can certainly help.

The first thing to avoid is sugar in all forms, which includes refined, brown, molasses, honey, maple syrup and all artificial sweeteners. A little concentrated fruit juice can be used as a sweetener instead and if you cannot cut sugar out altogether then try to reduce the amount as much as you can.

Chocolate is another culprit and many women have extreme cravings during PMS or before their periods. This may be because it contains magnesium, a mineral which can be deficient in a diet which is high in processed foods and low in fresh fruit, vegetables and whole grains. Taking magnesium with calcium in supplement form may alleviate the craving and has many health benefits.

Caffeine and alcohol can also be triggers for PMS and are best avoided or drastically reduced as they can increase irritability and destroy important nutrients. Alcohol also decreases magnesium levels and affects the liver and blood-sugar levels which can contribute to a number of PMS-like symptoms.

With PMS some people find that their eating pattern may alter before their period, due to blood-sugar changes. The levels of blood sugar can be kept more stable by eating small amounts more frequently and avoiding large amounts of refined carbohydrates and heavy meals. Snacks could include sunflower seeds, nuts and fruit. It is helpful to eat plenty of green leafy vegetables, fruit, whole grains, nuts and seeds and cut down on fried foods and saturated fats. A good supplement regime would include vitamin B complex, vitamin B5, B6, C and bioflavonoids, A, E, inositol, choline and the minerals calcium, magnesium, zinc and chromium. See the general introduction for more dietary suggestions. Regular, gentle exercise is also beneficial.

Evening primrose oil can help a number of reproductive system disorders, and DLPA may help with the depression that some

REPRODUCTIVE SYSTEM

people suffer. Please see under Menstrual Cramps for some important cautions on the use of DLPA.

Lecithin granules can be added to the diet to supply the nutrients choline, inositol and methionine which help the liver's important role in breaking down hormones. Small amounts of cold pressed and unrefined vegetable oils every day will provide essential fatty and linoleic acids. For more information see the chapter on Vitamins and Minerals.

The herb agnus castus appears to help correct hormone imbalances and also encourages progesterone production.

With PMS, supplements of the amino acid histadine should be avoided or used with caution as they can worsen some of the symptoms.

For help with nervousness, anxiety, headaches and herpes please see the chapter on Natural Remedies.

There are a number of self-help and support groups around the country and two useful addresses are given below:

PMS Help
PO Box 160
St Albans
Herts, AL1 4UQ

When writing, please send a stamped addressed envelope for reply.

The Women's Nutritional Advisory Service
PO Box 268
Hove
East Sussex, BN3 1RW
(01273) 771366

The service provides general and individual nutritional advice for women with PMS, menopausal symptoms or problems with the birth control pill. For details of their postal advisory service, or London clinic, write with stamped, addressed envelope.

NATURAL REMEDIES FOR COMMON AILMENTS AND SIDE-EFFECTS

A number of side-effects can be very unpleasant, but some of them can be helped or alleviated without the further use of drugs. If used properly natural remedies do not contribute further side-effects and often have the added benefit of aiding the healing process.

Common ailments and side-effects can result from a variety of causes including nutrient loss or deficiency. Quite a number of side-effects may be the body's response to drugs decreasing or impairing the absorption or effects of nutrients, causing them to be used too quickly or eliminated in greater amounts and more rapidly than is normal. Common ailments can frequently be the result of marginal nutritional deficiencies caused by factors such as eating the wrong foods or exposure to environmental pollutants and stress. They are often treated with non-prescription medicines, but the right supplements and herbs can often help without the risk of any side-effects.

The liver and kidneys are the organs which detoxify and eliminate drug residues so it is essential to give them all the help you can to perform this task. Check that your diet contains plenty of vitamins C and E and the trace element selenium. Raw garlic or garlic capsules are helpful and lecithin is also important because it contains choline, inositol and methionine. If you try to eat fewer processed, artificially coloured and flavoured foods, drink less alcohol and decrease the amount of cigarettes or tobacco smoked then the liver and kidneys will be better able to detoxify and eliminate drug residues.

The suggestions offered here are designed to help generally with your condition, but it is very important that you do not try to treat yourself. If you suffer severely or regularly from a particular complaint, any serious disorder, or are pregnant then you should not use these remedies before discussion with a doctor. Always report any side-effects and seek medical advice before trying natural remedies and if within a period of one week there has been no improvement then you should consult your doctor. For more individual advice on natural medicine you should consult an alternative/complementary practitioner.

It is possible that certain remedies, supplements or foods could react dangerously with the drugs you are already using so you must check with the fact sheet relating to your medicine to avoid interactions. Please note that it is not advisable to gather your own herbs unless you are sure they are free of any chemicals or pollutants and you can positively identify the correct variety. Always make sure that supplements or natural remedies are taken two to three hours apart from any drugs.

If while reading you come across a particular word or term that is unfamiliar to you please look in The Fact Finder; information on nutrients will be found in the chapter on Vitamins, Minerals and their Food Sources and details of practitioners are in the chapter on Alternative/Complementary Medicine and Therapies.

NATURAL REMEDIES

ANXIETY AND NERVOUSNESS

A soothing herb tea can be made by putting an eighth of a teaspoon each of sage, chamomile, catnip, lemon verbena and rosemary into a teapot and pouring boiling water over them. This should be steeped for about three minutes and drunk 2-3 times a day. It can be flavoured with lemon and a little honey if desired.

Tryptophane is an amino acid which has a calming and relaxing effect. It is important that it is taken on an empty stomach 2-3 hours after food or half an hour before eating.

High potency vitamin B complex including B5 and B6 has been found helpful when taken two to three times per day with food. The B complex vitamins are important for healthy functioning of the nervous system and include inositol which has a calming effect on the brain similar to that of tranquillizers. Inositol is present in lecithin and if used in this form should be balanced with calcium to offset its high phosphorus content. It is generally not advisable to take B complex in the evening as it can keep some people awake. Most B complex tablets colour the urine a bright yellow, due to their B2 content, but this is a harmless reaction. Other nutrients which can be calming are the bioflavonoids including rutin and these are best taken with vitamin C.

Calcium and magnesium are also important in the proper functioning of the nervous system and have a calming effect on the body. They are often used in equal ratio doses ranging from 500-1000mg per day. Up to 30mg of zinc a day may also prove beneficial.

NATURAL REMEDIES

275

Homoeopathic Gelsemium 6x is often helpful for general feelings of anxiety, including visits to the dentist and stage fright.

Many people find that the Bach flower rescue remedy helps them in situations where they experience nervousness or anxiety. The remedies can be chosen according to emotions and personality and you may find others from the Bach flower remedies which are particularly suited to you. More information on them will be found in the chapter on Alternative/Complementary Medicine and Therapies.

A very powerful relaxing herb tea can be made from a combination of no more than a sixteenth of a teaspoon each of valerian, lady's slipper, skullcap and hops mixed together and placed in a teapot. Pour boiling water over the herbs and allow them to steep for about three minutes. One cupful can be sipped throughout the day as needed, leaving a little for a bedtime drink but do not drink more than one cup of this mixture per day and avoid using it for more than a week without guidance from a herbalist. This mixture does not have a very pleasant taste or smell and honey and lemon can be added if required. If you are using this tea then valerian and hop tablets must not be taken in conjunction with it; however, they can be taken instead of the tea as their calming effects may be helpful.

Try to avoid alcohol, foods and beverages high in caffeine, sugar and refined or processed foods which can all rob your body of important nutrients, especially B complex vitamins and zinc.

Relaxation techniques and tapes can be very beneficial and information on Relaxation for Living can be found in the chapter on Alternative/Complementary Medicine and Therapies.

APPETITE LOSS There are a number of supplements and herbs which can help this condition, amongst them are the B complex vitamins and B12, zinc, the amino acid DLPA, and the herbs ginseng and fenugreek. There are some cautions to be noted with DLPA. It should be used with care if you have high blood pressure as it may be increased in susceptible people. Children under the age of eight should not be given DLPA unless recommended by a practitioner, because although it is not dangerous to adults, its safety in the young has not yet been established. If you are pregnant or suffer from phenylketonuria or are taking MAOI's then DLPA must only be taken under supervision.

Small frequent meals are best and fruit, vegetables and wholefoods are important to maintain good levels of nutrition. The herbal yeast tonic Bio Strath is also very helpful.

Homoeopathic lycopodium is taken when there is some appetite, but only small amounts of food can be taken before feeling full.

ARTHRITIS AND RELATED DISORDERS

See How to Help Yourself in the chapter on Pain and Inflammation.

ATHLETE'S FOOT AND FUNGAL NAIL INFECTIONS

Athlete's foot is a fungal infection which occurs as painful or itching skin between the toes and on the feet. Ensure that the feet are washed frequently every day and dried thoroughly. Wear cotton socks and avoid shoes which cause your feet to perspire. Pure tea tree oil can be applied to the affected areas, including the nails, 2-3 times a day. Powdered green clay can be used as a healing dusting powder for the feet and it also helps to absorb moisture. A homoeopathic remedy is the tissue salt Kali. Sulph. which can also help. For dietary advice on thrush, fungal infections and candida see How to Help Yourself in the chapter on Infections and Parasites. Fungal nail infections can be helped in the same way and tea tree oil should be applied to the nails 2-4 times a day.

BITTER TASTE IN MOUTH

This may be helped with the homoeopathic tissue salt Nat. Phos.

BURNING TONGUE OR MOUTH

Homoeopathic Nat. Sulph. 6x or Aconite 6x are often found helpful for this condition. A high potency vitamin B complex taken once or twice a day with food can also be of assistance and it is important to have a good quantity of B12 in the diet. If taken late in the day, B complex can keep some people awake. Vitamin B2 present in B complex tablets colours the urine a bright yellow which is a harmless reaction.

COLD SORES AND CANKER SORES

See Mouth Ulcers.

CONSTIPATION

If constipation persists you should consult your doctor. Laxatives or laxative herbs should not be taken on a regular basis or taken to relieve abdominal pains, nausea or cramps. Any sudden change in bowel habits, constipation alternating with diarrhoea or the sudden onset of pain or bleeding must be reported to your doctor.

A raw beetroot and carrot grated and eaten with each meal is an excellent source of vegetable fibre and vitamins and minerals which are important to the healthy functioning of the whole digestive system. Try to include a fresh salad in your diet every day. Vegetables should be steamed or lightly cooked and their cooking water should be used to make soups, gravies and savoury drinks so that nutrients which are important to digestion are not thrown away.

NATURAL REMEDIES

Papaya melon helps your body digest proteins and is helpful for digestion and elimination as it contains an enzyme called papain. Papaya can be eaten with each meal or as a snack. Also include plenty of fresh and dried fruit but remember that all dried fruit should be soaked overnight before eating.

Fluid intake is important and if enough water is not consumed digestion and elimination is likely to suffer. It has been recommended that up to eight glasses of water or liquids are drunk a day, but it is best to drink only the highest amount of fluids that you feel comfortable with. A glass of warm water and lemon juice can be drunk every morning before breakfast. Some people find this has a slight laxative effect, and it helps cleanse the body and wake up the digestive system.

About 6-8oz of plain 'live' yogurt once a day can be helpful because the bulgaricus bacteria, which cause yogurt to ferment, also feed and encourage the growth of acidophilus bacteria in the intestines. These bacteria are important for the health and function of the entire digestive system.

Chewing a couple of teaspoons of linseeds well once or twice a day is generally helpful to the digestive system and the slippery quality of linseed can help the transit of wastes through the bowels. Linseed also contains important vitamins, minerals and oils. For extra vitamins, minerals and fibre, pumpkin and sunflower seeds can be eaten as snacks or ground up and added to baked potatoes and salads.

Natural practitioners often suggest the use of psyllium seeds as an aid to elimination. These can be mixed with water to form a harmless bulk which helps carry wastes through the body.

Taking molasses is sometimes helpful for constipation. It is a source of inositol which can have a relaxing effect on muscles and nerves.

Homoeopathic tissue salts Nat. Mur. and Calc. Fluor. are helpful for digestive disorders. Nat. Mur. is used to promote hydrochloric acid production in the stomach and also helps when fat is hard to digest. Calc. Fluor. promotes good muscle tone and may help the peristaltic action of the bowel which moves material along.

Vitamins and minerals are also crucial for proper digestion and elimination. A diet containing a good variety of fresh whole foods is important. The following nutrients are particularly helpful and have been used therapeutically to help improve digestion and therefore elimination:

NATURAL REMEDIES

High potency B complex in doses ranging from 25-100mg per day can help the digestive system to stay healthy, and B5 also helps ensure proper peristaltic movement of the bowel. It is generally not advisable to take B complex in the evening as it can keep some people awake. Most B complex tablets colour the urine a bright yellow, due to their B2 content, but this is a harmless reaction.

Acidophilus, the healthy intestinal bacteria, is often used by natural practitioners because of its assistance in digestion and elimination.

There are a variety of herbal laxative formulas available in health food stores, but you may find that if cascara is taken alone it may cause uncomfortable cramping and the same can happen with senna pods if they are soaked in hot water. Soaking senna pods overnight in cold water will avoid this effect.

Regular exercise and fresh air are very important for healthy functioning of the digestive system and elimination. Try to avoid refined foods, excessive amounts of rice, matzos and supplemental iron which is not from food sources or yeast.

CYSTITIS   See How to Help Yourself in the chapter on Infections and Parasites.

DEPRESSION (transitory)   Depression may be a serious side-effect of some medicines and should be reported to a doctor if it persists for more than three days.

Food allergies, drugs and chemicals can sometimes trigger bouts of depression and a natural practitioner may be able to help if you suspect these may be contributing to depression.

Women often find that depression may be triggered in the pre-menstrual week and the birth control pill can also have the same effect. Zinc, manganese, calcium and vitamins C and B6 may help and the herb agnus castus appears to help regulate hormone levels and may also be useful. Women prone to depression or PMS should avoid the amino acid histadine or use it with caution as it may make them worse.

B complex vitamins, particularly B3 and B6, are important for the healthy function of the nervous system and if they are in short supply some people are prone to depression. B3 seems to work best in the form of niacin, not niacinamide, but it is likely to cause a harmless flushing and tingling sensation of the skin accompanied by a slight itching which may last from 5-20 minutes. Because of this effect it should be avoided by anyone with painful skin complaints or certain other conditions, details of which will be found in the notes section on B3 in the chapter on Vitamins and Minerals. It is generally not advisable to take B complex in the evening as it can keep some people awake. Most B complex tablets colour the urine a bright yellow, due to their B2 content, but this is a harmless reaction.

Tryptophane is an amino acid which can sometimes help depression. It is important that it is taken on an empty stomach. DLPA is another amino acid which may help some forms of depression but there are some cautions to be noted. It should be used with care if you have high blood pressure as it may be increased in susceptible people. If you are pregnant or suffer from phenylketonuria or are taking MAOI's then DLPA must only be taken under supervision.

Kelp is a good source of minerals, including some important trace elements, and it may help in some cases of depression. However, if you are taking any kind of thyroid medication or if you have thyroid disorders then you should take kelp only under supervision. Minerals such as zinc, calcium and magnesium also need to be generously suppled in the diet.

The homoeopathic tissue salt Kali. Phos. has been found helpful for some forms of depression.

A high intake of sugar, refined foods, coffee, alcohol and copper have all been found to increase depression in susceptible people.

See also Anxiety and Nervousness in this section.

DIARRHOEA

Diarrhoea which persists for more than three days must be reported to your doctor. Diarrhoea alternating with constipation, any sudden change in bowel habits, sudden onset of pain or bleeding should also be reported and if the remedies make the condition worse or cause pain consult your doctor immediately. Because of the danger of dehydration you should never attempt to treat diarrhoea in babies, infants, the elderly or debilitated but should always contact your doctor for advice. If you have diverticulosis or colitis do not use these remedies.

Dehydration and loss of vitamins and minerals are the two major dangers of diarrhoea and it is very important to have a diet which is high in nutrients. Potassium, sodium, zinc and magnesium are just a few of the important minerals which can be lost during diarrhoea. A good intake of fluid is also essential although coffee, tea and alcohol should be avoided. Lactose can aggravate diarrhoea so it is best to avoid milk and milk products during an acute attack.

Kelp is a good supplemental source of many minerals but do not add it to your diet if you are taking any kind of thyroid medication or if you have any thyroid disorders.

Sometimes diarrhoea can result from an upset in the balance of the bacteria in the digestive system, when the harmful bacteria become too prolific. Acidophilus tablets or powder can help to correct this and work more efficiently if taken with natural 'live' yogurt.

Langdale's Cinnamon Essence has an antiseptic effect and can help the body to fight infection. It can be added to warm water to make a pleasant but rather fiery drink and is available from chemists.

Bananas and carob powder are rich in pectin, which has binding qualities, and they are a good source of minerals and other important nutrients which are lost with diarrhoea. Carob powder can be used as a beverage or added to food.

A tablespoon of rice or oat bran added to yogurt and eaten with each meal for 2-3 days may be enough to help regulate the bowels and brown rice and cooked carrots are a folk remedy for diarrhoea.

Homoeopathic Arsen. Alb. is a helpful remedy for a number of types of diarrhoea.

ECZEMA, SKIN RASHES, DERMATITIS AND HIVES

A number of skin complaints can be helped with the external application of vitamin E. The contents of a 100-600IU capsule can be squeezed on the affected area once or twice a day, avoiding the eyes as it may cause a stinging sensation which could last for several hours. Do not allow the oil to come into contact with clothing as it will stain anything it touches. Because of its soothing and healing properties it may also help to apply aloe vera gel or juice to the affected area as often as needed.

The herb chickweed can be infused by adding 2 teaspoons to a cup of boiled water and steeping for 10-15 minutes. It should be applied externally by soaking a cloth in the mixture and using as needed.

Vitamin A is sometimes called the skin and anti-viral vitamin and works well when taken in conjunction with zinc. Cod liver oil is a good source of vitamins A and D and has traditionally been given to children to help prevent skin problems and infections.

Vitamin B rich foods and supplements can help some skin complaints and PABA, choline, inositol and B5 can be particularly helpful for some skin conditions. Lecithin is a good source of choline and inositol. It is generally not advisable to take B complex in the evening as it can keep some people awake. Most B complex tablets colour the urine a bright yellow, due to their B2 content, but this is a harmless reaction.

Vitamin C and bioflavonoids are important for helping the body overcome internal and external allergic reactions; they are also integral to growth and repair of skin tissue. Supplements ranging from 250-500mg taken 2-4 times a day with food have been used to help skin complaints. If this amount of vitamin C is used then dietary calcium, magnesium and B12 should be adequately supplied.

It will be helpful to avoid sugar, coffee, all dairy products, citrus fruit and processed foods for a while. However you do need calcium rich foods and these should be supplied from other dietary sources, or it may be advisable to supplement your diet with 1000mg of calcium and 500mg of magnesium a day.

If the skin problem is aggravated by detergents then clothing should be washed in a gentle soap and rinsed extremely well. Sometimes manufacturers change washing powder formulas and you may be allergic to an additional or different chemical. A mild biodegradable cleanser such as Ecover washing powder or wool wash may help, but it can take up to three or four washes before the clothes are free of the original residues. Synthetic fabrics can also cause problems and it may be worth trying 100 per cent cotton clothing which will allow the skin to breathe.

FATIGUE OR LETHARGY

Unusual tiredness or fatigue may be a serious side-effect of a number of medicines and must be reported to a doctor if there is no improvement within five days.

Fatigue may be helped with a good supply of B complex either from the diet or in supplement form. It is generally not advisable to take B complex in the evening as it can keep some people awake. Most B complex tablets colour the urine a bright yellow, due to their B2 content, but this is a harmless reaction. Often B12 and potassium are depleted by drug therapy and this can lead to fatigue. If this is the cause then you should ensure that the diet contains foods which are rich in these nutrients.

Kelp is a rich source of trace elements and minerals which can help some people overcome fatigue, but it should not be used by anyone taking thyroid medicines or who have thyroid disorders.

Vitamin C and B5 are important for the healthy function of the adrenal glands which play an important part in energy levels. Ginseng can also help to increase stamina and energy but it should be taken three hours apart from vitamin C supplements. If you feel that a tonic is needed then Bio Strath is a specially grown yeast containing numerous nutrients and can help to restore energy and well being.

The homoeopathic tissue salts Calc. Phos., Kali. Phos. and Ferr. Phos. can be used together to help fatigue and lethargy.

In some cases it is worth checking on what you eat daily as there may be some hidden food allergies which could be contributing to the fatigue. In susceptible people some items in the diet such as tea, coffee, refined foods, sugar, excess salt, colas, chocolate and alcohol can also contribute to fatigue.

FLATULENCE OR WIND

If the problem is a temporary or intermittent one there are several options to try. Health food stores sell digestive enzyme tablets like papaya and bromelain or herbal formulas, and these work as a temporary measure to improve digestion and decrease problems of flatulence. Charcoal tablets are effective for flatulence but they should only be used for temporary relief. They work by absorbing wind in the intestines but because of this they may also absorb important minerals, vitamins and bacteria found in the intestinal tract.

If the flatulence is acute then a pungent and fiery remedy can be made by adding 3-4 drops of peppermint essence to warm water and sipping it slowly.

If the problem lies in an upset of the balance of bacteria in the digestive tract then acidophilus powder or capsules may help, especially if taken with live natural yogurt.

If you suffer from indigestion and flatulence try chewing all food well and try to relax whilst eating. Yeast or supplements which contain it may increase flatulence in some people.

See also How to Help Yourself in the chapter on the Digestive System.

FUNGAL INFECTIONS, THRUSH OR CANDIDA

See How to Help Yourself in the chapter on Infections and Parasites.

GUMS, SORE OR BLEEDING

Bleeding gums may be one of the first signs of folic acid, vitamin C and bioflavonoid deficiency. The pith or white fleshy part of citrus fruit, found under the skin, is a good source of bioflavonoids and rutin tablets are also helpful. It is important to ensure that the diet contains enough protein, vitamin B complex, calcium, magnesium and zinc.

Goldenseal powder and myrrh can be mixed together and used as a toothpaste to help bleeding or sore gums. Goldenseal has a very bitter taste and can stain any fabrics it comes into contact with. Weleda make a natural mouthwash concentrate containing herbs, including myrrh, which is healing and antiseptic.

HEADACHE (Transitory)

Herbs have long been used to help headaches and a traditional remedy is tea made from the herbs rosemary and sage. A quarter of a teaspoon of each steeped in a cup of boiled water for about three minutes can be drunk when needed. Valerian and hops are other folk remedies for headaches and tension, but because of their taste they are most palatable taken as capsules or tablets.

Before aspirin was synthesized extract of white willow bark was used for pain and inflammation. This natural form of aspirin is quite effective and does not have the side-effects attributed to its synthetic cousin. If your medication interacts with aspirin, willow bark or willow extract should not be used.

Feverfew is often used for migraine headaches and can be eaten fresh or taken in capsule form. The homoeopathic tissue salts Nat. Phos., Mag. Phos., Nat. Mur. and Silicea are used for migraine headaches.

Vitamins such as C and bioflavonoids and the B complex can help with some types of headache and calcium and magnesium may be helpful for muscle tension. A good shoulder and neck massage can help to relieve tension associated with some headaches.

Many things have been blamed for contributing to headaches and migraine: coffee, alcohol, chocolate, salt, sugar and refined foods, greasy or fried foods, and smoking. If you suspect any of them, it could be worth trying to eliminate them on a trial basis from your diet.

See also Anxiety and Nervousness in this chapter.

HEARTBURN

Antacid tablets are often a high source of sodium or aluminium which many people would prefer to avoid. Papaya melon or papaya tablets are an effective alternative and can help indigestion and acid conditions quickly and naturally.

Another very effective and handy remedy is a raw potato. Grate it, strain through a clean, well-rinsed cloth and drink the juice which is very alkaline. Ensure the potato has no green colouring on it and if it does, do not use it. Cut off any sprouts before using as they contain a poisonous chemical called solanine.

To help over-acid conditions and heartburn, 2 teaspoons of aloe vera gel or juice can be taken up to twice a day. Seaweed extract, sodium alginate, if taken with a little milk has been found helpful by some people.

As a preventive measure it is important to avoid large meals, especially in the evening, and lying down immediately after a meal. Other culprits can be sugar, alcohol, smoking, some types of vinegar, caffeine, also fatty, spicy or fried foods. Details of caffeine containing items are in The Fact Finder.

INSOMNIA

Exercise may be a good antidote to insomnia and ensuring that the diet contains a good percentage of the B complex vitamins, including the calming nutrient inositol, throughout the day can also help. B complex taken late in the day can prevent some people from sleeping so it may not be advisable to take it in supplement form after four o'clock in the afternoon. The B2 present in B complex supplements colours the urine a bright yellow but this is a harmless reaction.

Calcium, magnesium and B6 supplements have a calming effect on the nervous system and can help prevent muscle cramps in the feet and legs* which can also keep some people awake. The amino acid tryptophane is often used for insomnia and has been found most effective when taken about an hour before retiring. It should be taken on an empty stomach with water or fruit juice only, approximately 2-3 hours after eating.

Valerian and hops are useful herbs for insomnia or tension and are most palatable taken as capsules or tablets, just before going to bed. Chamomile is the country standby for sleeplessness and combined with catnip makes a good night-time tea. Half a teaspoon of each can be steeped in a cup of boiled water for up to three minutes and sipped before retiring.

The homoeopathic tissue salt Kali. Phos. helps some cases of insomnia.

Certain food items may be responsible for keeping some people awake, among them are caffeine, sugar, heavy protein such as red meat and rich foods generally. Details of caffeine containing items are in The Fact Finder.

See also Anxiety and Nervousness and Muscle Cramps and Restless Legs* in this chapter.

ITCHING, HIVES AND NETTLE RASH

If you have an aloe vera plant you can break open a leaf and use the watery gel on the affected area of skin. It is very soothing and healing and often helps itching or rashes very quickly. Aloe vera juice is also available commercially.

Vitamin E can be applied by breaking open a capsule and this can have soothing and healing effects. Try to avoid getting it into the eyes as it can cause a burning sensation which may last for several hours. If it comes into contact with clothing it can stain it permanently.

Rectal itching can be helped by external application of vitamin A, vitamin E or aloe vera gel. Like vitamin E, vitamin A can also stain the clothing. The homoeopathic tissue salt Calc. Phos. is also helpful for rectal itching.

Supplements or foods high in vitamin C and bioflavonoids, vitamins B complex, E, A and the mineral zinc have been found helpful for skin complaints. Vitamin C, 250mg up to 4 times a day taken with up to 500mg of B5, can help allergic itch and nettle rash.

It is possible to develop an allergic reaction to washing powders and if the skin problem is aggravated by detergents then clothing should be washed in a gentle soap and rinsed extremely well. Sometimes manufacturers change washing powder formulas and you may be allergic to an additional or different chemical. Changing to a mild biodegradable cleanser such as Ecover washing powder or wool wash may help, but it can take up to three or four washes before the clothes are free of the original residues. Synthetic fabrics can also cause problems and it may be worth trying 100 per cent cotton clothing which will allow the skin to breathe.

Food additives, some prescription or non-prescription drugs, including aspirin, can sometimes be responsibile for hives in sensitive people.

MOUTH ULCERS, CANKER SORES, COLD SORES AND FEVER BLISTERS

Deficiency of vitamin A is often associated with these conditions and as this nutrient has antiviral properties it can help fight the herpes simplex virus which is responsible for herpes cold sores and fever blisters. Daily supplements of beta carotene or fish liver oil A in dosages up to 2,500IU with up to 400IU of vitamin D can be taken until relief is obtained. The addition of acidophilus powder or capsules to the diet helps prevent further outbreaks and this is best taken with natural live yogurt.

A vitamin B12 deficiency may also contribute to these conditions and the diet should be adequately supplied with this nutrient. Some vegans or vegetarians may be more prone to this problem unless B12 intake is carefully monitored.

A vegetarian diet may also be higher in the amino acid arginine and lower in lysine and this appears to encourage the herpes simplex virus which is responsible for the painful herpes fever blisters or cold sores. Arginine levels are high in almonds, cashews, carob, chocolate, coconut, gelatin, oats, peanuts and peanut butter, pecans and seeds, soya beans, wholewheat and white flour and wheatgerm. Arginine is also found in smaller quantities in garlic, ginseng, peas and untoasted cereals. Although a number of these foods also contain a significant amount of lysine, this is offset by their arginine content. Arginine should be avoided in supplement form by any one who suffers from herpes simplex.

A diet which is high in arginine should be offset with lysine rich foods and supplements. Beans, beef, brewer's yeast, cheese, chicken, fish, lamb, milk, mung sprouts and most fruit and vegetables are good sources of this amino acid.

A high potency vitamin B complex supplement taken every day in conjunction with a diet rich in zinc, folic acid and iron appears to be important in the prevention and healing of mouth ulcers and sores. It is generally not advisable to take B complex in the evening as it can keep some people awake. Most B complex tablets colour the urine a bright yellow, due to their B2 content, but this is a harmless reaction.

A little aloe vera juice or gel swilled around the mouth approximately every half-hour helps painful mouth ulcers or canker sores. It is not necessary to swallow it.

A small amount of bicarbonate of soda on a cotton bud, dabbed inside the mouth on ulcers or canker sores, two or three times a day will help stop pain. Try not to swallow the soda.

Tea tree oil applied externally to cold sores, approximately every hour, helps reduce pain and hastens healing. If it is applied at the onset of a blister developing, it can help shorten its duration.

Existing sores can be aggravated by the acid reaction in the body of foods such as coffee, sugar, alcohol and refined foods. Eating plenty of fresh vegetables and a salad every day helps carry acid wastes from the body.

MUSCLE CRAMPS AND RESTLESS LEGS

Muscle cramps are sometimes helped when lost minerals are restored to the body through diet or supplementation. An excessive salt intake could contribute to muscle cramping by causing the body to excrete excess potassium. Calcium and magnesium, zinc and potassium rich foods are among the most important to help prevent muscle cramps. The diet can also be supplemented with calcium and magnesium tablets, kelp and high potency vitamin B complex with B6 and B5. During an actual cramping episode the supplements may work quite quickly to stop the discomfort.

Menstrual cramping pains can be helped by 500-1000mg of calcium and magnesium, taken in supplement form at bedtime for a week before the period is due and up to three times a day during menstruation. For more information on menstrual cramping and disorders see How to Help Yourself in the chapter on the Female Reproductive System and Endocrine Glands.

Temporary but speedy relief may be obtained by firmly massaging cramping muscles with Olbas, linseed or castor oil or Weleda's massage oil which contains arnica, lavender and rosemary oil. If the cramp is in the legs follow by stroking the legs upwards from the ankle.

The homoeopathic tissue salt Mag. Phos. is used to help muscle cramps and the homoeopathic remedy Arnica can help if the cramp is due to stress or tiredness. Nux. Vom. can help night cramps.

Natural vitamin E may be especially beneficial in night cramps, and other types of muscle cramping. It has been used successfully in doses ranging from 200-400IU per day. If you have rheumatic heart disease, mitral valve prolapse or are taking certain heart medicines vitamin E should not be taken in supplement form except under supervision. If you are susceptible to high blood pressure then vitamin E can be taken in supplement form, but must be started at a very low dosage and gradually increased and again is best done under supervision.

Restless legs may be helped with a diet which is rich in folic acid and iron. Supplements of natural vitamin E may also help, but see the previous paragraph for important warnings about vitamin E. It is important to encourage circulation to the area so massage and the use of hot and cold water can help. The affected area should first be immersed in hot and then cold water, alternating for periods of one minute. This can be done with a shower, or bowls of hot and cold water for a period of up to four minutes, ending with cold water and then towelled briskly dry. For added benefit you can put a tablespoon of mustard powder or teaspoon of cayenne pepper into the hot water. Do not add them if you have any cuts, sores or rashes on the area which you are immersing. This can also help ordinary muscle cramping.

NAUSEA, VOMITING OR TRAVEL SICKNESS

Nausea which persists for more than two or three days or vomiting which lasts for more than 24 hours must be reported to your doctor.

Traditionally herbs have been used to help nausea and vomiting. A mixture of an eighth of a teaspoon each of chamomile, basil, peppermint and clove should be steeped in a cup of boiled water for about three minutes and then sipped slowly.

Ginger root powder or fresh ginger can be made into a very effective but fiery tea by steeping a quarter of a teaspoon in a cup of boiled water for about three minutes. It should be sipped slowly. If the tea is unpalatable to you, capsules of ginger can be taken instead and are available from health food stores. Ginger is used for travel sickness too, and 2-4 capsules taken with B6 and B complex are remarkably effective. Ginger can also be added to the mixed herb tea mentioned previously.

Homoeopathic remedies Nux. Vom. 6x or petroleum are effective remedies in tablet form which are dissolved under the tongue.

Vitamin B complex especially B6 is used to help digestion and prevent nausea and vomiting. It is generally not advisable to take B complex in the evening as it can keep some people awake. Most B complex tablets colour the urine a bright yellow, due to their B2 content, but this is a harmless reaction. The herb ginseng can also help some types of nausea or vomiting and it can aid digestion generally.

NEURALGIA

The homoeopathic tissue salts Mag. Phos. and Calc. Sulph. are used for neuralgia which occurs in the head or the side of the face.

PALPITATIONS OR ABNORMALLY RAPID HEARTBEAT

Palpitations may be a sign of a serious disorder and must be discussed with a doctor before any attempt is made to use natural remedies. If palpitations persist after trying a natural approach for 2-3 days then please consult your doctor.

Half a teaspoon of the herb rosemary steeped in a cup of boiled water for about three minutes makes a helpful tea which can be drunk 3-4 times a day.

The homoeopathic tissue salt Ferr. Phos. is used to help this condition.

A good dietary intake of B complex vitamins including B6, B5, B12 and minerals such as calcium, magnesium and especially potassium can sometimes help palpitations. It is generally not advisable to take B complex in the evening as it can keep some people awake. Most B complex tablets colour the urine a bright yellow, due to their B2 content, but this is a harmless reaction.

NATURAL REMEDIES

NATURAL REMEDIES FOR COMMON AILMENTS AND SIDE-EFFECTS

Plunging your face into a basin of cold water for about 15-20 seconds, although it sounds unlikely, has the temporary effect of helping palpitations, but should not be attempted if you have any type of heart disorder or before it has been discussed with a doctor.

Some items that can worsen or cause palpitations are a high salt intake, alcohol, sugar, smoking, and caffeine. Details of caffeine containing items are in The Fact Finder. Eating large quantities of natural liquorice can contribute to palpitations as it decreases potassium in the body.

SKIN RASH   See Itching, Hives and Nettle Rash.

SORE THROAT   Sore throat may be a serious side-effect of some drugs and must be discussed with a doctor before any of the remedies are tried. Very painful sore throat accompanied by bleeding could be very dangerous if not treated by your doctor and if any sore throat persists for more than 2 days you should seek medical advice.

For those who enjoy raw garlic, a piece can be cut from a clove and sucked for an effective remedy for most sore throats.

Zinc helps the body to fight infection and sore throats are helped by sucking a zinc lozenge or a chelated zinc tablet. It is not recommended to exceed the dosage stated on the bottle unless specifically advised by a practitioner.

Propolis, which is produced by bees, has an antiseptic quality and when sucked or chewed can be helpful for sore throats.

A soothing herbal tea for sore throats is made from half a teaspoon of any one of the following herbs steeped in boiled water for about three minutes: sage, stinging nettle, eucalyptus or fenugreek. The herbs can be mixed in any combination you prefer and fresh lemon juice and honey can be added.

An eighth of a teaspoon each of cayenne pepper and goldenseal root powder placed in a cup with boiling water, should be sipped slowly when it has cooled a little. Although it is fiery, this tea can help increase the circulation of blood to the throat and fight infection. If there is any undissolved cayenne pepper in the bottom of the cup, throw it away, do not try to swallow it as it is extremely hot. Diabetics, or anyone with serious blood-sugar disorders should avoid taking goldenseal. Anyone suffering from hiatus hernia should avoid cayenne pepper.

Vitamin C supplements are often taken in 250-500mg doses 3-4 times a day for 2-3 days to help the first signs of sore throat or infections. As a high intake of vitamin C can decrease vitamin B12, calcium and magnesium, these should be generously supplied in the diet. Gradually decrease the amount of vitamin C you are taking when you begin to feel better. Some people respond to vitamin A with vitamin C or find that vitamin A works best without vitamin C. You may wish to experiment to see which suits you best.

SUNBURN

If the burn is severe, consult your doctor. Natural remedies will help soothe the aftermath of less severe burns.

A homoeopathic remedy for blistering and pain is Cantharis and there is also a burn ointment which quickly soothes pain and hastens healing. If you do not have this homoeopathic ointment you can apply a slice of raw potato to the affected areas and follow with honey which is sticky but soothing and healing.

To help take the pain out of the burn, add 4-6 ounces (110-175ml) of apple cider vinegar to cool bath water and soak for about ten minutes.

If you have an aloe vera plant, break open a leaf and apply the gel to the burned skin every thirty minutes until the burn is soothed, then apply 2-3 times per day until the burn is healed. Bottled aloe juice can also be used liberally on the affected area to help healing and soothe the burn.

Vitamin E squeezed from a capsule or pure lavender oil can be applied liberally to the affected area of minor burns, where the skin is not broken. Contact with the eyes should be avoided or you may experience a burning sensation which can last for several hours. Clothing can be stained permanently with oils so try to prevent it from coming into contact with them. Vitamin E can also be used internally for burns. For important warnings on the use of vitamin E please see the chapter on Vitamins and Minerals.

Cold tea's tannic acid content is very soothing for burns and can be used effectively to help reduce the pain.

It would be a good idea to drink plenty of fluid and eat foods high in protein, vitamin A and zinc which are important for healing. 500mg of vitamin C with bioflavonoids can be taken in supplement form for a few days to help the skin heal.

TASTE, LOSS OF SENSE OF

There are some nutrients which can help restore a lost sense of taste and these are zinc and vitamins A, B6 and B12. Homoeopathic remedies which can help this condition include Nat. Mur., Nat. Phos., and Silicea.

THRUSH OR FUNGAL INFECTIONS

See How To Help Yourself in the chapter on Infections and Parasites.

ULCERS

See How To Help Yourself in the chapter on the Digestive System.

VITAMINS AND MINERALS
INTRODUCTION

A good diet is the basis of health, and the vitamins and minerals in food are essential to life. Minerals must be supplied in the diet as we are unable to synthesize them ourselves. They are important for the majority of metabolic processes and for the building of body structure. Vitamins generally act as catalysts, helping the body perform a multitude of functions.

A healthy person is able to synthesize small amounts of vitamins B12, B5, B3, D, K, inositol, folic acid and biotin. The fat soluble vitamins, E, A, K and D require the presence of fats in the digestive system in order to be absorbed, used and stored. Vitamins C, B complex and bioflavonoids are water soluble and are dissolved and utilized with the presence of water in the digestive tract.

Because of the way foods are produced, handled, stored and processed our diets often contain fewer nutrients than nature intended. Add stress, environmental pollution, the use of medicines, drugs and other substances which deplete nutrients and it is easy to see that sub-clinical deficiencies can develop. Transient headaches, digestive complaints, lack of energy and skin disorders are all too common and may arise as a result of eating food which does not supply all of our nutritional needs and a lifestyle which depletes nutrients even further.

VITAMINS AND MINERALS
INTRODUCTION

Careful preparation of food is important to retain vital nutrients and enzymes. Vegetables are best eaten raw, cooked in a pressure cooker or steamed. Cooking water should be saved to make broths and soups or to cook grains. The key to preserving nutrients is to chop vegetables as little as possible to reduce nutrient 'bleed', use the minimum amount of water and heat as is practical and always cover the saucepan with a tight fitting lid. Adding bicarbonate of soda to cooking water may make vegetables look more attractive but its alkalinity quickly robs foods of a number of vitamins and minerals. Fruit is always best eaten fresh and whole grains retain much of their nutrition when cooked in a pressure cooker.

Supplements are just that — something to add to our foods to enhance them. Eating a poor diet and hoping to make up for it with a handful of tablets unfortunately does not work. For an individual assessment of which nutrients you may be lacking or for long-term supplemental requirements it is best to consult a practitioner who is trained in their use, as a number of vitamins or minerals could be detrimental in large doses or can act to cancel out each other's benefits.

Vitamin supplements can lose some of their potency with time, but minerals are less affected. If a bottle of vitamins has been opened and stored correctly its shelf-life is about one year, if unopened then it can be up to two years. It is important to keep them away from damp, light and heat although it is not necessary to store them in a refrigerator. All vitamin tablets should be taken with food or immediately after but alkaline minerals such as magnesium will disrupt digestion and should be taken up to three hours before or after meals.

Because so many vitamins and minerals are affected by drug treatments it is important to know from where they are obtained in the diet and the following section gives some significant food sources. It is important to note that the nutrient content of food depends on the soil where it was grown and the lists should only be considered as a guide.

VITAMINS & MINERALS

VITAMIN A

Vitamin A is a fat soluble vitamin which is not significantly destroyed by ordinary cooking temperatures; however, it can be destroyed by light and oxygen and by cooking in iron or copper pans. It is produced in the tissues of animals and fish, and can be absorbed in the digestive tract in the presence of fats and minerals. The liver is the site of vitamin A storage. There are two types of vitamin A: pro-vitamin A known as carotene is found in yellow, orange, and green vegetables and fruits and is converted to vitamin A by the body. The second type is retinol, known as pre-formed A which can be found in foods of animal origin.

SOME SIGNIFICANT FOOD SOURCES

PRE-FORMED A
- butter
- cheese
- egg yolks
- fish liver oils
- liver
- whole milk

PRO-VITAMIN A
- beet greens
- broccoli
- carrots
- dark green leafy vegetables
- mangoes
- olives
- papaya
- parsley
- pumpkin
- spinach
- sunflower seeds
- tomatoes
- watercress
- watermelon

REQUIRED FOR
- resistance to infections
- respiratory system health
- skin, hair and eye health
- formation of visual purple for night vision
- healthy mucous membranes
- growth and development
- protection against UV radiation
- protection against heavy metal toxicity
- protection against oxidation and free radicals
- production of digestive juices
- protein synthesis
- protection against air pollution
- prevention of anaemia

DEFICIENCY MAY LEAD TO
- skin or scalp disorders
- poor night vision, conjunctivitis, cloudy vision, itching or burning eyes, dry eyes, inflamed eyelids, red eye rims

poor finger or toe nails
excessive mucus production

IMPORTANT
CO-NUTRIENTS

B complex
vitamin C
vitamin D
vitamin E
vitamin F
calcium

inositol
phosphorus
selenium
manganese
zinc

REQUIREMENTS
INCREASED DUE TO

fever
infection
air pollution
smoking
alcohol
ultra violet light
a diet extremely high in
    protein

liquid paraffin
antacids
gout drugs
aspirin
* oral contraceptives
* oestrogens

lipid lowering drugs

*See How to Help Yourself in the chapter on the Female
Reproductive System for important information about vitamin
A's interaction with these hormones.

TOXICITY

The recommended amount for adults is 750IU a day in the UK
and 800-1000IU in the USA. Taking more than ten times that,
in supplements of pre-formed vitamin A, i.e. 7500-10,000IU, for
an extended period of time is thought to produce toxicity. Doses
of pre-formed vitamin A over 25,000IU taken for an extended
period of time have produced toxicity.

If excessively large amounts of pro-vitamin A, as in the form
of supplements or carrot juice, are consumed then an orange
pigmentation may appear on the palms of the hands and soles
of the feet. This is harmless and will disappear in a few days
when the source of carotene is withdrawn.

TOXICITY SYMPTOMS

nausea
headaches
vomiting
brittle nails
diarrhoea
skin rash
weight loss
blurred vision
hair loss
dry scaly lips, skin or scalp
enlargement of liver and spleen

VITAMINS AND MINERALS
VITAMINS

B COMPLEX VITAMINS The B group of vitamins consists of nutrients which include B1, B2, B3,B5, B6, B12, biotin, choline, folic acid, inositol, and PABA. B complex supplements consist of all these in combination. Each of these separate vitamins is dealt with individually under this B complex heading.

VITAMIN B1

Thiamine, also known as aneurine, is a water-soluble vitamin. It was first isolated from rice polishings in 1926 and has been dubbed 'the morale vitamin' because of its positive effect on the nervous system. It is lost into cooking water and decreased during roasting, braising and frying. B1 is destroyed by alkalis like baking soda or powder, sulphites such as sulphur dioxide, and avidin which is found in raw egg white. This vitamin is quickly absorbed in the upper and lower intestine, and can only be stored in very small amounts in the body.

SOME SIGNIFICANT FOOD SOURCES

brewer's yeast and extract
dandelion leaves
egg yolk
heart, kidney and liver
most vegetables and fruits

oranges and nuts
peas and beans
rice bran, wheat bran
seafoods
whole grains, wheatgerm

REQUIRED FOR

nerve function
digestion of starches and sugars and their conversion to glucose for energy
digestion and the production of digestive juices
growth and development
normal appetite

DEFICIENCY MAY LEAD TO

tiring easily
appetite loss
irritability
impaired carbohydrate digestion
bowel disorders
lack of concentration
nerve disorders
numbness and tingling in arms and legs
muscle disorders, tenderness or weakness
loss of co-ordination

heart failure, rapid pulse
water retention
shortness of breath
extreme weakness and paralysis
anaemia
emaciation

IMPORTANT CO-NUTRIENTS

other B complex vitamins
vitamin C
vitamin E
manganese

magnesium
sulphur
zinc

REQUIREMENTS INCREASED DUE TO

pregnancy
breast feeding
fever
surgery
stress
strenuous activity

large consumption of:
raw fish
shellfish
alcohol
raw egg white
caffeine

foods containing phytic acid
refined foods
smoking
oral contraceptives
oestrogens
antacids
sulphur drugs
penicillins
other antibiotics
urinary tract anti-infectives
aspirin
NSAI's

TOXICITY

Excess B1 is excreted by the body and there is no known toxicity.

Note:
Diabetics who are receiving drugs or insulin should take B1 only under medical supervision.

VITAMIN B2

Riboflavin is also known as vitamin G or lactoflavin. B2 was recognized in yeast in 1932 and isolated from milk whey in 1933. It has a yellow colour which is often used as a food colouring and when taken in supplement form causes the urine to appear very yellow but this is harmless. It can be found in the kidneys and liver, but is not stored by the body. It is a water and alcohol soluble vitamin which is absorbed through the walls of the small intestine. Cooking is not destructive to B2 unless alkalis are present such as baking soda or powder, but it is lost into cooking water and destroyed by light.

SOME SIGNIFICANT FOOD SOURCES

brewer's yeast and extract
eggs and cheese
fish
green leafy vegetables
lean meat

liver and kidney
seeds and nuts
soya flour
wheatgerm
whole milk

REQUIRED FOR

formation of enzymes
production of energy from the conversion of glucose, amino acids and fatty acids
growth and repair of body tissues
maintenance of healthy red blood cells
conversion of the amino acid, tryptophane, to B3
healthy skin, hair and nails
the nervous system
normal growth and development
light tolerance or adaption to changes in light

DEFICIENCY MAY LEAD TO

EYES:

sensitivity to light
eye fatigue
changes in the cornea
bloodshot
blurred vision
burning or gritty sensations under the eyelids
cataracts

SKIN:

dermatitis
scaling of skin around the face and head
oily skin
cracks around corners of the mouth
glossy and inflamed tongue

CENTRAL NERVOUS SYSTEM:

depression
lack of energy
headaches
insomnia

dizziness
trembling
learning difficulties

IMPORTANT CO-NUTRIENTS

other B complex vitamins
vitamin C
manganese

phosphorus
zinc

REQUIREMENTS INCREASED BY

alcohol
breast feeding
fever

pregnancy
smoking
stress

antacids
antibiotics
antidepressants

oestrogens
oral contraceptives
penicillins

TOXICITY   There are no known toxic effects as B2 is water soluble and excess is excreted by the body. If an excessive amount of B2 is taken in supplement form symptoms such as numbness, itching or burning sensations may occur and will disappear when the dose is reduced or withdrawn.

Note:
All B vitamins should be taken together, never separately, to prevent deficiency symptoms developing.

VITAMIN B3

B3 is also known as niacin, nicotinic acid, nicotinamide, niacinamide and antipellagra vitamin or PP factor. It is a fast acting vitamin which is soluble in hot water and alcohol and not easily destroyed by light or ordinary cooking temperatures although it is lost into cooking water. The body is able to manufacture B3, from the amino acid tryptophane, and absorption takes place in the intestines. The liver is the main storage area for this vitamin.

SOME SIGNIFICANT FOOD SOURCES

beans and peas
brewer's yeast and extract
eggs
fish
green leafy vegetables

lean meat
liver
sunflower seeds
wheatgerm
whole grains

REQUIRED FOR

digestive processes
breakdown of fats, carbohydrates and proteins into energy
cell and tissue respiration and function
activating enzymes which nourish brain
nerves, skin and hair
production of hormones such as cortisone, insulin, thyroxine, and the sex hormones
regulating blood pressure and cholesterol levels

DEFICIENCY MAY LEAD TO

gastro-intestinal upsets
difficulty swallowing
dermatitis
rashes

coarseness, roughening or darkening of the skin
exhaustion
insomnia
irritability
depression
dementia
disorientation
confusion
poor memory
loss of attention
tremors

IMPORTANT CO-NUTRIENTS

other B complex vitamins
vitamin C
manganese

phosphorus
zinc

REQUIREMENTS INCREASED DUE TO

a diet which is very high in corn and corn products such as cornflour, cornmeal and sweetcorn
excessive consumption of refined sugar
vigorous exercise
large consumption of alcohol

oral contraceptives
oestrogens
anxiolytics
sleeping tablets
aspirin

TOXICITY

No actual toxicity has been reported with B3 but if extremely large doses are taken liver function may be affected and depression can occur. Nicotinic acid and niacin can have a vasodilatory effect at doses of approximately 100mg and over. This is not dangerous and is characterized by flushing, heating, prickling and itching of the skin. Occasionally headache or abdominal cramps and nausea may be experienced, although this is generally when extremely large doses are taken. These symptoms may disappear within 15 minutes to an hour and do not occur with niacinamide or nicotinamide.

Note:
B3, niacin and nicotinamide should not be taken by those with gout or high uric acid, or a history of these conditions. B3 competes with uric acid for excretion and may cause it to rise rapidly, worsening gout and causing nausea or vomiting. Avoid niacin or nicotinic acid if you have any form of peptic ulceration, glaucoma or itching skin rash. If you are receiving treatment for diabetes, cardiovascular disease or high blood pressure

consult your doctor before using more than 50mg a day of niacin or nicotinic acid. During the first two months of pregnancy large doses of B3 should be avoided.

All B vitamins should be taken together, never separately, to prevent deficiency symptoms developing.

Never give niacin or nicotinic acid to infants, young children or animals as the flushing sensation which may occur could be very frightening.

VITAMIN B5

B5, also known as pantothenic acid and calcium pantothenate, is a water-soluble vitamin found in all cells and produced in the intestines by bacteria. B5 is known to play a role in preventing depression, and is called an anti-stress vitamin. It is lost into cooking water, destroyed by heat or freezing and acids or alkalis such as vinegar or baking soda.

SOME SIGNIFICANT FOOD SOURCES

brewer's yeast and extract
egg yolks
milk, yogurt and cheese
nuts
organ meats
peas and beans
royal jelly
soya flour
wheatgerm and bran
whole grains

REQUIRED FOR

production of steroid hormones
antibodies which fight infection
cholesterol and fatty acids metabolism
carbohydrate, protein and fat metabolism
nervous system function
skin health
adrenal glands' production of hormones
resistance to stress, shock and allergies
decreasing side-effects of certain drugs
protection against radiation-caused cellular damage

DEFICIENCY MAY LEAD TO

abdominal discomfort
cramping in legs
fatigue, depression and insomnia
increased susceptibility to infections and stress
indigestion, vomiting or appetite loss
pins and needles
burning sensation in the feet

IMPORTANT CO-NUTRIENTS	other B complex vitamins vitamin C manganese	sulphur zinc
REQUIREMENTS INCREASED DUE TO	stress and allergies strenuous activity heavy coffee intake antacids antibiotics	anxiolytics and sleeping tablets aspirin diuretics sulphur drugs
TOXICITY	There are no known toxic effects with B5, but very high doses may cause some people to experience diarrhoea.	

Note:
All B vitamins should be taken together, never separately, to prevent deficiency symptoms developing.

VITAMIN B6

B6, also known as pyridoxine, is a water and alcohol soluble vitamin crucial to many body processes. It is de-activated by heat, sunlight or air and is lost into cooking water. B6 helps to balance the sodium and potassium levels in the blood, assists with the conversion of the amino acid tryptophane to niacin and acts as a natural diuretic.

SOME SIGNIFICANT FOOD SOURCES	bananas brewer's yeast and extract green leafy vegetables meat molasses	rice bran soya flour wheat bran wheatgerm whole grains
REQUIRED FOR	manufacture of red blood cells and haemoglobin fighting infection regulating cholesterol levels nervous system function preventing convulsions helping with depression maintaining balance of minerals utilization of B12 maintaining female fertility production of digestive juices and HCl prevention of vomiting and nausea	

**DEFICIENCY
MAY LEAD TO**
depression
irritability
weakness
tiredness
memory loss
loss of concentration
dermatitis around mouth, eyes and nose
cracked lips
sore tongue
loss of appetite
nausea or vomiting
nervousness
headaches
menstrual disorders
breast tenderness

**IMPORTANT
CO-NUTRIENTS**
magnesium
potassium
other B complex vitamins
vitamin C
manganese
zinc

**REQUIREMENTS
INCREASED DUE TO**
alcohol
dieting
pregnancy
breast feeding
severe vomiting of early pregnancy
smoking
stress
strenuous activity
large intake of choline over a long period of time

antacids
diuretics
hydralazine antihypertensives
oral contraceptives and oestrogens
some antibiotics
isoniazid antituberculosis drugs

TOXICITY
There is no known toxicity but high doses taken late in the day may cause night restlessness and vivid dream recall.

Note:
All B vitamins should be taken together, never separately, to prevent deficiency symptoms developing.

VITAMIN B12

B12 is a water and alcohol soluble vitamin, also known as cyanocobalamin as it contains the mineral cobalt. It was isolated from liver in 1948 and can be grown on moulds or bacteria or by fermentation but it is not produced synthetically because of its complex structure. It is unstable if cooked with acids or alkalis such as vinegar or baking soda and is lost into cooking water. B12 is needed by every cell in the body, especially red blood cells, muscle, nerve, and gastro-intestinal cells. It is not easily absorbed from food and requires calcium and a substance called intrinsic factor, which must be present in the digestive juices, for its assimilation. When supplementation is necessary doctors may give B12 by injection or it can be taken in tablet form under the tongue. Some B12 can be manufactured in small amounts in the body and it is stored in the liver.

SOME SIGNIFICANT FOOD SOURCES	cheese and milk products
	egg yolks
	fermented foods such as
	  yogurt, miso and
	  tempeh
		kelp
		organ meats, especially
		  liver
		sardines
		spirulina (plant plankton)

REQUIRED FOR	production of red blood cells prevention of anaemia maintenance of normal bone marrow growth and development in children muscle energy nervous system health utilization of iron, B5, vitamin C and some amino acids metabolism of fats, proteins and carbohydrates	
DEFICIENCY MAY LEAD TO	depression irritability mental sluggishness mood swings loss of short term memory numbness and tingling in the extremities tremors tiredness anaemia sore tongue or inflammation of tongue or mouth menstrual disorders	
IMPORTANT CO-NUTRIENTS	other B complex vitamins vitamins C, E and A potassium	manganese sodium zinc

REQUIREMENTS INCREASED DUE TO

alcohol
digestive disorders and parasites
malabsorption in the elderly
high intake of vitamin C, over 750mg a day
high and consistent intake of comfrey
pregnancy
smoking
some vegan or vegetarian diets
lack of intrinsic factor and HCL in the digestive juices

antacids
anticonvulsants
anxiolytics and hypnotics
aspirin
certain antibiotics
oral contraceptives and oestrogens
some antiparkinsonian drugs
urinary tract anti-infectives

Note:
A deficiency of B12 can go undetected for some time. Damage to the nervous system and spinal cord may occur during this time and pernicious anaemia may develop.

TOXICITY

There is no known toxicity although a very high supplementary intake may mask the signs of pernicious anaemia.

Note:
All B vitamins should be taken together, never separately, to prevent deficiency symptoms developing.

BIOTIN

Biotin is a water soluble vitamin also known as vitamin H and co-enzyme R. It is important, as a co-enzyme, for the production of proteins and fats and the oxidation of carbohydrates and fatty acids. The bacteria in the intestinal tract produce biotin, and small amounts can be stored in the kidneys, adrenal glands, liver, and brain. Some is lost into cooking water.

SOME SIGNIFICANT FOOD SOURCES

brewer's yeast and extract
egg yolk
liver
meat
molasses

fish
fresh vegetables
nuts
whole grains
yogurt, cheese and milk

VITAMINS AND MINERALS
VITAMINS

REQUIRED FOR	bone marrow growth and development metabolism of carbohydrates, fats and proteins nerves oil, sweat producing and sex glands skin and hair
DEFICIENCY SYMPTOMS IN ADULTS	decreased haemoglobin anaemia depression insomnia dermatitis increased cholesterol levels in blood loss of appetite muscle aches or pains nausea or vomiting pallor of skin sore mouth and lips
DEFICIENCY SYMPTOMS IN BABIES	abnormal redness of skin dermatitis diarrhoea
IMPORTANT CO-NUTRIENTS	other B complex vitamins especially B12, B5 and folic acid vitamin C manganese sulphur zinc
REQUIREMENTS INCREASED DUE TO	alcohol large intake of raw egg white antibiotics urinary tract anti-infectives oral contraceptives and oestrogens sulphur drugs
TOXICITY	There is no known toxicity of biotin.

Note:
All B vitamins should be taken together, never separately, to prevent deficiency symptoms developing.

CHOLINE

Choline is a water soluble member of the B complex vitamins. It is part of a group of fats known as phospholipids which are found in both animal and plant cells and it can be synthesized by the interaction of B12 and folic acid with methionine. Choline, combined with fatty acids and phosphoric acid within the liver, forms lecithin. It can be lost into cooking water.

SOME SIGNIFICANT FOOD SOURCES	beans and peas beef liver and heart brewer's yeast and extract corn egg yolk	green leafy vegetables lecithin soya flour wheatgerm whole grains

REQUIRED FOR
myelin sheaths of the nerves
transmission of nerve and brain impulses
regulation of liver and gall bladder functions including elimination of toxins and drugs
preventing accumulation of fats in the liver, other organs and vascular system
cell membranes
metabolic reactions

DEFICIENCY MAY LEAD TO
nerve degeneration
cirrhosis or fatty deposits in the liver
kidney disorders
increased susceptibility to infections such as streptococcal sore throat
high cholesterol levels
hardening of the arteries
high blood pressure

IMPORTANT CO-NUTRIENTS
other B complex vitamins especially inositol and B12
vitamin A
linoleic acid
manganese
zinc

REQUIREMENTS INCREASED DUE TO
alcohol
diabetes
diuretics
oral contraceptives and oestrogens

TOXICITY
There is no known choline toxicity but large doses over a prolonged period of time may increase B6 requirements.

Note:
All B vitamins should be taken together, never separately, to prevent deficiency symptoms developing.

VITAMINS & MINERALS

INOSITOL

Inositol is a water soluble member of the B complex vitamins, also known as lipotropic factor. It is found in both animal and plant tissues and in cereals is present as phytic acid and is phosphorus based. The body's intestinal bacteria are able to produce inositol from glucose. Some may be lost into cooking water.

SOME SIGNIFICANT FOOD SOURCES	bananas	molasses
	brewer's yeast and extract	nuts
	citrus fruit	soya lecithin and flour
	green leafy vegetables	wheatgerm
	liver and beef heart	whole grains

REQUIRED FOR
liver function
fat transport and utilization
prevention of fatty accumulation in the liver, other organs and vascular system
calming the nervous system
hair and skin health

DEFICIENCY MAY LEAD TO
hair loss
fatty accumulations in the liver and other organs and/or the vascular system. These are advanced deficiency symptoms.

IMPORTANT CO-NUTRIENTS	B complex vitamins	manganese
	choline	zinc
	linoleic acid	

REQUIREMENTS INCREASED DUE TO
alcohol
large consumption of coffee
pregnancy or lactation

diuretics
oral contraceptives and oestrogens

TOXICITY
There are no known toxic effects.

Note:
If you supplement your inositol primarily from soya lecithin, it would be wise to include plenty of mineral rich foods in your diet, especially high calcium foods or supplements of calcium and magnesium. Lecithin's high phosphorus level may upset the body's mineral balance.

All B vitamins should be taken together, never separately, to prevent deficiency symptoms developing.

FOLIC ACID

Folic acid is a water soluble vitamin also known as folate, folacin, vitamin M, vitamin Bc and pteroylglutamic acid. Folic acid takes its name from 'foliage' as it was first found in dark green, leafy vegetables. It is destroyed by high temperatures, cooking with acids such as vinegar and is decreased when stored for long periods at room temperature or when exposed to light. A large percentage of this vitamin is lost into cooking water. Folic acid is not produced by the body but the liver converts it to folinic acid, with vitamin C's assistance, and can store it.

SOME SIGNIFICANT FOOD SOURCES	asparagus beans, peas and avocado brewer's yeast and extract eggs and fish green leafy vegetables	nuts organ meats and liver parsley watercress wheatgerm

REQUIRED FOR
- production and development of blood cells
- the formation of haem, the iron containing substance found in haemoglobin
- formation of RNA and other nucleic acids which are needed for growth and the reproduction of body cells
- breakdown and utilization of proteins
- pregnancy and lactation

DEFICIENCY MAY LEAD TO
- poor growth and development disorders in children
- inflammation of the tongue
- digestive disorders
- megaloblastic anaemia
- tiredness
- weakness
- irritability
- insomnia
- forgetfulness

IMPORTANT CO-NUTRIENTS	B complex vitamins
	  especially biotin,
	  B12 and B5
	vitamin C
		manganese
		PABA
		zinc

REQUIREMENTS INCREASED DUE TO	ageing alcohol illness injury	lactation pregnancy stress smoking

aspirin
isoniazid antituberculosis drugs
lipid lowering drugs
oral contraceptives and oestrogens
phenytoin*
primidone anticonvulsants
pyrimethamine anti-infectives
sulphonamides*
triamterene and other diuretics
trimethoprim anti-infectives*

*Supplemental folic acid can decrease the effectiveness of these drugs and should only be taken with them under supervision.

TOXICITY No actual toxicity has been reported but intakes over 15mg a day may cause nausea, wind, irritability and loss of appetite in susceptible people. High daily intake of folic acid may mask the symptoms of B12 deficiency which can lead to nerve degeneration if not corrected.

Note:
All B vitamins should be taken together, never separately, to prevent deficiency symptoms developing.

PABA

PABA is an abbreviation of the full name Para-aminobenzoic acid and is a water soluble vitamin which occurs as a component of folic acid, although it is usually referred to as a separate B complex vitamin. PABA is synthesized by intestinal bacteria and is stored in body tissues. It is believed that PABA also stimulates intestinal bacteria to help form folic acid, which then stimulates the production and utilization of B5. Externally PABA is used as a sunscreen in some suntan lotions. When PABA is taken with sufficienct zinc, manganese, B5 and B6 it has been found helpful for some cases of vitiligo, a skin condition which appears as patches of light coloured skin.

SOME SIGNIFICANT FOOD SOURCES
brewer's yeast   molasses
eggs   wheatgerm
liver   whole grains

REQUIRED FOR a co-enzyme in the metabolism of proteins and the production of blood cells
skin and hair health

DEFICIENCY MAY LEAD TO There are no specific symptoms associated with PABA deficiency although it may be involved in digestive disorders or nervous tension.

IMPORTANT CO-NUTRIENTS

folic acid   manganese
other B complex vitamins   zinc
vitamin C

REQUIREMENTS INCREASED DUE TO

alcohol

oral contraceptives and oestrogens*
sulphur drugs**

*Extremely large supplemental doses of PABA can increase the activity of oestrogen and may increase the side-effects of oestrogen drugs or the Pill.

**PABA should not be taken when sulphonamide drugs have been prescribed as it may counteract their therapeutic effects. See Sulphonamides for more information.

TOXICITY High doses of PABA over prolonged periods may cause nausea and vomiting or a skin rash. It could also have a toxic effect on the liver, kidneys or heart.

Note:
All B vitamins should be taken together, never separately, to prevent deficiency symptoms developing.

VITAMIN C

Vitamin C, also known as ascorbic acid, is a water soluble vitamin which is easily destroyed by heat, light, air, and oxidation. When cooking in iron and copper utensils there is a greater loss if alkalis such as baking powder or soda are used. Vitamin C is also lost into cooking water. Very little is lost when foods are quick frozen. Most animals manufacture their own vitamin C but humans are not able to do so and must rely on dietary sources. Vitamin C is absorbed from the gastro-intestinal tract into the blood stream and eliminated in the urine and perspiration. It is stored in the body only to a limited extent.

VITAMINS AND MINERALS
VITAMINS

SOME SIGNIFICANT FOOD SOURCES

blackberries/blackcurrants | kale
brussels sprouts | papaya
citrus fruit | parsley
green peppers | rosehips
honeydew melons | watercress

Most fruit and vegetables contain a certain amount of vitamin C.

REQUIRED FOR

the production of connective tissue
healing of wounds and burns
production of digestive enzymes
utilization of fats, carbohydrates and proteins
glandular activity
brain and nerve function
formation of teeth and bones
strength and health of blood vessels
ability to cope with stress
production and activity of infection fighting white blood cells
lubrication of joints
absorption of iron, and conversion of folic acid to folinic acid
controlling cholesterol levels in the blood
protection of cells and B complex, A and E vitamins from oxidation
minimizing the effects on the body of environmental pollution

DEFICIENCY MAY LEAD TO

swollen, red or bleeding gums
loose teeth
slow wound or fracture healing
abnormal bruising or bleeding
weakness
iritability
joint or muscle pains or swelling
increased susceptibility to infection
shortness of breath
impaired digestion
anaemia
an increased risk of atherosclerosis, heart attack and stroke

IMPORTANT CO-NUTRIENTS

bioflavonoids | vitamin A
calcium | manganese
magnesium

REQUIREMENTS INCREASED DUE TO

baking soda or powder | smoking*
diabetes | strenuous physical activity
alcohol | stress
high fever | surgery
menstruation | injury
petrol fumes | dental treatment

*Up to 25mg of vitamin C can be destroyed by each cigarette smoked, and similar losses apply to cigars and loose tobacco.

antacids	barbiturates
antibiotics	cortisone
anticonvulsants	diuretics
antihistamines	oral contraceptives and
aspirin and other pain	oestrogens
killers	sulphur drugs

TOXICITY There are no known toxic effects of vitamin C, although with daily doses of 500mg or more some people may experience slight burning during urination, loose bowel movements or skin rashes. Over 750mg of vitamin C can decrease B12 absorption. Long term large doses of vitamin C can affect laboratory tests so it is important to tell the person in charge if this applies to you. If B6 and magnesium are not supplied adequately in the diet then a very large intake of C may cause kidney stones to form, especially in those with hyperoxaluria. If you suffer from gastric ulcers it is best to take vitamin C as calcium ascorbate, so it will not be so irritating.

During pregnancy it is not advisable to take doses of vitamin C over 750mg a day because it could be detrimental to the foetus.

Note:
Large amounts of chewable vitamin C can cause damage to tooth enamel.

VITAMIN D

Vitamin D is a fat soluble vitamin which is not destroyed significantly by cooking, processing or refrigeration. Vitamin D2, ergocalciferol, can be synthesized by the exposure of yeast to light. Vitamin D3, cholecalciferol, is found naturally in animal tissues. In humans it is formed in the skin when ultraviolet light activates the conversion of a form of cholesterol to D3; because of this it is often referred to as the 'sunshine vitamin'. Dietary vitamin D is absorbed through the intestinal walls with the help of bile salts, converted by the liver and kidneys into a form the body can use, and stored in the liver.

**SOME SIGNIFICANT
FOOD SOURCES**

dairy products
egg yolk
fatty fish

fish liver oils
liver

REQUIRED FOR

the absorption and metabolism of calcium and phosphorus
bone and tooth formation
functions related to calcium and phosphorus metabolism such
    as those of the nervous system, heart and blood clotting
growth in children and normal calcification of bones and teeth
formation of hormones by the thyroid gland

**DEFICIENCY
MAY LEAD TO**

faulty utilization of calcium and phosphorus
irritability
weakness
tooth malformation
rickets in children; symptoms are bone malformation or
    softening, muscle weakness and nervous irritability
osteomalacia in adults; symptoms are softening of the bones,
    muscle weakness, pains in the limbs, spine and pelvis
tetany, which is spasm of the arms and legs

**IMPORTANT
CO-NUTRIENTS**

choline
vitamin A
vitamin C
vitamin F

magnesium
calcium
phosphorus

**REQUIREMENTS
INCREASED DUE TO**

lack of exposure to sunlight, in conjunction with a diet which
    is low in vitamin D

anticonvulsants
laxatives such as liquid paraffin
lipid lowering drugs

TOXICITY

Vitamin D may be toxic in doses over 400IU a day if taken
regularly.

TOXICITY SYMPTOMS

increased urination
appetite loss
nausea or vomiting
diarrhoea
weakness of muscles

headache
dizziness
thirst
calcification of organs and
soft tissue

VITAMIN E

Vitamin E is a fat soluble vitamin made up of seven compounds called
tocopherols: alpha which is the most active, beta, delta, gamma, epsilon,

zeta and eta. Dl-alpha tocopherol is the synthetic form of vitamin E. This vitamin is destroyed by cooking in open pans, and particularly by deep frying. Some may also be lost during commercial deep freezing. Absorption of vitamin E takes place in the intestines with the help of bile salts. High concentrations of vitamin E are found in the liver, fat storing tissues, muscles such as the heart and the adrenal, pituitary and sex glands. Excess vitamin E is excreted in the urine.

SOME SIGNIFICANT FOOD SOURCES
avocado
dark green vegetables
egg yolk
safflower oil
sesame seeds and tahini
soya and sesame oils
sunflower seeds and oil
vegetable oils
wheatgerm, wheatgerm oil
whole grains

REQUIRED FOR
protection of cells, fatty acids and certain vitamins from oxidation
decreasing the oxygen requirements of organs and muscles
promoting normal blood clotting
preventing or dissolving blood clots
maintaining cardiovascular health
detoxification of pollutants in the body
maintaining normal function of the adrenal and pituitary glands
preventing vitamin A and saturated fats from breaking down into harmful substances in the body
protecting sulphur-containing amino acids in the body
release of insulin from the pancreas
maintaining normal function of the reproductive glands
regeneration of skin and the healing of burns
prevention of scar tissue formation
increasing the levels of 'good' cholesterol in the body
protecting against calcification of bones, joints and soft tissue

DEFICIENCY MAY LEAD TO
decreased fertility
fatigue or decreased energy
irritability
leg cramps
muscle weakness

IMPORTANT CO-NUTRIENTS
inositol
selenium
sulphur containing amino acids
vitamin A
vitamin C
vitamin F
vitamin B complex
manganese
zinc

REQUIREMENTS INCREASED DUE TO
stress
pregnancy and lactation
menopause

VITAMINS & MINERALS

high consumption of refined foods
pollutants, including lead
strenuous activity
malabsorption disorders
high intake of polyunsaturated oils or fats
rancid cooking oils and rancid oil in nuts and seeds
infections
diabetes
high oxygen intake, such as in medical treatment
drinking chlorinated water
smoking

liquid paraffin and other laxatives
lipid lowering drugs
oral contraceptives and oestrogens

Note:
Supplemental iron and vitamin E should be taken eight hours apart as they can hinder each other's absorption.

TOXICITY   Vitamin E is not toxic although large doses may cause fatigue, muscle weakness and possibily gastro-intestinal upsets.

Warning:
Vitamin E should be taken under supervision in doses over 1000IU a day. If you have rheumatic heart disease, mitral valve prolapse or are taking certain heart medicines vitamin E should not be taken in supplement form except under supervision. If you are susceptible to high blood pressure then vitamin E can be taken in supplement form, but must be started at a very low dosage and gradually increased and again is best done under supervision. If you are taking digitalis drugs, beta blockers, or other medicines for the heart it is important that you consult your doctor before taking vitamin E supplements.

Insulin dependent diabetics must consult a doctor before taking vitamin E as the insulin dose may need to be adjusted in accordance with the amount of vitamin E.

VITAMIN K

Vitamin K is a fat soluble vitamin and because of its ability to help in the formation of prothrombin, which is needed for blood clotting, it has been called the 'anti-haemorrhagic' vitamin. K1, also called phytomenadione is found in food sources, K2 or menaquinone is formed by bacteria in the intestines, and K3, menadione is water soluble and produced synthetically. Bile and bile salts help with the absorption of vitamin K in the upper intestinal tract and the liver uses it for the production of proteins which contribute to the clotting mechanism of blood. Only a small amount of this vitamin is stored in the body. Vitamin K is destroyed by light and acids and alkalis such as vinegar or baking soda or powder.

SOME SIGNIFICANT FOOD SOURCES

cauliflower	kelp
cow's milk	liver and other meats
eggs	molasses
fish liver oils	polyunsaturated oils
green vegetables	tomatoes

REQUIRED FOR

conversion of carbohydrates to glycogen
aids in normal liver function
carbohydrate storage in the body
formation of a protein which binds calcium
synthesis of proteins involved in blood clotting
promotes normal functioning of the circulatory system
helps to prevent strokes

DEFICIENCY MAY LEAD TO

increased blood clotting time
easy bruising and excessive bleeding

IMPORTANT CO-NUTRIENTS

No data found

REQUIREMENTS INCREASED DUE TO

high intake of acids such as vinegar, or alkalis like baking soda
air pollution
decreased secretion of bile by the liver
destruction of, or inadequate 'good' intestinal flora
diarrhoea
gall bladder disorders
high intake of rancid oils
surgery
X-rays
excessive doses of vitamin E

antibiotics	sulphur drugs
anticonvulsants	salicylates and aspirin
laxatives and liquid paraffin	tuberculosis antibiotics
lipid lowering drugs	

TOXICITY

Natural vitamin K produces no toxicity. Very large doses of synthetic vitamin K3 especially injections or intravenous administration may cause toxicity symptoms such as facial flushing, breathing disorders, sweating and low blood pressure.

VITAMIN P, BIOFLAVONOIDS

The bioflavonoids are sometimes called flavones and may also be called vitamin P because of their effect on the permeability of capillaries. Bioflavonoids are a group of water soluble substances which comprise a number of factors including hesperidin, myrecetin, nobiletin, rutin, tangeritin and quercetin. Vitamin P was first discovered in the white part of citrus fruits and the flavonoids are responsible for making the yellow and orange colour in citrus fruits. Absorption takes place in the intestinal tract. Bioflavonoids are found with vitamin C in foods and work with it. They are destroyed by boiling and by exposure to air.

SOME SIGNIFICANT FOOD SOURCES	apricots cherries blackcurrants grapes and plums blackberries papaya and rosehips buckwheat** skin and pith of citrus fruit* cantaloupe melon

*Bioflavonoids are found in the whole of the lemon, including the juice.

**Buckwheat is an excellent source of rutin.

REQUIRED FOR	maintaining the health of capillaries and blood vessels, in conjunction with vitamin C resistance to infection preventing oxidation of vitamin C in the body enhanced function of vitamin C
DEFICIENCY MAY LEAD TO	easy bleeding or bruising bleeding gums small areas of bleeding under the skin
IMPORTANT CO-NUTRIENTS	vitamin C
REQUIREMENTS INCREASED DUE TO	petrol fumes diuretics stress oral contraceptives and oestrogens aspirin and NSAI's
TOXICITY	There are no toxicity symptoms reported with bioflavonoids.

CALCIUM

Calcium is the chief mineral in the body and is stored in the bones; it is a major component of bones and teeth. The parathyroid glands in the neck help to regulate the storage of calcium and if dietary intake of calcium is less than the body requires then they release a hormone which, with vitamin D, moves calcium from the bones into the blood to maintain a steady level. If, on the other hand, the blood level of calcium is too high then the thyroid and parathyroid glands release a hormone which sends excess calcium to the bones for storage. We only absorb about 20-30 per cent of the calcium we eat and it depends on a number of factors for its breakdown and absorption, including adequate hydrochloric acid in the stomach. Calcium is excreted in the urine and stools.

SOME SIGNIFICANT FOOD SOURCES

brewer's yeast
carob
cheese and milk
nuts
pumpkin seeds
seaweeds such as hijiki
sesame seeds and tahini
vegetables
wheatgerm
yogurt

REQUIRED FOR

absorption of fats by activating pancreatic lipase
normal blood clotting
bones and teeth
firmness and elasticity of tissues
healing and building of tissues
immune system
maintaining the pH of the blood
muscles including the heart
nerves
preventing toxic heavy metal build-up
production and release of certain hormones
production of digestive juices including intrinsic factor and bile
storage of glycogen
the body's enzyme system

DEFICIENCY MAY LEAD TO

cramps
depression
insomnia
nervousness
spasms in legs and feet, especially at night
grinding of teeth in sleep
tremors
twitching of muscles

319

VITAMINS & MINERALS

IMPORTANT CO-NUTRIENTS		
B complex vitamins	phosphorus*
B6	selenium
fluorine	vitamin D
iron	vitamin E
lactose	vitamin C
magnesium	vitamin A
manganese	zinc

*Should be in a ratio of two and a half times more calcium than phosphorus.

REQUIREMENTS INCREASED DUE TO

stress
immobilization
excessively high or low protein intake
sugar, but not milk sugar
imbalanced vitamin D intake
high intake of phosphorus
alcohol
high intake of phytic acid
high intake of oxalic acid
high intake of saturated fats
pregnancy and lactation
menstruation
excessive fluid intake
kidney damage
malabsorption disorders
lactose intolerance
hormone imbalances
insufficient hydrochloric acid
infection
fever or sweating
insufficient intake of magnesium in the diet

antacids
aspirin
cortisone
liquid paraffin

TOXICITY

Calcium is not actually toxic and a healthy body excretes it in the urine and stools, although hypercalcaemia results when there is too much calcium in the blood. This can occur if too much calcium is absorbed, excessive vitamin D is taken or if there is an increase in the thyroid gland's production of parathormone. This can result in calcification of bones, joints, blood vessels and damaged areas of the body.

CHROMIUM

Chromium is a trace element. It is found in small amounts throughout the body, but is present in significant amounts in the bone, kidneys, muscles, fatty tissues, skin and adrenal glands. Both the brain and adrenal glands require chromium. The insulin mechanism relies on GTF, the glucose tolerance factor, and chromium is an essential factor in this and metabolism. Chromium is excreted in the stools and urine.

SOME SIGNIFICANT FOOD SOURCES

brewer's yeast
cheese
liver

molasses
nuts
whole grains*

*Except corn and rye. Trace amounts of chromium are found in fruit, meat and vegetables.

REQUIRED FOR

glucose tolerance factor
glucose metabolism and activation of insulin
control of blood sugar levels in the body
healthy immune system and white blood cells
conversion of foods to energy in the body
normal cholesterol levels in the blood
formation of glycogen
increase in HDL levels
protein synthesis
brain
nerves

DEFICIENCY MAY LEAD TO

blood sugar disorders
impairment of glucose tolerance
nervous disorders
rise in blood cholesterol

IMPORTANT CO-NUTRIENTS

B3
the amino acids glutamine, glycine, and cysteine

REQUIREMENTS INCREASED DUE TO

alcoholism
dieting
foods grown on chromium-poor soils
high intake of refined foods
insulin dependent diabetes
pregnancy
stress
surgery

TOXICITY   Chromium is a trace mineral and therefore, large supplemental intake over 200mcg a day is not recommended unless under supervision. Exposure to chromium as a pollutant in the air and cigarette smoke appears to be more toxic than ingestion from food or supplements.

COPPER

Copper is a trace element which is found in all the tissues of the body. A high concentration is found, first, in the liver and secondly in the brain. It is also found in the muscles, bones, heart and glands. Copper is absorbed in the stomach and upper intestine. It is excreted by the liver via the bile and the faeces and a small amount is also lost in the urine.

SOME SIGNIFICANT FOOD SOURCES

brewer's yeast	meat
cereals and whole grains	nuts and seeds
cocoa and chocolate	oysters
curry powder	tea
liver	vegetables

REQUIRED FOR

blood
bones
brain and nerve transmission
formation of the colouring pigment of skin and hair
immune system
iron absorption
protein metabolism
synthesis of phospholipids
tissue formation

DEFICIENCY MAY LEAD TO   Copper deficiency is extremely rare as most of us actually ingest far too much copper from food, water pipes, pesticides and fungicides. Copper cooking utensils and taking the Pill also raise copper levels. If deficiency does occur as a result of malnutrition, malabsorption or disease, the symptoms include:

anaemia	decreased resistance to
irritability	infection
weakness	pale skin and hair
skin sores	diarrhoea.
brittle nails and bones	

IMPORTANT CO-FACTORS

cobalt	zinc
iron	

REQUIREMENTS
INCREASED DUE TO

deficient dietary intake
excessive phytic acid intake
malabsorption disorders

prolonged diarrhoea
some medical treatments
  such as dialysis

TOXICITY

Extreme copper toxicity symptoms include abdominal pain, nausea and vomiting, diarrhoea, mental disorders and anaemia. It is rarely that this occurs, but higher blood copper levels may usually only be found where the following occur:

abnormal copper
  metabolism
deficiency of zinc
epilepsy
high blood cholesterol

child hyperactivity
rheumatoid arthritis
schizophrenia
some heart disorders
users of oral contraceptives

Note:
It is important to ensure that dietary zinc, manganese and vitamin C levels are adequate as they are important in preventing copper excess.

IODINE

Iodine is a natural trace element from the sea which is also found in the soil. Most of the body's iodine is stored in the thyroid gland and is used to make thyroid hormones which regulate the metabolism of the entire body. Iodine is excreted in the urine. Food content of this mineral varies greatly depending upon the soil where it was grown and, with the exception of fish, seafoods, seaweed and sea vegetables, levels may fluctuate quite dramatically.

SOME SIGNIFICANT
FOOD SOURCES

eggs
fresh fruit
fruit
garlic
kelp and dulse seaweeds

milk
other sea vegetables
seafoods
vegetables
whole grains

REQUIRED FOR

excretion of radioactive iodine
production of thyroid hormones which are involved in:

metabolism
production and regulation of cholesterol
growth
immune system

skin, hair and nail health
conversion of carotene to vitamin A
synthesis of protein

**DEFICIENCY
MAY LEAD TO**

coarse skin
drowsiness
enlargement of the thyroid gland at the front of the neck
lack of energy
low resistance to infections
muscle weakness
poor quality hair and skin
sensitivity to cold
slow mental reactions
weight gain

**IMPORTANT
CO-NUTRIENTS**

No data found.

**REQUIREMENTS
INCREASED DUE TO**

pregnancy
growth
adolescence
stress
low dietary iodine intake
high intake of goitrogens of antithyroid foods
oral antidiabetics
para-aminosalicylic acid antituberculosis drugs

TOXICITY

Extremely large iodine intake, usually from iodine prepared as medicine, can inhibit the production of thyroid hormones and may lead to hyperthyroidism or thyrotoxicosis. If asthmatics are receiving long-term therapy with iodine, then hypothyroidism may occur.

IRON

Iron is the oxygen carrier. It energizes cells by transporting oxygen to them in haemoglobin, the substance which makes blood red. Approximately 90 per cent of the body's iron is contained in the blood stream. It is absorbed from food in the small intestine and is passed, via the blood stream, to the bone marrow where it is used to make haemoglobin. Iron is conserved by the body or recycled when red blood cells break down. The recycled iron is stored in the liver, spleen and bone marrow until needed.

SOME SIGNIFICANT FOOD SOURCES	brewer's yeast and extract cherries dried fruit egg yolk green leafy vegetables	liver and other lean meat molasses parsley watercress wheatgerm

The liquid iron supplement, Floradix, is an excellent source of iron from plant and fruit sources. In the diet, it is generally true that the darker the fruit or vegetable, the higher its iron content.

Note:
Although grains and spinach contain iron it is rendered insoluble by their phytic or oxalic acid content; most of this iron is lost in the faeces.

REQUIRED FOR

the breakdown of carbohydrates, protein and fats into glucose
destruction of toxic metabolic products
haemoglobin formation and development of blood cells
oxygen reserve in muscles
production of white blood cells
removal of carbon dioxide waste
resistance to disease
tissue respiration

DEFICIENCY MAY LEAD TO

ANAEMIA: EARLY SYMPTOMS	inside of eyelids pale pale skin	paleness under the fingernails tiredness and fatigue
ANAEMIA: ADVANCED SYMPTOMS	chronic fatigue continual headaches easily become breathless giddiness	heart rhythm disorders loss of appetite opaque and brittle nails pins and needles
IMPORTANT CO-NUTRIENTS	B12 copper* folic acid manganese* vitamin C	zinc phosphorus selenium calcium

*Copper is needed in minute amounts only for the absorption of iron; too much can lower iron levels. Excessive amounts of manganese can decrease iron storage.

**REQUIREMENTS
INCREASED DUE TO**

bleeding ulcers
childbirth
haemorrhage or heavy bleeding
infections
laxatives
menstruation
strenuous physical activity
excessive phosphorus intake
high intake of comfrey
excessive use of olive oil for long periods

Note:
Supplemental iron and vitamin E should be taken eight hours apart as they can hinder each other's absorption. Tea and coffee consumed with a meal can reduce the absorption of iron, but drinking coffee an hour before a meal does not seem to prevent absorption to the same degree.

TOXICITY

The body conserves and recycles iron very efficiently and if too much iron is taken it may be difficult for it to get rid of the excess. Too much iron can cause damage to tissues and in certain individuals may result in accumulation of excessive iron containing pigment in organs especially the liver and spleen and body tissues.

MAGNESIUM

Magnesium is considered an antispasmodic and anti-stress mineral. The parathyroid glands influence the rate of magnesium absorption from the small intestine and the adrenal hormone, aldosterone, regulates its excretion in the urine via the kidneys. Over 50 per cent of the body's magnesium is stored in the bones.

**SOME SIGNIFICANT
FOOD SOURCES**

apples
avocado
bananas
beans, peas and lentils
blackberries
brewer's yeast
black grapes, raisins

green leafy vegetables*
fish and seafoods
most nuts and seeds
soya flour
wheatgerm
whole grains

*Spinach, swiss chard and beet greens are not considered a good dietary source of magnesium as they contain oxalic acid which can decrease magnesium absorption.

REQUIRED FOR
bones and teeth
brain function and health
cardiovascular system health
cell strength
co-enzyme to many biochemical processes
co-factor in B1 and B6 function
digestive enzyme, HCL and bile production
DNA duplication
growth and repair
hormones and hormone synthesis
immune system
maintaining blood pH
metabolism
muscles
nervous system function and health
preventing blood clotting
removal of ammonia and other metabolic waste from the body
cell production of proteins

DEFICIENCY MAY LEAD TO

abnormal blood clotting
abnormal calcium deposition
appetite loss
blood sugar disorders
cardiovascular disorders
child hyperactivity
confusion and disorientation
convulsions or seizures
fatigue

insomnia
involuntary rapid eye
   movements
irregular heartbeat or
   palpitations
muscle cramps
nervousness
tremors, spasms or tics

IMPORTANT CO-NUTRIENTS

B5
B6
calcium

natural vitamin D
phosphorus
vitamin C

REQUIREMENTS INCREASED DUE TO

abnormally high or low protein intake
appetite loss
breast feeding
burns
chronic diarrhoea
diabetes and diabetic insulin treatment
excessive urination or perspiration
excessive vitamin D intake, especially D2
fatigue
heart, kidney, pancreas and liver diseases
high intake of phosphorus
high coffee or tea intake
high alcohol intake

high intake of sugar and refined carbohydrates
malabsorption disorders
pregnancy
high intake of foods containing oxalic acid
stress or shock
surgery

aminoglycoside antibiotics given generally by injection
anticonvulsants
aspirin
colchicine antigout drugs
diuretics
oral contraceptives and oestrogens

TOXICITY Excessive magnesium intake can cause diarrhoea. The symptoms of extreme magnesium toxicity are generally only found in those with kidney failure who are given excessive magnesium. The cardiovascular and respiratory systems may be seriously affected and will require medical treatment.

Note:
Because magnesium is an alkaline mineral it should not be taken with food, or less than 15 minutes before meals. If taken after food then 2-3 hours should be allowed to elapse.

MANGANESE

Manganese is an essential trace element required by the brain and nervous system. It is absorbed slowly from the small intestine and a high concentration is stored in the bones, kidneys, liver, pancreas and heart. Manganese is excreted via the bile, faeces, urine and perspiration.

SOME SIGNIFICANT FOOD SOURCES

avocados
blueberries/blackberries
dulse seaweed
kidney beans
nuts and seeds

olives
organ meats
raisins, other dried fruit
watercress
wheatgerm
wholegrains

Note:
Ordinary tea contains a high amount of manganese but this is offset by its high tannin content which prevents manganese absorption.

REQUIRED FOR

activation and utilization of vitamins B, C and E
activator of enzymes involved in the formation of urea
building and breakdown of protein and nucleic acids
co-factor in production of thyroxine hormones
female hormones
glycogen formation
helps in protein production
immune system
lipid metabolism
metabolism
necessary for normal blood clotting
nervous system and brain
normal skeletal development
normal blood sugar levels
red blood cell production
transport of oxygen

DEFICIENCY MAY LEAD TO

blood sugar disorders
convulsions
ear disorders
failure of muscle co-ordination

Note:
Myasthenia gravis and schizophrenia have been linked with manganese deficiency in some individuals.

IMPORTANT CO-NUTRIENTS

B1
calcium
vitamin E
phosphorus

REQUIREMENTS INCREASED DUE TO

high tannin intake
high intake of processed foods
large intakes of calcium and phosphorus
low intake of fresh fruit and vegetables

TOXICITY

Toxicity from dietary intake is rare and most cases of toxicity have been reported from industrial poisoning where manganese dust has been inhaled. The symptoms of poisoning include weakness, apathy, muscular and movement disorders, loss of appetite, headaches, lung disorders, nerve degeneration similar to Parkinson's disease, tremors and schizophrenic behaviour.

VITAMINS & MINERALS

PHOSPHORUS

The mineral phosphorus is part of every cell and chemical reaction which takes place in the body. It occurs in plant and animal cells as phosphate and is the second most abundant mineral in the body after calcium. A high percentage is found in the bones, teeth, and muscles. Phospholipids are compounds of phosphorus found in tissues, the lymphatic system, brain and nerves. Phosphorus is only slightly soluble in water but dissolves in oils and alcohol and its absorption takes place in the intestine. Main excretion is via the urine.

SOME SIGNIFICANT FOOD SOURCES

almonds and walnuts
beans and peas
brewer's yeast
cocoa and chocolate
eggs and dairy products
lentils

liver and other meats
other nuts and seeds
soya products/lecithin
wheatgerm/bran
wholegrains

Note:
Soft drinks and refined or processed foods are high in phosphorus and may contribute to an excessive amount of phosphorus in the diet.

REQUIRED FOR

energy
equilibrium in body tissues
fatty acid transport in the body
hair, nail and eye health
maintenance of pH balance in blood and digestive juices
metabolism of carbohydrates, fats and proteins
muscle contractions
nervous system and brain
nucleic acids to maintain and repair cells
phospholipid production in the liver
protein synthesis
teeth and bones

DEFICIENCY MAY LEAD TO

appetite loss
bone and tooth disorders
cramps and aching muscles
fatigue
heart disorders

irritability
loss of weight
pins and needles
tremor
weakness

IMPORTANT CO-NUTRIENTS

calcium
iron
manganese

vitamin E
vitamin D
vitamin A

REQUIREMENTS INCREASED DUE TO

deficiency of vitamin E
excessive consumption of alcohol
excessive iron and aluminium intake
malabsorption disorders
X-rays

aluminium hydroxide antacids
antithyroid drugs
aspirin
cortisone
diuretics
laxatives

TOXICITY

Excessive phosphorus may lead to diarrhoea. If too much of this mineral is ingested, which is possible if the diet is high in processed or refined foods and soft drinks, then the body's stores of calcium may be depleted and calcification of joints and soft tissues may occur. There is also the possibility of kidney and gall stones developing. Iron, zinc, and magnesium may also be depleted by excess phosphorus levels.

POTASSIUM

Potassium is an alkaline mineral found in all body tissue and after calcium and phosphorus it is the third most prevalent mineral. Potassium is absorbed through the walls of the small intestine and excreted mainly in the urine although a small amount is normally lost in the faeces and a little through the sweat glands. Potassium works in partnership with other minerals, especially sodium, in many of the body's functions. Some potassium may be lost into cooking water.

SOME SIGNIFICANT FOOD SOURCES

fresh and dried fruit
green leafy vegetables
kelp seaweed
molasses
nuts and sunflower seeds

potatoes*/other vegetables
soya flour
vegetable and fruit juices
watermelon
wheatgerm
wholegrains

*Especially in the half inch below the skin.

REQUIRED FOR

cells and cell metabolism
energy metabolism
maintaining pH
muscle contraction
nerve impulses

osmotic pressure
protein synthesis
regulating water balance
the brain
the heartbeat

**DEFICIENCY
MAY LEAD TO**

constipation
drowsiness or dizziness
electrocardiogram changes
excessive thirst
fatigue
insomnia
loss of appetite
mental confusion and apathy

muscle weakness and cramps
pins and needles
respiratory failure
skin and hair disorders
slow or irregular heartbeat
urinary system disorders
vomiting

**IMPORTANT
CO-NUTRIENTS**

magnesium
sodium
vitamin B6

**REQUIREMENTS
INCREASED DUE TO**

blood sugar disorders
eating mainly processed or refined foods
excessive intake of alcohol, sugar, protein, coffee or natural
    liquorice
inadequate magnesium intake
insufficient or excessive sodium or salt intake
malabsorption disorders
prolonged diarrhoea or vomiting
severe burns
some surgical or medical procedures
strenuous exercise
stress or illness including influenza

antibiotics and antifungals
aspirin
carbenoxolene ulcer drugs
corticosteroid drugs
digitalis drugs
intravenous saline drip used long-term
laxatives
non-potassium conserving or containing diuretics

TOXICITY

Excessive potassium intake can lead to many of the same
symptoms as potassium depletion especially vomiting, muscular
weakness, cramps and apathy. Potassium supplements are not
recommended except under supervision as high oral doses can
irritate the stomach and cause discomfort or pain. Potassium
supplements which are enteric coated may stimulate the
production of ulcers in the small intestine.

Note:
Because potassium is an alkaline mineral, it should not be taken
with, or less than 15 minutes before, meals. If taken after food,
2-3 hours should elapse.

SELENIUM

Selenium is an essential trace element and is one of the scarcest and most poisonous minerals. It is a water soluble chemical element resembling sulphur and occurs abundantly in those areas which contain volcanic ash. Modern farming methods, loss of topsoil and food processing have contributed to its scarcity in much of our food. Some may also be lost into water when cooking. The highest concentrations of selenium are found in the liver and kidneys and men require more than women as almost half of their selenium supply is found in the testicles and seminal ducts. Selenium is excreted in the urine and may be lost with male seminal fluid.

SOME SIGNIFICANT FOOD SOURCES	asparagus bran and germ of cereals brewer's yeast brown rice eggs	fish garlic onions organ meats tuna

REQUIRED FOR
- blood cells
- cardiovascular system
- chelating and removing toxic heavy metals from the body
- insulin
- eye, skin and hair health
- glutathione's role in the regulation of carbohydrate metabolism
- immune system
- protection against oxidation and free radicals
- iron recycling in the body
- male reproductive system
- prostaglandin production
- protection of fat soluble vitamins from oxidation
- protection against certain types of cancer
- protein production

DEFICIENCY MAY LEAD TO
- accelerated ageing
- degenerative diseases
- lack of energy
- low resistance to infection
- male infertility
- poor quality hair, skin and nails

IMPORTANT CO-NUTRIENTS
- vitamin E

REQUIREMENTS INCREASED DUE TO
- diet high in processed and refined foods
- diet high in foods grown on selenium deficient soils
- environmental pollution

TOXICITY The maximum recommended daily dosage of selenium is 200mcg. Organically bound selenium such as selenium yeast is less toxic than other supplements. Selenium toxicity can occur from an excessive dietary intake or by inhalation. If you work close to a copying machine please note that selenium may be found in the environment around it if its plates are selenium. You can offset this by ensuring that your diet contains sulphur rich foods such as garlic, onions, cabbage, eggs, fish or meat.

The symptoms of selenosis or selenium poisoning include decreased sense of smell, respiratory disorders, skin rash, irritability, fatigue and poor quality hair and nails.

SODIUM (SALT)

Sodium is present in body fluids especially those which surround the cells, lymph, serum and blood. It is also found in body tissue and bone. The stomach and small intestines are the sites of sodium absorption and excretion is mainly from the kidneys via the urine. A small amount is also lost in the faeces and through the sweat glands. Sodium has an alkaline reaction in the body and works closely with other minerals especially potassium.

SOME SIGNIFICANT FOOD SOURCES

bacon
baking soda or powder
bouillon, gravy and stock
certain food additives
cheeses

most canned/packaged food
most processed foods
olives
smoked fish
table, rock and sea salt
yeast extracts

SOME NATURALLY OCCURRING SODIUM SOURCES

beetroot
carrots
celery
coconut
cucumber
dandelion leaves
fresh and dried fruit

kelp and other seaweeds
milk whey
most other vegetables
poultry and meat
unsmoked fish, seafood

Sodium occurs to some degree in most vegetables.

SOME DRUG SOURCES

certain antacids
sodium cromoglycate used for asthma
sodium nitroprusside used for angina

sodium picosulphate laxatives
sodium valproate used for epilepsy

REQUIRED FOR
hydrochloric acid production
keeping other minerals soluble in the blood
maintaining correct osmotic pressure
muscle contraction including the heart
nerve stimulation and impulse transmission
regulation of blood pH
removal of carbon dioxide from the body
transportation of glucose
transportation of nutrients between cells via the blood and other
   fluids*

*This function is the reason why tears, urine, blood and perspiration are salty.

DEFICIENCY MAY LEAD TO

craving for salt	nerve disorders
excessive urination	poor digestion and flatulence
loss of weight	rapid pulse
low blood pressure	weakness
muscle cramps	

IMPORTANT CO-NUTRIENTS
chlorine
potassium
vitamin D

REQUIREMENTS INCREASED DUE TO

certain diseases	severe diarrhoea or vomiting
excessive laxative use	lack of chlorine
excessive sweating	lack of potassium

TOXICITY
Too much sodium may be due to excessive dietary intake or alcoholism, diabetes, kidney failure and other diseases.

TOXICITY SYMPTOMS

cramps	irregular heartbeat
decreased potassium levels	raised blood pressure
dizziness	water retention
fatigue	

ZINC

Zinc is a water soluble trace element which is essential to many body functions and is found in almost all tissues especially the thyroid gland, pancreas, reproductive organs especially the prostate gland in men, liver, kidney, bones and muscles. It is absorbed in the upper part of the small intestine and excreted in the faeces, urine, sweat and semen. Because it is water soluble it may be lost into cooking water.

SOME SIGNIFICANT FOOD SOURCES

brewer's yeast
brown rice
eggs and dairy products
herring
liver and other organ meats

most vegetables
pumpkin seeds
rye bread
seafood
wheatgerm
wholemeal bread

REQUIRED FOR

blood cells
bones and joints
carbohydrate metabolism
cholesterol production
circulatory system
digestive and metabolic enzymes
general health of the reproductive system
glandular function
growth, development and functions of the reproductive organs
healing of wounds, ulcers and burns
immune system
insulin release and storage
liver function
nervous system
production of sperm and ova
protein production
release of vitamin A from liver stores
synthesis of nucleic acids
tissue respiration
vision and eye health

DEFICIENCY MAY LEAD TO

apathy
bleeding gums
brittle hair and hair loss
increased susceptibility to infections
loss of sense of taste and smell
pica
post natal depression
reproductive system disorders
skin lesions
slow wound, ulcer or burn healing
white spots on the nails

IMPORTANT CO-NUTRIENTS

B6
calcium*
copper*

phosphorus
vitamin A

*Too much copper or calcium are zinc antagonists.

**REQUIREMENTS
INCREASED DUE TO**

breast feeding
cooking solely with copper utensils
diabetes
eating mainly refined or processed foods
excessive perspiration
excessive intake of calcium, copper, iron or manganese
high phytic acid intake
high carbohydrate, low protein intake
high alcohol intake
liver and kidney disease
malabsorption disorders
porphyria
pregnancy
lack of phosphorus, or an excessive phosphorus intake

digitalis drugs
long-term or high dosage corticosteroid treatment
oral contraceptives and oestrogens
penicillamine chelating agents
thiazide diuretics

Note:
If you are vegetarian or vegan then your diet may be high in phytic acid which can decrease your body's absorption of zinc. Fermented foods such as miso contain the enzyme phytase which can offset phytic acid's effects. Sourdough or breads which have risen with yeast do not contain phytic acid so the zinc in the grains is available to the body.

TOXICITY

Dietary zinc is not toxic and any excess is excreted in the urine. However, it is not necessary to take more than 25mg a day unless it has been recommended by a doctor or practitioner. A high intake of zinc may interfere with copper metabolism and increase the need for vitamin A rich foods. Industrial inhalation from smelting plants and ingestion of acidic liquids stored in galvanized containers may result in zinc poisoning which may manifest as fever, nausea and vomiting.

ALTERNATIVE/COMPLEMENTARY MEDICINE AND THERAPIES

Natural healing is not a new idea, although it seems as if it has only been attracting attention during the last few years. It has actually been with us in different forms since the first attempts were made at finding materials in nature to control or relieve disease. For centuries many civilizations have used food and herbal remedies medicinally and a large number of today's alternative/complementary therapies were major means of restoring health prior to the era of drug therapy that has been developed during the twentieth century.

Alternative/complementary medicine is a generic name for a number of therapeutic techniques, all of which avoid the use of orthodox drugs in their treatment. Health and disease are looked at in terms of the whole person, body, mind and spirit and each individual's different and unique needs are taken into account. The root of natural medicine is the treatment of the cause of disease rather than symptoms. Natural practitioners work on the basis that, if given the chance and the right help, the body can often work to heal itself.

At the turn of this century Thomas Edison said, 'The doctor of the future will give no medicine, but will interest the patient in the care of the human frame, in diet and in the cause and prevention of disease.' The importance of preventive measures and an understanding of nutrition's relationship with medicine is increasingly evident, together with a greater awareness of the need to become more involved in personal health care. Natural medicines are a valuable facet of that health care which, as Thomas Edison foresaw, are part of the medicines of the future.

GENERAL INFORMATION

Included in this chapter are brief descriptions of systems which are therapeutic in their own right and may be used in conjunction with alternative/complementary medicine. Information relating to the more commonly used therapies appears in this chapter, but because of the scope of therapies in this field it is not possible to include all of them. Further details on other aspects of natural medicine or therapies not listed here may be found in The Fact Finder. General information on practitioners and allied associations will be found at the end of this chapter.

Please note that the names and addresses which appear in this chapter are intended as information sources and are not intended as endorsements.

ACUPUNCTURE

Acupuncture is part of the traditional medicine of China where it has been practised for over 5000 years. Acupuncturists believe that health is a state of total harmony between the physical, emotional and spiritual aspects of the individual and that illness and symptoms are associated with an imbalance or blockage of the body's vital energy. To reach a diagnosis an acupuncturist will make a detailed examination of disease symptoms, and take into account age, medical history, and physical and emotional traits. Physical examination includes the unique Chinese reading of the twelve pulses in the wrist and examination of the tongue. Acupuncturists seek to re-establish a proper balance and flow of vital energy in the body by inserting very fine needles into particular points on the body. Each point has a precise location and a specific therapeutic action. The burning of a dried ball of the herb mugwort on the shaft of a needle is called moxibustion. This has the effect of heating the needle and reinforcing its action of stimulating vital energy and restoring balance. Traditionally acupuncture is used to prevent illness as well as to restore and maintain health. It is also effective for relieving pain and has been used successfully for anaesthesia, during childbirth, and with smoking, drug addiction and weight problems.

The Council for Acupuncture has been formed as an umbrella society representing the associations listed below and the International Register of Oriental Medicine (UK). One of the main concerns of the Council is the protection of the public regarding hygiene, needle sterilization and codes of practice. They can be contacted at the same address as the Research Council for Complementary Medicine, Suite 1, 19a Cavendish Square, London, W1M 9AD, and their telephone number is (01) 409 1440.

WHO TO CONTACT

The British Acupuncture Association and Register
34 Alderney Street
London, SE1 4EU

All enquiries should include a stamped addressed envelope.

ALTERNATIVE/COMPLEMENTARY MEDICINE AND THERAPIES

Traditional Acupuncture Society
1 The Ridgeway
Stratford upon Avon
Warwickshire, CV37 9JL

Send a stamped addressed envelope for details of local practitioners. A Register of Practitioners costs £1.50.

The Register of Traditional Chinese Medicine
19 Trinity Road
London, N2 8JJ
(0181) 883 8431

Send a stamped addressed envelope for any general enquiries and details of their members.

BACH FLOWER REMEDIES

The Bach flower remedies are made by infusing specific flowers in pure water warmed by sunlight. Practitioners work on the premise that worry, fear, loneliness, exhaustion, impatience and other emotions deplete the body's ability to resist disease. The remedies are chosen according to the emotional state and personality of the individual and are used to restore a harmonious balance in the body.

Remedies and advice on their use are available from:

The Bach Flower Centre
Mount Vernon
Sotwell
Wallingford
Oxon, OX10 0PZ

Please enclose a stamped addressed envelope with all enquiries and note that the centre does not have a list of practitioners.

CHIROPRACTIC

Chiropractic is a manipulative technique which specializes in the diagnosis and treatment of mechanical disorders of the spine and the joints and their effects on the nervous system. Chiropractors may place emphasis on the nervous system in their treatments and use a direct approach, adjusting a particular part of the spine in a particular direction. X-rays and a range of diagnostic techniques are also used. Chiropractors can also help remove spasm and tension and improve nerve and blood flow throughout the body. This can result in the relief of a range of other complaints including headache and menstrual disorders.

ALTERNATIVE/COMPLEMENTARY MEDICINE AND THERAPIES

WHO TO CONTACT

British Chiropractic Association
29 Whitley Street
Reading
Berkshire, RG2 0EG
(01734) 757557

A Register of Members and further information is available; please send a stamped addressed envelope with all enquiries.

McTimoney Chiropractic Association
21 High Street
Eynsham, Oxon OX8 1HE

With enquiries about chiropractic or for a descriptive leaflet, please send a stamped addressed envelope. If you also require a directory of practitioners then send an A5 or larger stamped addressed envelope and a postal order for £1.50.

HERBALISM

Herbalists look beyond a patient's symptoms and evaluate the overall balance of the body's systems to discover disharmonies. Specially selected remedies appropriate to individual circumstances are recommended; therefore two patients apparently suffering from the same complaint may receive two entirely different remedies. Unlike orthodox medicine, herbal practitioners do not use isolated substances from plants as they believe their powerful constituents are balanced making them readily accessible to the body. Herbal remedies provide trace elements, vitamins and medicinal substances. Plant remedies used by herbalists are characterized by low toxicity, few side-effects and absence of withdrawal symptoms. They are also non-addictive.

WHO TO CONTACT

The General Council and Register of Consultant Herbalists
Grosvenor House
40 Seaway
Middleton-on-Sea
Sussex, PO22 7SA

For a list of practitioners please send a stamped addressed envelope and state the enquiry is for a herbalist.

National Institute of Medical Herbalists
56 Longbrooke Street
Exeter, Devon, EX4 6AH

For a list of practitioners please send a stamped addressed envelope addressed to the Hon. Secretary.

ALTERNATIVE/COMPLEMENTARY MEDICINE AND THERAPIES

HOMOEOPATHY

Homoeopathy is based on the principle of 'like cures like' and homoeopaths treat the whole person rather than the disease; considering the personality of the patient as well as the physical symptoms in order to select a remedy. Homoeopathic remedies are derived from mineral, plant and animal sources and are selected on the basis of their similarity to the patient's symptoms. Substances are prescribed in a diluted form which in normal amounts would cause the same symptoms as the patient is exhibiting. A special process called potentisation leaves only the therapeutic properties of the remedies which stimulate the body's natural healing mechanism and initiate the process of healing. Each treatment usually consists of one remedy which is specific to the individual. Homoeopathic remedies do not interfere with the body's natural processes and aid in restoring health as rapidly and gently as possible.

WHO TO CONTACT

British Homeopathic Association
27a Devonshire Street
London, W1N 1RJ
(0171 935 2163)

Please send a stamped addressed envelope with all enquiries.

Society of Homeopaths
2 Artizan Road
Northampton, NN1 4HU
(01604) 21400

Please send a stamped addressed envelope with any enquiries.

NATUROPATHY

The aim of naturopathy is to restore vitality and energy to the body by building up its natural capacity for health. It seeks to promote health by stimulating and supporting the body's inherent power to regain harmony and balance and it does this by creating the most favourable conditions for the healing power of nature. The naturopath focuses on the complete person, rather than on specific symptoms, treating the body, mind and spirit as a whole. Treatment aims at restoring health and balance to the body and educating patients in maintaining their own health. A naturopath may use many different forms of therapy, always taking into account environmental and emotional factors. Treatments include diet and nutrition, herbal remedies, hydrotherapy, manipulation of joints, acupressure or acupuncture, stress control techniques and massage.

ALTERNATIVE/COMPLEMENTARY MEDICINE AND THERAPIES

WHO TO CONTACT
General Council and Register of Naturopaths
Frazer House
6 Netherhall Gardens
London, NW3 5RR

They produce a register of practitioners and you may be able to obtain it at your local library. If not, send £1.00 and a 9½ × 6½ inch (240 × 165mm) envelope, stamped with 20p, for a copy of the Register and two free leaflets.

For other naturopathic associations or schools contact The Institute for Complementary Medicine which is listed under General Information.

OSTEOPATHY AND RELATED THERAPIES
Osteopathy is a manipulative therapy which uses massage, or soft tissue massage techniques and places emphasis on the relationship of blood circulation to healthy tissue. Osteopaths use a system of spinal manipulation including stretching and massage which is intended to re-align structural abnormalities and to correct any interrupted blood or nerve supply within the body. The purpose of osteopathic treatment is to balance the spine and relax any tension found there or in other parts of the body. Cranial osteopathy uses special manipulative techniques to align bones in the skull including the jaw. Treatment aims to restore normal movement to the whole body and because of its ability to improve blood and nerve flow it is not limited to helping solely back or joint problems; many other disorders such as headaches or menstruation difficulties may also respond. Osteopathic manipulation is also often used to help with the lower back problems that can be associated with pregnancy.

WHO TO CONTACT
The Secretary
General Council and Register of Osteopaths
56 London Street
Reading, Berks RG1 4SQ
(01734) 576585

Send a stamped addressed envelope with any enquiries.

ALTERNATIVE/COMPLEMENTARY MEDICINE AND THERAPIES

The London and Counties Society of Physiologists
100 Waterloo Road
Blackpool,
Lancs, FY4 1AW
(01253) 408443

Information on practitioners of remedial massage and manipulative therapy can be obtained by telephoning or writing to the society and including a stamped addressed envelope with all enquiries.

For other osteopathic schools or associations contact The Institute for Complementary Medicine, details of which are listed under General Information in this chapter.

POLARITY THERAPY

Polarity therapy is a blend of western and eastern healing techniques which was developed by Dr Randolph Stone, an American osteopath, chiropractor and naturopath. It is a holistic therapy concerned with balance. Polarity therapists believe that health is based on the balanced and free flow of vital energy and that if it is obstructed, disorders or illness can result. Touch is used both as a therapeutic tool and also to gather information about energy flow. Foods which aid the body cleanse and function at a more vital level are an integral part of the therapy along with a special system of exercises to help stimulate the release of blocked energy. Also, through a system of counselling, emotional balance is sought.

WHO TO CONTACT

Polarity Therapy Association UK
Monomark House
27 Old Gloucester Street
London, WC1N 3XX
(01483) 417714

You can obtain a list of qualified and registered practitioners or more information about polarity therapy by writing to the above address and including a stamped addressed envelope.

REFLEXOLOGY

Reflexology focuses on nerve endings where deposits of uric acid and calcium may form. Reflexologists apply gentle thumb pressure to reflex points on the feet and hands to break up these deposits, thus allowing them to be reabsorbed into the bloodstream and at the same time stimulating the nerve endings. Reflexology can be helpful in a wide range of complaints and is used for relaxing tension and improving blood and nerve supply. As in acupressure and acupuncture, considerable attention is paid to the energy flow of the body and its influence on balance and healing.

WHO TO CONTACT

The British Reflexology Association
Monk's Orchard
Whitbourne
Worcester, WR6 5RB
(01886) 821207

For more information please telephone or write, enclosing a stamped addressed envelope. A register of members of the British Reflexology Association is available.

SPIRITUAL HEALING

Spiritual healing involves touch, or the laying on of hands and/or prayer. A transfer of energy takes place from the healer to the patient which can be healing or calming and patients may experience a cool or hot current through the healer's hands. Spiritual healers may also help the patient in other ways; they may use therapies such as chromotherapy, which is the use of colour for healing, or homoeopathy or dietary changes. The healer takes time to give caring attention and may encourage patients to play their part in the healing by practising relaxation and visualization. Spiritual healing is not confined to any one particular religious persuasion or faith.

WHO TO CONTACT

National Association of Spiritual Healers
Old Manor Farm Studio
Church Street
Sunbury on Thames
Middlesex, TW16 6RG
(019327) 83164

ALTERNATIVE MEDICINES

ALTERNATIVE/COMPLEMENTARY MEDICINE AND THERAPIES

Please send a stamped addressed envelope for general enquiries or for explanatory leaflets.

T'AI-CHI CH'UAN

T'ai-chi ch'uan is a Chinese method for becoming one with nature. There are thirteen basic self defence postures which are used to unlearn bad habits of the body, mind and spirit which can cause disharmony. It emphasizes the relationship of mind and body and the importance of the natural and unimposed flow of energy. T'ai-chi is excellent even for those who usually cannot take part in exercise as its gentle movements can help with tension, weak muscles and circulation.

WHO TO CONTACT

The International Taoist Society
426 Charter Avenue
Canley
Coventry, CV4 8BD

Please send a stamped addressed envelope with any enquiries.

YOGA AND RELAXATION

Yoga is a holistic system of development integrating mind, body and spirit. It includes postures, breathing, diet, exercise, relaxation and meditation. Energy is consciously directed towards sustaining health and vigour and the postures can have beneficial effects upon the body's function. The ultimate goal is to attain self-realization where individual consciousness evolves.

WHO TO CONTACT

British Wheel of Yoga
1 Hamilton Place
Boston Road
Sleaford, Lincs NG34 7ES

Please write, enclosing a stamped addressed envelope, for more information or for a list of local teachers.

The Yoga for Health Foundation
Icwell Bury
Northill
Near Biggleswade
Beds, SG18 9ES
(01767) 627271

For more information or details of the Ickwell Bury Centre and the courses available, please telephone or write enclosing a stamped addressed envelope. Information on a worldwide network of Yoga for Health Clubs is also available.

For information about relaxation contact:

Relaxation for Living
29 Burwood Park Road
Walton-on-Thames
Surrey, KT12 5LH

This registered charity organizes small group relaxation classes throughout the country, and correspondence courses for those out of reach of a teacher. They also publish and distribute self-help leaflets and cassettes. Please send a large stamped addressed envelope for more information.

INFORMATION ON PRACTITIONERS

The associations listed in this section can help you locate other practitioners and their associations which are not listed in this book. If you need advice and information about practitioners in your area it is best to contact their recognized colleges or associations.

Institute for Complementary Medicine
PO Box 194
London SE16 1QZ
(0171) 2375165

They can give information on practitioners and complementary medicine on a national or local level as well as details of special courses for medical students, nurses, and other groups. There is also a clinic which has a team of highly trained complementary practitioners and a medical doctor. Please send a stamped addressed envelope with all enquiries.

Alternative Action
Carlton House
11 Marlborough Place
Brighton
East Sussex, BN1 1UB

They have details of qualified practitioners in the Sussex area and information on natural medicine generally, as well as producing a bi-yearly Natural Medicine Directory. Please send a stamped addressed envelope with any enquiries.

The Health Information Centre
Green House
Bangor, Gwynedd
LL57 1AX

ALTERNATIVE/COMPLEMENTARY MEDICINE AND THERAPIES

For information about practitioners' names and addresses, natural healing, women's health, and facilities and activities at the Health Information Centre, please send a stamped addressed envelope.

HEALTH CARE AND OTHER ASPECTS OF NATURAL MEDICINE

Marylebone Health Centre
17 Marylebone Road
London, W1
(0171) 935 6328

The Centre has an educational unit which holds programmes and lectures on health and self-care.

Council for Complementary and Alternative Medicine
Suite 1
19a Cavendish Square
London, W1M 9AD
(0171) 724 9103

The Council provides a forum for communication and co-operation between professional bodies representing acupuncture, chiropractic, homoeopathy, medical herbalism, naturopathy and osteopathy.

Research Council for Complementary Medicine
Suite 1
19a Cavendish Square
London, W1M 9AD

An independent charitable organization sponsoring and publishing research into complementary medicine. Please send a stamped addressed envelope with any correspondence.

British Holistic Medical Association
179 Gloucester Place
London, NW1 6DX
(01743) 261155

The BHMA do not have details of alternative/complementary practitioners, but will provide information on self-care, and organize seminars, conferences, and workshops in this field. Information leaflets are available for a small charge. Please send a stamped, addressed envelope with any enquiries.

College of Health
14 Buckingham Street
London, WC2N 6DS
(0171) 839 2413

ALTERNATIVE/COMPLEMENTARY MEDICINE AND THERAPIES

Information is available about self-care and self-help, keeping healthy and using the National Health Service effectively. The College can also give details of voluntary organizations, and they publish a guide to alternative medicine, price given on request. Please send a stamped addressed envelope with any enquiries.

The Patients Association
Room 33
18 Charing Cross Road
London, WC2H 0HR
(0171) 240 0671

This association promotes and protects the interests of patients generally and gives advice or information on handling health problems. Information leaflets and a quarterly bulletin *Patient Voice* are also available. A directory of national organizations concerned with various diseases and handicaps called *Self Help and the Patient* is also available, price given on request. Please send a stamped addressed envelope with all enquiries.

Community Health Foundation
The East West Centre
188–194 Old Street
London, EC1V 9BP
(0171) 251 4076

The foundation has a programme of regular activities such as yoga, meditation, shiatsu, macrobiotic cookery, healthy eating, t'ai-chi, Alexander technique and many others. If you write for details of courses, please send a stamped addressed envelope.

The Natural Medicines Society
Information Office
95 Hagley Road
Edgbaston
Birmingham, B16 8LA

A public society formed to work for freedom of choice in medicines. If you contact them for information and membership details then please enclose a stamped addressed envelope.

THE FACT FINDER FOR MEDICAL AND ALTERNATIVE/COMPLEMENTARY TERMS

A

ABSORPTION   The process by which nutrients are passed into the blood stream via the intestines.

ACID FOODS   Those foods which produce acid when broken down in the body. The kidneys excrete these acids via the urine and an excessively acidic diet and some drugs may cause its acidification. Acid forming foods include breads, cereals, cheese (including cottage cheese), chocolate, cocoa, corn, cranberries, eggs, fish, flour and grain products, lentils, meats, nuts (including brazils, hazelnuts and walnuts), oats, pasta, peanuts, peanut butter, pearl barley, plums, prunes, sugar, wheatgerm, tea, coffee, most meats, fowl, rye bread, wholemeal bread. Prunes, prune juice and citrus fruits and juices contain acids but do not produce acid when broken down in the body.

ACUTE   Brief and relatively severe.

ADDISON'S DISEASE   The inadequate secretion of corticosteroid hormones by adrenal glands. It is characterized by loss of energy, weakness, low blood pressure and dark pigmentation of the skin.

ADRENAL GLAND   Triangular shaped gland next to each kidney which produces cortisone and epinephrine (adrenalin).

ALEXANDER TECHNIQUE   Aims to overcome patterns of bodily misuse that interfere with poise and free movements by learning how to stand and move so that an appropriate relationship exists between the neck, head and back.

ALKALINE FOODS   Foods broken down by the body into alkali. The kidneys excrete alkali via the urine and an excessively alkaline diet and some drugs can cause its alkalinity. If urine becomes too alkaline then the excretion of certain drugs may be slowed, leading to a possible increase in side-effects and a build-up of the drug in the body. Alkaline forming foods include almonds, beet greens, buttermilk, chestnuts, coconuts, cream, fruit except for cranberries, fresh plums and prunes, milk, molasses, soya flour, vegetables except corn, yeast, yogurt, herb teas, fresh tomatoes, potatoes, lettuce and watercress.

ALLERGY   A reaction by body tissues to a specific substance.

ALUMINIUM   Found in aluminium hydroxide antacids, deodorants, baking powder, aluminium cookware and foil, plant fertilizers, animal foods. Signs of aluminium toxicity are constipation, colic, loss of appetite, nausea, loss of energy, skin ailments, twitching leg muscles.

AMINO ACIDS   Organic compounds commonly known as the 'building blocks' of protein.

AMNESIA   Memory loss.

AMPHETAMINES   Stimulants which were used for slimming because of their appetite suppressant qualities, but not now, due to their addictive potential. In some cases they are used to prevent constant sleepiness in elderly people.

ANAEMIA   A reduction in the normal number of red blood cells or too little haemoglobin in the red blood cells.

ANAEMIA, HAEMOLYTIC   Anaemia caused by shortened life-span of red blood cells. The body is unable to manufacture new cells fast enough to replace old cells.

ANAEMIA, IRON DEFICIENCY   Anaemia caused when the iron necessary to manufacture red blood cells is not available.

ANAEMIA, PERNICIOUS   Anaemia caused by vitamin B12 deficiency.

ANALGESIC   Medicine used to relieve pain without reducing consciousness.

ANAPHYLAXIS OR ANAPHYLACTIC SHOCK   Severe allergic reactions, resulting from introduction of a substance to which an individual is, or has become, sensitive. Symptoms include wheezing, itching, rash, nasal congestion, intense burning of hands and feet, collapse, loss of consciousness and cardiac arrest. Symptoms appear within a few seconds or minutes after exposure. Death may occur if emergency treatment is not given.

ANEURYSM   Balloon-like swelling in the wall of a blood vessel which may be due to weakness of the blood vessel wall or disease or may have been present since birth.

ANGINA PECTORIS   Severe attacks of pain around the heart, caused by insufficient supply of blood to the heart.

ANGIONEUROTIC OEDEMA   Allergic condition producing transient or persistent swelling of areas of skin accompanied by itching which may possibly be severe. Caused by allergy to food substances, drugs or other allergens. May be precipitated by heat, cold or emotional factors. See also Urticaria.

ANGITIS   Inflammation of a blood or lymph vessel.

ANKYLOSING SPONDYLITIS   Inflammation of the backbone and sacroiliac joints which are in the lower back. It may sometimes appear in the shoulder and hip and in severe cases the spine may become rigid.

ANOREXIA   Severe and prolonged loss of appetite or refusal to eat which occurs mainly in young women. It can also occur in older women and men but is less usual.

ANTAGONIST   Something which works against something else.

ANTHELMINTIC   Drug(s) used in the treatment of parasitic intestinal worms.

ANTI-EMETIC   Medicine(s) used to prevent vomiting.

ANTIOXIDANTS   Substance(s) capable of uniting with oxygen to protect other substances from being destroyed or modified by exposure to oxygen. Nutrients such as vitamins A, E, C and bioflavonoids, zinc, selenium, and amino acids such as cysteine and methionine which contain sulphur can help control or suppress the rate of oxidation. See also Free Radicals.

ANTIPLATELET MEDICINES   Used to prevent blood from clotting internally.

APPENDICITIS   An inflammation of the appendix. The symptoms are abdominal pain which can be severe, nausea, vomiting, fever, increased pulse rate rising with the fever and tenderness in the lower right side of the abdomen.

AROMATHERAPY   The use of essential oils from herbs, flowers, trees and resins to treat the skin, cause stimulation or relaxation, prevent infection or maintain bodily resistance to disease.

ARRHYTHMIA   Irregular heart beat.

ARTERIOSCLEROSIS   Loss of elasticity in the artery walls due to thickening or hardening.

ARTERY   Blood vessel carrying blood away from the heart.

ARTHRITIS   Inflammation of a joint, usually accompanied by pain and swelling.

ASTHMA   Recurrent attacks of breathing difficulties caused by a decrease in the diameter of the air passages. This decrease is the result of spasm of the bronchial tubes or swelling of their mucous membranes.

ATHEROSCLEROSIS A form of arteriosclerosis which may be caused by the accumulation of fats, lipids, calcium deposits, carbohydrates, blood, and blood products on artery walls.

B

BENZODIAZEPINES Used principally to treat anxiety.

BIOFEEDBACK A procedure which allows individuals to become aware of their mental and physical reactions so that they can learn how to control them. Biofeedback machines are connected to the skin and monitor changes in electrical activity which reflect increases in muscle tension. These changes are registered electronically by lights, sounds or a meter, allowing subjects to respond to processes occurring in their bodies.

BLOOD COUNT Laboratory studies to count white and red blood cells, platelets and other elements of the blood.

BLOOD PRESSURE, DIASTOLIC Blood pressure recorded when the heart muscle is relaxed and the heart is resting and refilling. This gives the lower reading when blood pressure is taken.

BLOOD PRESSURE, SYSTOLIC Blood pressure recorded when the heart muscle contracts and ejects blood, producing the maximum pressure in the larger arteries. This gives the higher reading when blood pressure is taken.

BLOOD SUGAR Formed during digestion, from starches, and absorbed from the intestines into the blood in the form of glucose, the simplest form of sugar.

BLOOD SUGAR DISORDERS See Hypoglycaemia, Hyperglycaemia, and Diabetes.

BREAKTHROUGH BLEEDING Spotting of blood in-between menstrual periods.

BROMELAIN An enzyme found in pineapple which digests protein. Like niacin, evening primrose oil, borage oil and blackcurrant seed extract it can stimulate the production of prostaglandin E1.

THE FACT FINDER FOR MEDICAL AND ALTERNATIVE/COMPLEMENTARY TERMS

BRUXISM   Grinding of the teeth.

BURSITIS   Inflammation of the bursa especially in the shoulder and knee. Some common forms include tennis elbow, housemaid's knee, bunions and painful shoulder.

C

CAFFEINE   An alkaloid drug which dilates or opens up the blood vessels, stimulates the heart, increases the flow of urine, and may interfere with sleep. Caffeine can be found in the following: coffee, ordinary tea, chocolate, guarana, colas, maté and yerba santé tea, some cold remedies and medicines.

CANDIDA ALBICANS   A yeast-like fungus which is commonly part of the normal flora of the mouth, skin, intestinal tract, and vagina. Formerly called monilla albicans.

CAPILLARY   An extremely narrow blood vessel, one of many which connect the arteries and veins.

CARBOHYDRATES   Starches and sugars found mostly in vegetables, fruits and grains which provide most of the body's energy requirements.

CARCINOGEN   A cancer causing substance.

CARDIAC GLYCOSIDES   Digitalis and derivatives used to treat heart failure.

CARDIOVASCULAR   Referring to the heart and blood vessels.

CATARACT   Clouding of the lens of the eye resulting in blurred vision.

CHELATION   Chelation refers to the surrounding of a mineral atom by a chelating agent, an amino acid. This process changes an inorganic mineral into an organic one and makes its passage through the intestinal walls easier so that the mineral is more readily absorbed into the blood stream and cells.

CHOLESTEROL   A fat-like substance which is found in all animal fats, bile, skin, blood, liver, kidneys, adrenal glands, spinal cord and brain tissue. It is also the principal constituent of most gall stones. It is synthesized in the liver and occurs in a number of foods and oils. It is a precursor of various sex hormones.

CHROMATOTHERAPY   See Colour Therapy.

CHRONIC   A long drawn-out disease.

CIRRHOSIS   Chronic liver disease characterized by scarred and destroyed liver tissue.

CNS   The abbreviation for central nervous system, which consists of the brain and spinal cord.

CO-ENZYME A   An important precursor in the manufacture of fatty acids.

CO-ENZYME Q   A substance which helps to transfer oxygen in the respiratory cycle and is present in all cells of the body. It is also known as ubiquinone.

COLITIS   Inflammation of the colon.

COLOUR THERAPY   Also known as Chromatotherapy, it is a technique for restoring imbalances by means of applying coloured light to the body. It may also focus on the influence of different coloured food, liquid, environment or clothing.

COMA   An abnormal deep stupor or unconsciousness often caused by injury or disease.

CONGENITAL   Decribes a condition that is recognized at birth or that is believed to have been present since birth.

CONVULSIONS   Violent, uncontrollable contractions of the voluntary muscles.

CORTICOSTEROIDS   Cortisone medicines used to treat severe attacks of asthma, skin complaints, inflammation and allergy.

COUMARIN   An anticoagulant found in sweet clover which is the basis for coumarin derivative anticoagulant drugs.

CROHN'S DISEASE   A condition in which segments of the alimentary tract become inflamed, thickened and ulcerated. Symptoms include pain, diarrhoea, malabsorption and fistulae — these are abnormal openings or passages.

CYSTITIS   Inflammation of the bladder.

THE FACT FINDER FOR MEDICAL AND ALTERNATIVE/COMPLEMENTARY TERMS

D

DERMATITIS Inflammation of the skin which may also be described as eczema.

DHA The abbreviation of docosahexaenoic acid. See EPA/DHA.

DIABETES Metabolic disorder in which the body does not use carbohydrates efficiently, leading to a dangerously high level of glucose in the blood.

DIASTOLIC PRESSURE See Blood Pressure.

DILATION Enlarge, widen or expand.

DIURETIC Increases the flow of urine from the body.

DNA The abbreviation of deoxyribonucleic acid which is present in chromosomes found in the nuclei of cells. It is the chemical basis of heredity and carrier of genetic information.

DOPAMINE FOODS AND BEVERAGES See Tyramine.

DOSAGE The amount of medicine to be taken at one time.

DUBIN JOHNSON SYNDROME A disorder similar to jaundice which is due to an inherited defect in bile metabolism.

DUODENUM The first 12 inches (30cm) of the small intestine.

DYSPEPSIA Indigestion accompanied by discomfort in the lower chest or abdomen.

E

ECZEMA Inflammation of the skin causing itching with a red rash, often accompanied by small weeping blisters.

EDEMA Fluid retention in the body which causes swelling.

ENDOCRINE GLANDS Ductless glands which secrete substances that are carried in the bloodstream or lymph and include the pituitary, thymus, pineal, thyroid, parathyroid, and adrenal glands, as well as the pancreas, ovaries, and testes.

EMBOLISM Obstruction of a blood vessel by a blood clot or foreign substance.

EMBOLUS A mass of undissolved matter present in a blood or lymph vessel, brought there by the blood or lymph flow.

ENTERIC COATED A tablet which is coated so that it dissolves in the intestine, not in the stomach.

ENTERITIS Inflammation of the intestines, particularly the small intestine. See Crohn's disease.

EPA/DHA Abbreviations of eicosapentaenoic and docosahexaenoic acids which are derived from fish liver oil. They may be used in supplement form for the prevention or treatment of cardiovascular diseases.

ERYTHEMA MULTIFORME Different shaped dark red spots usually on the extremeties with successive eruptions of short duration without pain or itching.

F

FAECES Waste material from the body which is made up of mucus, bacteria, food waste, and epithelium which is discharged via the anus.

FASTING Abstention from food, but not water, for a period of time. Fasting is used for resting the digestive system, encouraging the body to fight disease or discharge waste material and as an aid to meditation and mental and spiritual growth. It should not be practised except under the guidance of a qualified practitioner.

FATTY ACIDS See Linoleic Acid and GLA.

FIBRIN Protein formed by the action of thrombin and fibrogen which is the basis for blood clotting.

FREE RADICALS Unstable atoms or compounds which can react detrimentally with other compounds. A certain number of them are needed for normal metabolism but they can increase when oxidation takes place unchecked. There are two substances made by the body to control free radicals: superoxide dismutase and glutathione. Nutrients which control oxidation appear under anti-oxidants. Free radicals are associated with damage to cells and may also damage DNA and RNA. They can contribute to premature ageing by damaging the skin's collagen and cells and can lead to blood clots and cardiovascular disease by damaging arteries and depressing a hormone which regulates blood clotting.

G

GALL STONES   Hard mass composed of bile pigments, cholesterol, and calcium salts which can form in the gall bladder.

GAMMA LINOLENIC ACID   Also known as GLA, it is produced in the body by the conversion of linoleic acids and is one of the first steps in the production of prostaglandins which are important to many body functions. The conversion to GLA and the production of prostaglandins can be decreased or hindered by a diet high in saturated fats and processed foods, also by alcohol, stress, ageing and some disease conditions. Factors which help in the conversion are magnesium, zinc, selenium and vitamins B6, B3 and C. The use of evening primrose, blackcurrant seed and borage oils is a way of short-cutting the conversion process as they already contain GLA and a high percentage of cis-linoleic acid which is converted to prostaglandin E1. See also prostaglandins.

GASTRO-INTESTINAL   Referring to the stomach and intestines.

GENERIC NAME   Non-specific or general name. In the Fact Sheets it refers to the main pharmaceutical ingredient of the drugs in a particular group.

GLA   See Gamma Linolenic Acid.

GLAUCOMA   Eye disease caused by increased fluid pressure within the eyeball. Loss of vision can occur if it is left untreated.

GLUTATHIONE PEROXIDASE   Present in animal tissues and important in cell respiration.

GOITRE   An enlargement of the thyroid gland, causing a swelling in the neck.

GOITROGENS Substances which in very large quantities may prevent the thyroid gland from producing thyroid hormones, causing goitre or enlargement of the thyroid gland. Foods which contain goitrogens include brussels sprouts, cabbage, carrots, tapioca, kale, mustard and rape seed, peaches, turnips, soya beans and spinach. Kelp is also a source of goitrogens, but it contains a good supply of iodine as well which offsets its goitrogenic action. Cooking is thought to destroy a percentage of the goitrogens in food.

GOUT A malfunction in the metabolism of uric acid, causing inflammation of joints particularly in the knee or foot.

GUARANA Dried paste prepared from the seeds of paullinia cupana, a tree native to Brazil. It can be found in some slimming regimes or as a food supplement and has a high caffeine content. .

GYNAECOLOGY The study of diseases relating to women.

H

HALF-LIFE The time taken for half the amount of a drug to be metabolized or disappear from the blood stream. An important consideration used for determining the amount and frequency of drug dosage.

HDL The abbreviation for high density lipoprotein, a useful blood fat which is thought to carry cholesterol through the bloodstream to where it can be harmlessly eliminated.

HEAVY METALS Term for toxic metals such as cadmium, lead and mercury.

HEPATIC Referring to the liver.

HEPATITIS Inflammation of the liver.

HORMONE A substance which is secreted from an organ or gland into the bloodstream. From there it is carried to another part of the body in order to stimulate or increase function, or to increase secretion of another hormone.

HYDROGENATED FAT See Hydrogenation.

HYDROGENATION A process whereby oil is exposed to hydrogen, in the presence of a catalyst, to produce a solid fat. Margarines, hydrogenated and partially hydrogenated oils have been exposed to this process. Margarines and vegetable oils, theoretically high in polyunsaturated fats, become highly saturated when hydrogenated.

HYPERGLYCAEMIA   High blood sugar, or an increase of blood sugar, as in diabetes.

HYPEROXALURIA   High amounts of oxalic acid present in the urine.

HYPERTENSION   High blood pressure.

HYPERTHERMIA   Unusually high fever.

HYPOGLYCAEMIA   Low blood sugar, or a deficiency of sugar in the blood.

HYPOTENSION   Low blood pressure.

HYPOTHERMIA   Below normal body temperature.

I

IDIOPATHIC   Used to describe a condition whose causes are not yet known.

IMPACTION   The accumulation of hardened body waste in the rectum.

INSOMNIA   Inability to sleep.

J

JAUNDICE   Increase in bile pigment in the blood, causing yellowing of the skin, and eyes. Can be caused by disease of the liver, gall bladder, bile system or blood.

K

KIDNEY STONES   Small stones formed from calcium, cholesterol and other body chemicals.

KIRLIAN PHOTOGRAPHY
A method of photographing what appears to be an energy, or electrical force emanating from parts of the body, especially the hands and feet. Researchers are testing possible links between health patterns and the photographic images and much research has been done in Russia where the technique originated. Kirlian patterns have also been suggested as linking with acupuncture energy pathways called meridians.

KWASHIORKOR
A severe protein deficiency in children which can occur after the child has been weaned.

L

LDL, LOW DENSITY LIPOPROTEIN
Consists of proteins combined with cholesterol, phospholipids and triglycerides. It is thought that individuals with high levels of LDL may be more predisposed to coronary heart disease. See also HDL.

LEGUMES
Plants which have edible seeds within a pod, including peas, beans, lentils, and peanuts.

LINOLEIC ACID
Linoleic and linolenic acids are essential fatty acids from vegetable sources and vegetable and nut oils. They are prostaglandin precursors.

LIPIDS
Fatty substances which are not soluble in body fluids or water. Triglycerides and cholesterol are examples of lipids.

LUPUS ERYTHEMATOSUS
A serious disorder of connective tissue, primarily affecting women. It varies in severity with symptoms including skin eruptions, joint inflammation, low white-blood cell count and damage to organs especially the kidneys.

LYMPH GLANDS
Glands in the lymph vessels of the body that trap foreign and infectious matter and protect the blood stream from infection.

M

MACROBIOTICS
The use of specific foods to balance the body. Practitioners believe that illness arises when there is an excess of either yin or yang foods in the diet and work towards balance. Yin foods

are those grown above the ground, like fruit, and are considered feminine; yang foods are grown below the ground, like root vegetables, and are considered masculine. They also consider the dominant aspects of foods which have both qualities and believe that food should be consumed only during the season of its growth. Processed foods, milk products, eggs, meats, refined flour and sugar are avoided.

MALABSORPTION   A decrease in the absorption of nutrients mainly from the small intestines. This condition may result from surgery, infections, and some diseases.

MAOI'S   Abbreviation for monoamine oxidase inhibitor drugs used for severe depression. They are not commonly used because of their dangerous interactions with other drugs and tyramine containing foods, and the high incidence of side-effects. See also Tyramine and Dopamine Foods and Beverages.

MENOPAUSE   The age at which menstruation ceases to occur.

MENIERE'S SYNDROME   Recurrent and usually progressive group of symptoms including deafness, ringing in the ears, dizziness and sensations of fullness or pressure in the ears.

METABOLISM   All physical and chemical changes that take place within an organism to produce energy and assimilate new material for repair and replacement of tissues.

MIGRAINE   Recurring headaches which may be caused by constriction of the arteries to the head. Symptoms include severe pain, vision disturbances, nausea, vomiting and light sensitivity.

MUCOSA   Membrane lining passages and cavities communicating with the air such as the nasal passages or digestive tract.

MYASTHENIA GRAVIS   Progressive muscle disease usually confined to the face, lips, tongue and neck.

MYOCARDIAL INFARCTION   Heart attack.

N

NARCOTIC   A drug that in moderate doses relieves pain and produces sleep.

THE FACT FINDER FOR MEDICAL AND ALTERNATIVE/COMPLEMENTARY TERMS

In excessive doses it is usually addictive and may produce unconsciousness, stupor, coma and possibly death.

NAUSEA A feeling of sickness in the stomach, with the urge to vomit.

NEPHRO Referring to the kidney.

NSAI Abbreviation for non steroidal anti-inflammatories which includes drugs such as aspirin.

NUCLEIC ACIDS Formed in the body from phosphoric acid, sugar, and nitrogen bases and includes RNA and DNA.

O

ORGAN MEATS Liver, heart, sweetbread and kidneys.

OROTATES Minerals combined with orotic acid found mainly in milk whey, also in yams, sweet potatoes and some other root vegetables. Orotic acid helps transport minerals across cell membranes and therefore enhances the body's ability to utilize them. Studies show that 6-10 times more of the orotate mineral will be absorbed than from other mineral sources, which is why the elemental potencies look low on orotate supplement labels. Calcium orotate which supplies 50mg of elemental calcium is equal to 300-500mg of calcium from other sources.

OSMOTIC PRESSURE The force or pressure exerted by a dissolved substance against a membrane which only allows certain sized particles to pass through it.

OSTEOARTHRITIS Joint cartilage disease associated with secondary changes in the underlying bone; ultimately causing pain and impairing the function of the affected joint.

OSTEOPOROSIS Bone softening caused by a loss of minerals, especially calcium which is not replaced by normal reabsorption. Bones such as the spinal vertebrae and thigh bone become brittle and liable to fracture. Factors which can contribute to this condition are prolonged low dietary calcium intake, long-term use of corticosteroid and other drugs, immobility, menopausal hormonal changes and increased urinary loss of calcium due to high protein diets.

THE FACT FINDER FOR MEDICAL AND ALTERNATIVE/COMPLEMENTARY TERMS

OXALIC ACID FOODS   Those which contain a significant amount of oxalic acid such as rhubarb, spinach, beetroot leaves, cranberry, swiss chard, and gooseberries.

OXIDATION   The chemical process by which a substance combines with oxygen. See also antioxidants.

P

PALPITATIONS   Rapid heartbeat.

PAPAIN   A proteolytic enzyme resembling pepsin which is found in the tropical melon papaya. Like bromelain, which is found in pineapple, it digests protein and protein based substances. Chymo-papain is sometimes used in medicine to help dissolve herniated spinal discs which are causing nerve compression. Papaya also contains an enzyme called carpain, thought to be like digitalis, which is believed to affect heart function.

PAPAYA   See Papain.

PARKINSON'S DISEASE   A disease of the central nervous system characterised by rigidity, tremor, loss of spontaneous movements, slower muscle movements, weakness and changed gait.

PEPTIC   Referring to the digestive tract.

pH   The measurement of acidity or alkalinity of a solution which uses a scale of 0-14. 0-7 is acidic, 7 is neutral, and over 7 is alkaline.

PHLEBITIS   Inflammation, pain and tenderness in a vein.

PHLEGM   Thick mucus secreted by glands in the respiratory tract.

PHOSPHORUS   A mineral, high sources of which are found in colas and other carbonated soft drinks, soya flour, high protein foods, yeast, milk and cheese.

PHOTOPHOBIA   An abnormal intolerance of light.

PHYTIC ACID   Phytic acid may bind with minerals making them insoluble and therefore unabsorbable. It is destroyed by the enzyme phytase which is found in many fermented grain and bean foods, especially miso and sour-dough bread, and by the leavening process where breads are made to rise with yeast. Phytic acid is found mainly in grains, unleavened bread such as matzo, and in some vegetables, nuts and legumes.

PICA   A craving for soil, dirt or other substances not generally fit to eat which may be associated with mineral deficiency. May occur in pregnancy or certain psychotic conditions.

PLATELET   Disc shaped element of the blood, necessary for clotting.

POLYP   A growth, usually non-cancerous, found on a mucous membrane.

POLYUNSATURATED FATS   See Unsaturated Fats.

PRECURSOR   A substance or substances that can precede another substance. A precursor can be used in the manufacture of another substance by the body, as in carotene, which is the precursor of vitamin A.

PROCTITIS   Inflammation of the rectum or anus.

PROGESTERONE   A steroid sex hormone secreted by the body.

PROGESTOGEN   A natural or synthetic hormonal substance that produces effects similar to those of progesterone.

PROPHYLAXIS   Prevention.

PROSTAGLANDINS   Hormone-like substances derived from fatty acids which help to stimulate the movement of smooth muscle in the body. Prostaglandins affect the heart rate and blood pressure and can encourage uterine contractions. Prostaglandin E1 is anti-inflammatory and has a beneficial effect on the cardiovascular system. It can also be helpful for pre-menstrual syndrome.

PROSTRATION   Absolute exhaustion.

PROTHROMBIN   A substance found in the blood which is essential in clotting.

PRURITIS   Itching which may be severe.

PSORIASIS   Chronic skin disease which can be a hereditary condition. It is characterized by itchy, scaly red patches of skin on many parts of the body.

R

RAYNAUD'S DISEASE Symptoms are cold hands and feet, pallor, numbness and discomfort in the fingers and toes. When the hands are cold the fingers go into spasm.

RAYNAUD'S PHENOMENON Similar to Raynaud's disease and may result from atherosclerosis, collagen diseases, ingestion of ergotamine drugs or the use of vibrating machinery such as road drills. Gangrene or ulceration may result from lack of circulation to the affected area.

REBOUND EFFECT The return of a condition, often with increased severity, following the withdrawal of a drug.

REFINED CARBOHYDRATES Those foods which have been put through the process of refining which may remove or destroy a number of nutrients. Some of these are white flour and its products such as breads, cakes, crackers, biscuits and some breakfast cereals and refined oils.

RENAL Referring to the kidney.

REYE'S SYNDROME A rare disease which is sometimes fatal and causes brain and liver damage in children. If a child infected with chickenpox or influenza is given aspirin or drugs containing it, or benorylate which is broken down into aspirin, then the risk of contracting Reye's syndrome is greatly increased.

RHINITIS Inflammation of the mucous membrane in the nose.

RNA Abbreviation for ribonucleic acid which transfers genetic information from DNA to the site of protein synthesis in the cells.

S

SALICYLATE FOODS Foods containing natural salicylates include almonds, apples, apricots, blackberries, cherries, cloves, cucumber, currants, gooseberries, grapes, raisins, mint, nectarines, oranges, peaches, plums, prunes, raspberries, strawberries, tomatoes, wines and wine products. Natural salicylates are also found in wintergreen, willow and meadowsweet.

SATURATED FATS Fat molecules which are filled with hydrogen. They can raise the level of cholesterol in the blood stream and some of the highest amounts are found in fats which are solid at room temperature such as butter, margarine, suet, lard and dripping. Saturated fats may also be found in cream, cheese, whole milk, fatty meats, and meat products, biscuits, cakes, pastries, chocolate. Fish, poultry, eggs and skimmed milk contain smaller amounts. See also Hydrogenation.

SEIZURE Brain disorder causing convulsions or changes of consciousness.

SINUSITIS Inflammation or infection of the sinus cavities of the skull.

SPIRULINA Plant plankton rich in vitamins, minerals, amino acids, fatty acids, proteins, and especially high in B12.

SPRUE A disease characterized by weakness, loss of weight, increased secretion by sebaceous glands, and digestive disorders. These can include impaired absorption of fats, vitamins and glucose and also fat appearing in the faeces.

STEVENS-JOHNSON SYNDROME See Erythema multiforme.

STOMATITIS Inflammation of the mucous membrane of the mouth.

STOOL See faeces.

STROKE Sudden paralysis as a result of an interruption to the flow of blood to the brain by a clot or by rupture of an artery wall.

STUPOR Almost in an unconscious state.

SUBLINGUAL Under the tongue.

SYMPATHOMIMETICS The action of these drugs mimics some of the effects of the naturally occurring body chemicals adrenaline and noradrenaline. Because of their action they may be used as nasal decongestants and bronchodilators.

SYMPTOMATIC RELIEF Short term relief of symptoms.

SYNTHESIS A process of building up or producing a more complex substance such as the synthesis of proteins from amino acids.

SYSTEMIC Referring to the whole body.

SYSTOLIC PRESSURE See Blood Pressure.

T

TANNIN An acid substance found in tea and coffee, and in smaller amounts in most herb teas, especially if they are steeped for more than 3 minutes. It is astringent and can be constipating.

TENDONITIS Inflammation of a tendon.

THIAZIDE DIURETICS Promote the excretion of water by the kidneys, prevent sodium and chloride reabsorption and promote potassium and magnesium excretion.

THROMBOEMBOLISM The blocking of a blood vessel by a thrombus that has become detached from where it was originally formed.

THROMBOPHLEBITIS The inflammation of a vein caused by the presence of a blood clot in it.

THROMBOSIS The formation, development or existence of a blood clot in the blood vessels.

THROMBUS A blood clot which obstructs a blood vessel or cavity.

THRUSH A yeast infection caused by candida albicans. Areas affected can be the mouth, throat and vagina.

THYROID A gland in the neck which manufactures and secretes several important hormones involved in metabolism.

TINNITUS Ringing or buzzing in the ears.

TOCOPHEROL Vitamin E is made up from seven compounds called tocopherols: alpha — which is the most active, beta, delta, gamma, epsilon, zeta and eta.

TOXICITY Refers to the point at which a substance becomes poisonous.

TRACE ELEMENTS There are 12 which are believed to be essential for animal life: chromium, cobalt, copper, fluorine, iodines, manganese, molybdenum, nickel, selenium, silicon, tin, and vanadium.

TRIGLYCERIDES Fats and lipids produced in the liver from carbohydrates. In excess, in the bloodstream, they can contribute to atherosclerosis.

TYRAMINE AND DOPAMINE FOODS AND BEVERAGES These include alcohol (especially beer, sherry and wines), aubergines, avocados, bananas, broad beans, chocolate, coffee, cola, liver, most cheeses, pickled herring, pineapple, plums, raisins, salami, sauerkraut, sour cream, soy sauce and other fermented soya bean products including tamari, shoyu and miso, yeast and extracts, yogurt.

U

ULCER Sore or lesion on the skin surface or internal mucous membranes.

ULCER, PEPTIC A break in the lining of the digestive tract produced by the digestion of the mucosa by pepsin and acid.

UNSATURATED FATS Those fats which are liquid at room temperature. They include a group known as polyunsaturated fats which have a slightly different chemical composition. Polyunsaturated fats are found in vegetable oils, from seeds and nuts such as sunflower, safflower and sesame. They are also found in fatty fish such as pilchards, herring, sardines and mackerel which also contain EPA/DHA, used to help decrease the risk of heart disease. Other sources include whole grains, cereals, wheatgerm, fresh green leafy vegetables and some other fresh vegetables. See also EPA/DHA. Mono unsaturated fats are found in olive oil and do not contribute to heart disease.

URETHRA Hollow tube through which urine and semen are passed.

URINARY TRACT Organs and ducts which secrete and eliminate urine. The urinary system consists of the kidneys, ureters, urinary bladder and urethra.

UTERUS A muscular organ, also known as the womb. It is a pear shaped hollow in which the foetus is contained during pregnancy.

V

VASCULAR Referring to the blood vessels.

VASODILATION — An increase in the diameter of the blood vessels due to a relaxation of their muscular coating. The dilation of the blood vessels allows an increase of blood flow within them.

VERTIGO — Sensations of dizziness and spinning, it may seem as if everything around, including yourself, is in constant movement.

VISUAL PURPLE — A protein also known as rhodopsin which is found in rods inside the retina of the eye. It becomes bleached in the presence of light and is restored by the lack of light.

W

WHITE BLOOD CELLS — Help to defend the body against disease and do not contain haemoglobin.

WILSON'S DISEASE — Defect in copper metabolism, present from birth. The result may be deposits in the liver which cause jaundice or cirrhosis, or in the brain which can cause mental retardation.

X

XANTHOPSIA — A vision disorder where objects are seen with yellow haloes around them.

XEROSIS — A condition of dryness of the skin or mucous membranes.

Z

ZOLLINGER-ELLISON SYNDROME — A peptic or duodenal ulcer caused by over-production of acid in the stomach.

INDEX OF DRUGS

Brand name drugs are listed with an initial capital and the generics are shown entirely in lower case, as in the Fact Sheets. The names of drug categories are shown in block capitals.

INDEX OF DRUGS

INDEX OF DRUGS

INDEX OF DRUGS

INDEX OF DRUGS

INDEX OF DRUGS

If you are not sure of the name of your medicine you can look up your particular condition here and you will be referred to the relevant fact sheet. A reference is also given to where you will find natural remedies and information on how to help yourself.

A

INDEX OF ILLNESSES AND AILMENTS

INDEX OF AILMENTS

C

INDEX OF ILLNESSES AND AILMENTS

INDEX OF AILMENTS

INDEX OF ILLNESSES AND AILMENTS

INDEX OF ILLNESSES AND AILMENTS

INDEX OF AILMENTS

INDEX OF ILLNESSES AND AILMENTS

INDEX OF ILLNESSES AND AILMENTS

INDEX OF ILLNESSES AND AILMENTS

INDEX OF ILLNESSES AND AILMENTS

BIBLIOGRAPHY

ABPI [Association of the British Pharmaceutical Industry] *Data Sheet Compendium, 1981-82, 1985-86, 1986-87*, Datapharm Publications Ltd.
Aspirin and Your Health, A.S. Freese M.D., Pyramid.
The Biochemic Handbook, Thorsons, 1984.
The Brain, The Human Body Series, Torstar Books Inc.
Breast Cancer, Carlton Fredericks, Grosset and Dunlap.
British National Formulary, No. 13, 1987.
Complete Guide to Prescription and Non-Prescription Drugs, 1986, H. Winter Griffith M.D., H.P. Books.
Consumer Drug Digest, American Society of Hospital Pharmacists/Facts on File.
Dictionary of Drugs, Richard B. Fisher Ph.D. and George A. Christie M.D., B.Sc., Paladin.
Dorland's Medical Dictionary, 24th edition, Saunders.
Dr Schuessler's Biochemistry, J.B. Chapman M.D., Thorsons, 1973.
Drugs and Nutrients, Vol. 21: The interactive effects, Drugs and the Pharmaceutical Sciences, Ed. Daphne A. Roe and T. Colin Campbell, Marcel Dekker Inc., 1984.
Drugs and Nutrition in the Geriatric Patient, Ed. Daphne A. Roe, Churchill Livingstone, 1984.
Drug Induced Nutritional Deficiencies, 2nd Edition, Ed. Daphne Roe.
Drug, Nutrient Interrelationships, Nutrition and pharmacology, an interphase of disciplines, Nutrition Society of Canada, McMaster University, Hamilton, 1974.
Essential Human Anatomy and Physiology, Barbara R. Landau, Scott, Foreman and Company.
Essentials of Homoeopathic Prescribing, H. Fergie Woods M.D., M.R.C.S., Health Science Press, 1970.
Gray's Anatomy, Bounty.
Homoeopathy, G. Ruthven Mitchell, W.H. Allen.
Human Hormones, Raymond Green, World University Library, McGraw Hill.
Iridology: The Science and Practice in the Healing Arts, Vols. 1 and 2, Bernard Jensen D.C., N.D., Bernard Jensen.
Martindale, 28th edition. The Pharmaceutical Press.
Medical Physiology, William F. Ganong M.D., Lange Medical Publications, 1981.
Medicinal Plants, Prof. Hans Fluck, Foulsham.
Mental and Elemental Nutrients, Carl Pfeiffer Ph.D., M.D., Keats, 1975.
Natural Healing, Mark Briklin, Rodale.
The Natural Health Book, Dorothy Hall, Angus and Robertson.
Nutrition Against Disease, Roger J. Williams M.D., Bantam.
Nutrition for Vegetarians, A.M. Thrash M.D. and C.L. Thrash M.D., Thrash Publications, Yuchi Pines Institute.
Oxford Concise Medical Dictionary, Oxford Medical Publications, 1980.
The Penguin Dictionary of Biology, Penguin.
The Penguin Medical Encyclopedia, Peter Wingate, Penguin, 1987.
Physician's Desk Reference, 40th edition, Medical Economics Company, 1986.
Potter's Cyclopaedia of Botanical Drugs and Preparations, R.C. Wren F.L.S., Health Science Press.
Psychodietetics, Cheraskin, Ringsdorf and Brecher, Stein and Day.
Taber's Cyclopedic Medical Dictionary, 15th Edition, Ed. Clayton L. Thomas M.D., M.P.H., F.A., Davis Company.

Magazines and Journals
British Journal of Pharmaceutical Practice
British Medical Journal
Geriatrics for GP's

BIBLIOGRAPHY

Journal of Alternative and Complementary Medicine
The Lancet
New England Journal of Medicine
New Scientist
Scrip

Quotes
'Among the Haida Indians of the Pacific Northwest . . .' *Another Roadside Attraction* by Tom Robbins. Reprinted by kind permission of W. H. Allen and Co. Plc.

'When you suffer an attack of nerves . . .' *The Lion of Boaz-Jachin* by Russell Hoban. Reprinted by kind permission of Faber and Faber.

'What we say is sexual reproduction . . .' *Sex in Human Loving*, Copyright © 1970, by Eric Berne. Reprinted by kind permission of Simon and Schuster Inc.

'Microbes is a vigitable 'an ivry one is like . . .' *Mr Dooley on Ivry Thing and Ivrybody* by Finley Peter Dunne. Reprinted by kind permission of Unwin Hyman Ltd.

'I am convinced digestion is the great secret of life.' Reverend Sydney Smith. *The Oxford Dictionary of Quotations 2nd Edition*, 1953. Reprinted by kind permission of Oxford University Press.

'I'm very brave generally . . .' *Alice Through the Looking Glass* by Lewis Carroll. Reprinted by kind permission of Penguin Books Ltd.

GENERAL INDEX